BIBLE Dreams
The Spiritual Quest

How the Dreams in the Bible
Speak to Us Today

SEYMOUR ROSSEL

Foreword by
Eugene J. Fisher

S.P.i. Books

New York

BIBLE DREAMS: The Spiritual Quest
How the Dreams in the Bible Speak to Us Today

Copyright © 2003 by **Seymour Rossel**

For further information contact:

S.P.I. Books
99 Spring Street, 3rd Floor
New York, NY 10012
(212) 431-5011 Fax: (212) 431-8646
Email: *sales@spibooks.com*
Web Address: *www.spibooks.com*

10 9 8 7 6 5 4 3 2 1
First Edition

An Ian Shapolsky Book

Copy editing by *Melvin Wolfson*

ISBN: 1-56171-939-0

Library of Congress Control Number: 2003092781

Printed in Canada

Contents

))

> *"This, then, is a book about dreams and visions recorded in the Bible, written by a Jewish explorer but not for Jews alone. It draws upon Jewish sources, but also upon spiritual sources from many ages and many cultures. It does not claim that one source is more sacred than another; instead, it assumes that all sources of spiritual growth flow from a single eternal fount."*

> *"If Freud or Jung had come to the conclusion that Elijah's visit to Sinai took place in a dream, they would have analyzed Elijah's dream as a reflection of the zeal of the prophet. No doubt, we would have read about how Elijah's angst led to his visions of fires and earthquakes and storms. The still, small voice might be portrayed as a metaphor for the deepest yearning of Elijah's faith to emerge from his subconscious world into his consciousness. No doubt, some commentaries would have stressed Elijah's repressed sexuality in terms of the conflicts of his drives for Eros and Thanatos—all of which would have been interesting from a scientific point of view, none of which*

would be relevant either to the probable purposes of the authors of the biblical account or to our ancient forebears themselves."

Dreamwork: *Using This Book*, 33

"We are most like our Creator, not when we create alone, but when we join others in the act of creation. God says, 'Let us...,' as if to say that in the course of creating together, shaping together, and building together we are acting in the image of God. As individuals, when we record a dream, we are performing an act of creation. Thus, there is an added holiness when we share our dreams with others, especially in the creativity we bring to interpreting our dreams and visions together."

Are We on the Right Path? *Abraham's Midlife Crisis*, 39

"The technology of dream induction was sometimes as simple as Gilgamesh's asking the mountain for a dream or Abraham's posing a question to God. But it could also be quite elaborate. It begins in the belief that dreams can be 'incubated,' or deliberately forced to serve our waking selves."

Dream Types: *Are All Dreams True?*, 65

"Dreams are, thus, a natural resource. If we ever truly appreciated how valuable a resource, Wall Street might trade them and the commodities markets might sell futures in them. Spiritual initiates, however, would find this suggestion somewhat ludicrous. Their inner awareness indicates that, even now, dreams and visions are the only things that Wall Street and the commodities markets ever offer to sell."

A Stairway to Heaven: *The Sages Interpret Jacob's Dream*, 85

"In interpreting Jacob's dream, the sages were interested in how its meaning might shape the future of the people. They had little regard for the dream's placement within the biblical narrative. And they

had little to say about what the dream meant to Jacob. They were intent on creating interpretations for the dream that would be 'true' for them. For us, the encounter between the Bible's most famous dream and the interpretations placed on it by the sages provides new clues for how the interpretation of dreams may ultimately shape destinies."

Paths of Interpretation: *The Art of Seeking Meaning*, 117

"It is the process of seeking meaning that seems to have the power to bring peace and healing to our inner and outer selves. The dreams we experience by night, the visions we experience by day, the myths we create with our lives—these are present for everyone, but not everyone becomes present for them."

To Awaken Transformed: *Jacob's Dream of Separation and Divorce*, 133

"From the evidence, it seems that both Abraham and Jacob incubated their dreams. They sought divine answers to moments of uncertainty and distress by initiating the dream process in a ritual way. In effect, they sent a question upward. In response, they received the inspiration and guidance they were seeking. Both the process and the dream were significant."

Preparing for Dreams and Visions: *Modern and Ancient Techniques*, 169

"There is infinite potential for wonder in the third of our lives that we spend sleeping. Should you close your eyes and sleep even while you are awake? Or should you open your eyes while you sleep and perhaps sense the astonishment that Jacob found?"

Coming Home: *Jacob's Dream of Reintegration*, 183

"If Jacob's staircase dream dealt with estrangement, divorce, and the path to salvation, the story of Jacob's wrestling match deals with maturity, self-image, and reintegration. Taking a reverse page from

Thomas Wolfe, this chapter might be called You Can Go Home Again, *provided that we add: but you will not be the same person who left, and home will not be the same as it was when you left it."*

"Now, if we count all of these forms—dreams, visions, and prophecy—as types of dreaming, the number of biblical texts available for dream interpretation multiplies exponentially. A wiser, more narrow, assertion might be: In the Bible, every dream or vision is a prophecy, but every prophecy is not necessarily a dream. The Bible makes it clear that we cannot say less than this."

"Where professional dream interpreters were available, most folk resorted to them to explain any but the most common dreams. This fact poses a difficulty. How did the people of Canaan manage to have their dreams explained? Joseph seems to suggest an answer when he points to God's part in dream interpretation. Many centuries later, the sages made a similar suggestion in regard to a recurrent motif in Genesis, God's statement to the patriarchs, 'And all the families of the earth shall bless themselves by you.'"

"In the mystic atmosphere of the Upper Galilee in the sixteenth century, a student of the Kabbalah proposed that the holiest among us create angels through the sounds we utter. An angel such as this, created out of human holiness, was called a maggid or 'interpreter' angel. Unlike God's angels, who are perfect in every way, angels created through human utterance are sometimes capable of deception, even as humans are."

For my beloved wife

Sharon L. Wechter

"They who dream by day are cognizant of many things which escape those who dream only by night" (Edgar Allan Poe).

A dream shared by two has no end;
and oft seems without beginning.
Who share it make it live;
and, once alive, it yields life meaning.
SR

Foreword

))

Seymour Rossel is on to something of great importance here, both for the field of biblical scholarship and, I believe, for the spiritual life of anyone, Christian or Jew, who believes the Bible to be a sacred text capable of speaking to us from generation to generation. Why not take the dreams and visions of the biblical patriarchs and matriarchs, prophets and sages, as seriously as did the biblical authors and their intended readers? Understand them precisely as they were intended to be understood—as dreams, visions of who we are and who we might become if we but follow the dreampath beckoning not just to "them" but also, and equally, to us.

Now this is a daring vision. Most biblical scholars employ a third-person, analytical methodology that is quite sound for its intended goal of determining a given text's original meaning within its historical context. Rabbi Rossel's grasp of modern biblical scholarship is quite solid, and he employs it here to good use. Solid, too, is his grasp of modern psychological theory, which he also employs to useful effect. But he stops with neither of these quite laudable scientific methodologies. These cognitive results are interwoven, drawn together, challenged, and finally transcended by engagement with the ancient, medieval, and modern insights of the masters of spirituality of a variety of religious traditions, though, for obvious reasons, he relies most heavily on Jewish and Christian tradition for it is their comments, from age to age, that have kept alive the dialogue between the people of God and God's book, the Bible.

In his innovative approach, Rossel is ironically at the same time deeply traditional, in the best sense of that term. Jews and Christians, mining the "inexhaustible riches" of the Hebrew Scriptures (to use the apt phrase of the Second Vatican Council) have from age to age affirmed that the sacred texts can have multiple meanings, ranging from the literal to the allegorical to the mystical. The "literal" (or, in Hebrew, the *peshat*) meaning, of course, is the historical-critical methodology mentioned above. The other possible meanings (what the rabbis would call the *derash* or "sought out") in one way or another apply the text to the life of the contemporary reader, what, in essence a good preacher does in one way and a good theologian does in another.

There is a rabbinic tale which explains why so many meanings can be valid at one and the same time, and yet be so different, addressing different areas of human life: philosophical, moral, spiritual, etc. A rabbi asks his students why, when Scripture of course does not waste a single inspired word, it is said "the God of Abraham, the God of Isaac, and the God of Jacob," when "the God of Abraham, Isaac, and Jacob" would suffice. They are baffled. "It is," he says, "because each generation must respond to God in its own way, and so appreciate God anew in every age."

Rossel's unique approach, combining traditional insights and contemporary science, thus has no precise precedent in either of our traditions, rich as they are, or modern scientific biblical scholarship. Yet it has paradoxically millennia of Jewish and Christian wisdom behind it. The Bible is always best read as "practical theology," God's way of telling us how to live the meaning of our lives, without quite telling us how. The name Israel means, in its root, "one who wrestles with God." Rossel's wrestling will not tell the reader exactly how to live their lives either. But he does show a way for us, a new path that can enlighten as it challenges us to think, and to pray, in new ways, to "wrestle" with what comes to us when we rest from all cares and have only our inner selves, the small, still voice within, to listen to.

I must admit that I, like many who will pick up this book and wonder whether it is worth purchasing, began with a bit of skepticism. But this is not "grocery store spirituality" or "new age mysticism" (whatever, indeed, they are). This is the real stuff. Here, the Bible itself speaks to each of us in a way most readers will have never been aware it could address our deeper concerns, anxieties, and hopes— the deeper fears and visions that we admit to ourselves only in our dreams, when we sleep and lay ourselves open to the quiet whisperings of the Spirit of God who dwells in our hearts.

Eugene J. Fisher, *Associate Director*
Secretariat for Ecumenical
    and Interreligious Relations
U.S. Conference of Catholic Bishops
Washington, DC
July 2002

BIBLE Dreams
The Spiritual Quest

How the Dreams in the Bible
Speak to Us Today

Introduction

THE PROMISE OF DREAMS

$\mathbb{)}$

We are such stuff as dreams are made on, and our little life is rounded with a sleep. — William Shakespeare, *The Tempest*, IV, I, 148

A holy man, one of the great masters, died. To provide sustenance for his widow, and to keep his memory fresh, his followers came to buy his clothing and other mementos by which to remember him. When nearly all of the small collection of worldly goods that had belonged to the master were gone, the widow noticed that the chief disciple of the master had bought nothing. "Surely," she said, "there is some keepsake that you would want. And, if you cannot afford to buy something, perhaps there is something that I can give you."

"You are kind," the disciple replied. "And, as you know, I come from an affluent family. Money is not the issue. But I had fixed my heart to bid on only one object, and I have not noticed it at all."

"Speak then," she said. "What is it that you wanted."

"I remember," said the disciple, "that the master spoke of having visions as he smoked his pipe. I had hoped to purchase that pipe for my own."

The widow said, "I intended to keep that memento for myself. It was precious to my late husband."

"Nevertheless," the disciple said, "it might sustain you in your old age. Name a high price, and allow me the privilege of purchasing it."

After a moment's thought, she answered in a tentative voice, "Perhaps, a hundred rubles would cause me to part with it."

The disciple smiled, "The price is high. I should be allowed to try the pipe to be certain that it is sound. Let me smoke it once, then, just to test it."

The widow opened a drawer and handed him the pipe. The disciple sat down, filled the pipe from his own pouch of tobacco, and lit the pipe.

As he drew upon the stem for the first time, the widow, the room, and the cottage disappeared. He found himself in the foyer of a great palace with marble columns stretching into the distance as far as the eye could see.

As he drew upon the stem yet again, the marble columns melted away like ice. A light brighter than any he had known heretofore forced him to shut his eyes tightly. Grasping the pipe tighter in his hand, he drew upon the stem a third time.

With the third puff of smoke, the light faded. He found himself in a wasteland beneath a night sky populated with a myriad of stars. Looking up, he saw the seven gates of Heaven and felt himself being wafting gently upward like the smoke itself.

The vision was so overpowering that he opened his mouth wide in astonishment. With that, the pipe dropped from his lips, landing in his lap. Its scattering ashes threatened to set him afire. Jarred back to mundane reality, he jumped to his feet, seized the pipe in one hand, and brushed the ashes from his clothes with the other. Then he smiled at the astonished widow and counted out the hundred rubles she had asked.

Arriving home, the disciple immediately filled the pipe and lit it again. He puffed once, but nothing happened. He puffed again, but still remained in his room, smoking the pipe before his hearth. Time and again he drew upon the pipe, but no vision appeared. "I have been tricked," he thought darkly.

Deeply perturbed, he sought out another learned disciple of the master and told his story.

"It is a simple matter," his friend said. "The first time you smoked the pipe, it still belonged to our departed master. You saw what the master saw when he smoked. But then you purchased the pipe and it became your pipe. You saw what you always see! In this life, the dreams and visions we are granted are those we are ready to receive. Make yourself worthy and the pipe will serve for you as it served for our master."

☽

This book owes its beginnings to a dream. The first time it came to me, it struck me as a kind of self-parody. But the dream returned a few months later, and then with greater frequency, until it took hold of me. It haunted me even in my waking hours. I caught myself sitting at my desk, star-

ing out my window at the stone towers guarding Man-
hattan's Central Park, seeing nothing of the scenery, only
revisiting my dream.

Slowly, I began to yield. I allowed myself to admit that
the dream might be seeking me. Finally, I put it into words.

> I am climbing a steep, rocky mountain. I am way
> above the tree line and struggling to catch my
> breath as I climb, when I chance upon an old man
> carrying a staff. He is sitting on an outcropping,
> staring up to the top of the mountain. I approach
> him and ask if I can help him up the mountain. He
> says, "No, that won't be necessary. You go on
> ahead. I have forty days and forty nights." So I keep
> climbing.

Even now, as I read the text again, I am amazed at how
few words it took to encompass what was less a dream than
an experience. Of course, the brief narrative hardly captures the dream's impact. Through its constant repetition,
and through my constant reflection on it, the dream had
taken shape as a message.

It awakened in me a curiosity about dreams and dreaming in general. I would tell my dream to a friend or share it
with a group in casual conversation. Amazingly, each time I
shared it I heard a new and fresh interpretation, or I was
asked a new and pertinent question, or I was treated to a
similar dream someone else had experienced. In fact, I discovered that most people I knew unconsciously enjoyed
taking part in this process of dream sharing.

I was thus surprised by how much of a subtext our
dreams supply. People are constantly and nonchalantly
swapping dreams. Sometimes dreams are attended to politely, then dismissed, as if they had not been told or not
been heard. Occasionally, however, a conversational men-

tion of a dream might evoke an entire interpretation, an explanation, or an extended sharing of dreams. What imparts this effect to the telling of some dreams and not to others? Is it something in the narrative, something in the way it is told, something in the dreamer, something in the listener, or something in the hearing?

Then, too, if we enjoy sharing our dreams, why do we share them so surreptitiously, couching them so often in casual conversation? After all, dreaming is an essential part of our nature, an inner natural resource. Dreams are experiences just as waking events are experiences. We constantly share waking events in our lives with others, why not dreams? Nearly all of us ask one another for help with things that happen in family life, in the workplace, in the society at large; why then do we tend to slip our dreams into conversations almost as an afterthought? Shouldn't we be more intentional about sharing our dreams?

In part, of course, we are constrained by a society that places a certain stigma on dreams. In our particular social milieu, in our particular moment in time, as in every time and place, we are bounded by a set of strictures that dictate what is "normative." Dreams do not fit our everyday lives as easily as waking events do, and visions are even less likely to be considered "normal" by our peers.

So, for example, if one of my coworkers were to spend the first part of every morning sharing dreams with office mates, he or she would not last long on the job. The job is considered important and essential; by comparison, dreams and visions are considered frivolous at best and, at worst, indicators of neurosis and psychosis. So we are socialized; so we behave.

Despite this apparent aversion to direct discussion, dreams and visions are as vital to us today as they were to our ancestors. In this regard, as a rabbi, I found myself at a special advantage. Spiritual inquiry is itself somewhat at odds with secular norms. It deals with the inner self, with knowledge that makes us not only more human but also more humane.

It was a natural progression, then, that led me to apply dream study to my work. I researched dreams through a wide variety of disciplines. I discussed dreams and the technology of dream study with a large number of people. After a while, I began to offer workshops both to share some of what I learned and also to learn more. And those who were open to seeking a deeper insight into their own spirituality responded with enthusiasm, sharing their dreams and visions with me. Writing this book was another means of sharing what I have discovered.

☽

This book centers on a handful of dreams and visions from the Bible. By Bible, I refer to what the Jewish people call the *Holy Scriptures*. Christians refer to it as the *Old Testament*. The people of Islam accept it as a precursor to their holy canon, the *Koran*. Both the *New Testament* and the Koran also contain rich accounts of dreams and visions. Each of these canons also deserves extensive exploration in the domain of dreams. But this is not a scholarly work, nor does it seek to be comprehensive. It takes certain dreams of the Bible as landmarks from which to explore spirituality, and seeks to explore the effect that dreams such as these can have on our personal lives. You might say that because it is founded on dreams in the Bible, it is religious, but you will soon see that it is not particular in its religion.

Dreams and visions transcend religious boundaries. The spiritual journey is a shared human endeavor, demanding a deep respect for the sacred no matter what garb the sacred chooses for its manifestation. Holy masters such as Mohandas Gandhi, Albert Schweitzer, and Mother Teresa rise above their particular religions to deliver spiritual messages vital to us all. In the same way, sacred texts—the Bible, the New Testament, the Koran, the Tao Te Ching, the Mahabharata, the Vedas, to name but a few—transcend the religions of their particular followers to deliver spiritual messages to the whole of humanity. Nevertheless, the universal messages and the universal messengers are always grounded in a particular venue. For our purposes, the Holy Scriptures serve as this venue.

This, then, is a book about dreams and visions recorded in the Bible, written by a Jewish explorer but not for Jews alone. It draws upon Jewish sources, but also upon spiritual sources from many ages and many cultures. It does not claim that one source is more sacred than another; instead, it assumes that all sources of spiritual growth flow from a single eternal fount.

As a guide, I hasten to point out to those who journey on the path of spirituality that the path opens to us as we open to it. Yet I also know that all of us, whether or not we seek the path, traverse parts of the journey in the course of our daily lives.

It is often the changing circumstances of our experiences that open us to forces beyond our understanding. Psychologists refer to such times as "moments of transformation." Dreams and visions play an especially important part in preparing us for moments of transformation. And, after moments of transformation pass, dreams and visions help us first to process the changes we have undergone and then to create new meanings for our life histories.

Even now, we are made of the same stuff as an Abraham, a Jacob, a Moses, a Miriam, a Deborah, a Solomon, an Ezekiel, or a Daniel. They had many dreams in the course of their lifetimes, just as we have. Yet the Bible chooses only a handful of dreams and visions to record and pass on to us. Without going into the mechanics of the Bible's development, it seems self-evident that those dreams and visions were not chosen at random. Indeed, they provide a map for our spiritual journey.

The dreams and visions included in the Bible share a common thread. To the extent that we can understand them, they seem to be guideposts to interpreting moments of transformation that occur not only in the lives of biblical characters but in our own lives as well. All of us walk similar paths through diverse experiences. All of us strive to mature—the milestones in our lives denoting a series of transformations. All of us seek our fortunes—the milestones in our lives denoting stages of success or failure. All of us suffer separations—the milestones in our lives denoting relationships left behind. The dreams and visions in the Bible offer guidance through these and similar moments of transformation in three ways:

First, they provide us with *meta-models*. Just as the characters in the Bible tend to be individuals writ larger than life, so their dreams and visions enable us to glimpse spiritual pathways broad enough for us to share. As we find ourselves in circumstances parallel to theirs, we can gain guidance for our personal moments of transformation from their dreams.

Second, the dreams in the Bible provide the *spiritual technology* to help us better understand our dreams. Though modern scientific technology may seem superior to the technology available in biblical times, our spiritual skills may have suffered setbacks due to the emphasis that modernity places on outward reality. Ancient spiritual technologies enable us to deal with outward reality in intriguing ways as we learn to open ourselves to inward truths.

Third, we can learn *new forms of interpretation*—means for opening our senses to the limitless potential that spiritual dreaming provides. Interpretation is the process by which we bring the meanings of dreams into our lives. We can learn to apply the techniques of interpretation employed by ancient and modern dream masters. And, through existing examples of dream interpretation, we can examine the spiritual lexicons of cultures other than our own.

In a sense, too, by exploring biblical texts, we can go beyond what the Bible teaches about dreams. This is possible because the kind of interpretation available to us today has never before been available. Imagine a pyramid formed entirely of human beings, a human ladder. The former generations are at the bottom, and each new generation climbs to the shoulders of the one before it. The view seen by the generation at the top is always unique, forever different from that seen by any beneath. Since we stand on the shoulders of those who came before us, we have their knowledge to guide us, while a new vista opens to our vision. Looking at a Bible dream envisioned and interpreted by a previous generation, we perceive it from a different vantage point. Of course, this requires some dexterity. We must balance ourselves on the past at the same time as we rely upon the sensibilities of the present. We can even anticipate what future generations will envision as they stand upon our shoulders.

☽

This book began with a dream. I offer that dream to you only as a point of departure. The wonderful thing about a spiritual journey is that it need never end. The things we possess in this life come and go. In the end, we ourselves depart, leaving most of them behind us. Throughout our lives, however, no matter what our physical gains or losses, the knowledge we accumulate remains. And, while it is easily demonstrated that we cannot take the things of this world with us when we depart, there is every reason to believe that our wisdom may remain inviolable. It certainly continues to exist in the world through the dreams and visions we pass on to our children and to the children of our children. Thousands of generations have believed that it continues to live on for us, as well, as we enter a world dimly glimpsed, where matter itself is transformed—a world where we may very well become our dreams and our visions.

Shattering Idols
BIBLE DREAMS AND OUR OWN

☽

There is a dream dreaming us. — proverb of the Kalahari
Bushmen[1]

To journey along the path of the dream seeker is to open
our selves to new possibilities. To grasp the way our biblical
ancestors viewed their world, however, we have to release
some modern preconceptions. It is commonly believed that
science will eventually explain all phenomena. Even many
who believe in extraordinary phenomena—astrology, extra-
sensory perception, natural healing, voodoo, telepathy, and
so on—are confident that these eventually will yield to scientific explanation.

By its very nature, however, the spiritual quest requires
us to consider the possibility that our world will always remain somewhat inexplicable. The journey of the spirit is a
pilgrimage toward the unknown, and, by definition, the unknown is bound to make us feel insecure, even confused.
Whatever we find on such a journey, we are not likely to un-

derstand it all at once. Moreover, the extraordinary phenomena encountered in the spiritual quest require little or no scientific understanding. As the eminent psychologist Roland Cahen notes:

> It may seem paradoxical to speak of the dream as involving us in reality, but this very paradox is the mainspring of our interest in dreams. The role played by the dream in our inner world is equivalent to that held by the object in the external world. I would even go so far as to say that dreams have an even greater immediacy than perceptions because they are within us from the start....[2]

In this chapter, we examine the immediacy of these internal perceptions taking the dreams of the charismatic early prophet Elijah as preeminent examples of how common understandings may not always be reliable in dealing with the dreams of the Bible.

$$\mathbb{)}$$

We all dream, yet most of us consider our dreams personal and unique. If this were true, the significance of dreams would depend entirely on our individual perceptions. At the same time, it is obvious that our dreams are conditioned by social norms, values, and images—by our culture. Intuitively, Native Americans tend to encounter animal spirit guides in their dreams, while people of European descent tend to encounter human spirit guides. Christians tend to encounter Jesus-like or Mary-like figures in their dreams; non-Christians often meet figures more reminiscent of their particular religions. We might state this in another way: Spirit guides seem to be a fairly constant and universal phenomenon in dreams, but *the particular shape the spirit guide assumes tends to differ depending on the norms of the dreamer's society.*

From the outset, then, we must admit that our dreams are not entirely personal and unique. We share images and dream objects on the most immediate level with our particular tribe or culture, then on broader levels with larger groups, and finally—on the broadest level—with all human beings. Culture affects our dreams and shapes our visions in ways that seem so transparent to us that we take them for granted.

Ironically, the cultural norms we take for granted are often the most difficult for us to define. Yet, trying to uncover our preconceptions is a little like being the deep-water fish that goes swimming off in search of the ocean. There is no science of the accepted. On the other hand, our notion of "the accepted" is often exposed when we contrast our beliefs with those held by other societies in other places and times, as when we compare the various kinds of spirit guides that people encounter in their dreams. Thus, to look directly at our selves and our prejudices, we need to take a sideways glance at what other societies believe or have believed about reality and about dreams.

In our Western model of reality, we conceive of our lives as a series of connected events. Compare this with the worldview of the Bushmen of the Kalahari Desert, who think of their lives as a series of visions by day and dreams by night. The Bushmen assert, "There is a dream dreaming us." They believe that what happens to them has neither an immediate cause nor a direct consequence. As in a dream, things happen to the Bushmen simply because they do. Their dreamlike existence places the whole matter of fate outside the control of the individual. Consequently, in the Bushmen society (as in many preliterate societies) there is little necessity to celebrate the importance of the individual, to revere what we call "personal consciousness" or "the continuity of the individual."

Before the twentieth century, Western civilization held a widely-shared perception of dreams. Shakespeare expressed this in *The Tempest* when he called us "such stuff that dreams are made on." He was being more than theatrical. In Shakespeare's era, dreams—waking or sleeping— were considered compelling events, exerting direct influence over the external world. Western society harbored a deep-seated, intuitive belief that dreams and visions held rich meanings, meanings that could alter the course of waking reality. Dreams, emanating from sources beyond human understanding, could seize and change us.

This is evident beginning even in the early literature of dreams. Studies of dreams and visions based on premodern understandings treat them as portents, as instruction from a benevolent or malevolent source, as inspiration from a personal "dream master," as visitations, or as prophecy. Many of the early texts on dreams and visions are either standardized explanations of dream symbols or recipe-like instructions for dream interpreters and would-be prophets. Most of these dream books are dictionaries of symbols providing us with "normative" meanings. (We shall have more to say on such dream books later.) Prior to the eighteenth century, nearly all dream literature took this dictionary-like form. In fact, these books remained popular even after new understandings about dreams began to take shape; and they continue to be popular today. No matter how recently they were composed—and even when they include explanations from modern psychological sources—they are usually borrowed in bulk from pre–eighteenth-century sources.

In short, throughout most of Western civilization's intellectual history, people believed in the formative power of dreams and visions. As Westerners, we never agreed with the Kalahari Bushmen who believed that dreams were real events in an unreal world. Nevertheless, we might have been willing to admit that they were unreal events influencing our real world.

))

Our biblical ancestors conceived of reality in a vastly different way. It was neither as haphazard as the nonsequenced lives of the Kalahari Bushmen, nor as ordered and regularized as Western reality. In the biblical world, extraordinary events were accepted as possessing layers of meaning. To introduce this kind of thinking, consider the story of Elijah and the ravens in I Kings:

> God's word came to [Elijah]: "Leave this place; turn eastward and hide by the Wadi Kherith, which is east of the river Jordan. You will drink from the wadi, and I have commanded the ravens to feed you there." He proceeded to do as God bid; he went, and he stayed by the Wadi Kherith, which is east of the Jordan. The ravens brought him bread and meat every morning and every evening, and he drank from the wadi" [I Kings 17:2–6].

Are we to take this literally? Did our biblical ancestors take this literally? Our difficulty is compounded when we attempt to find modern explanations for such phenomena.

A *wadi* is a dry riverbed through which water runs only during the rainy season. Such riverbeds abound near the Jordan River, and the Wadi Kherith could be any one of them. Or it could be none of them. The *wadi*'s name could be a wordplay.

The word *kherith* is associated with covenants. As a verb, it connotes "making an incision," "cutting off," or "cutting down." Surely, there is a dreamlike quality to the whole passage, even though it is reported as a historical incident in the life of the prophet. It may be that we have lost some association here that made it possible for our biblical ancestors to understand the story as a metaphor. Hold on to that thought for a moment and consider a second incident from Elijah's life:

> After a while, the son of the mistress of the house fell sick, and his illness grew worse, until he had no breath left in him. She said to Elijah, "What harm have I done to you, O man of God, that you should come here to recall my sin and cause the death of my son?" "Give me the boy," he said to her; and taking him from her arms, he carried the boy to the upper chamber where he was staying, and laid him down on his own bed. He cried out to God, saying, "O Eternal my God, will You bring calamity upon this widow whose guest I am, and let her son die?" Then he stretched out over the child three times and cried out to God, saying, "O Eternal my God, let this child's life return to his body!" God heard Elijah's plea; the child's life returned to his body, and he revived. Elijah picked up the child and brought him down from the upper room, and gave him to his mother. "See," Elijah said, "your son is alive." And the woman answered Elijah, "Now I

know that you are a man of God and that God's word is truly in your mouth" [I Kings 17:17–24].

This selection seems somewhat more "real" to us. From the text, we can easily speculate that Elijah performed mouth-to-mouth resuscitation on the child. Notice the emphasis the widow places on "God's word" being in Elijah's "mouth." We can theorize that "God's word" was a metaphor for the breath of life that God breathed into Adam in the first chapter in Genesis. So we can safely sit back and assume that we have a provided a plausible explanation for what actually transpired as Elijah "raised" the child from the dead. Maybe.

Nevertheless, the story still retains a dreamlike quality. The text explicitly states that Elijah required God's help to revive the child. So we could also reverse our understanding to ask a different question: When patients cease breathing and the Emergency Medical Technicians or the doctors take over to try to resuscitate them, would their success rate be greater if the doctors and the EMTs paused long enough to pray for God's help? Hold that thought for a moment and consider a third episode from the life of this extraordinary prophet:

> [Elijah] lay down and fell asleep under a broom bush. Suddenly an angel touched him and said to him, "Arise and eat." He looked around; and there, beside his head, was a cake baked on hot stones and a jar of water! He ate and drank, and lay down again. God's angel appeared a second time and touched him and said, "Arise and eat, or the journey will be too much for you." He arose and ate and drank; and with the strength from that meal he walked forty days and forty nights as far as the

mountain of God at Horeb. There he went into a cave, and there he spent the night.

Then the word of God came to him. God said to him, "Why are you here, Elijah?" He answered, "I am moved by zeal for the Eternal, the God of Hosts, for the Israelites have forsaken Your covenant, torn down Your altars, and put Your prophets to the sword. I alone am left, and they are out to take my life." "Come out," God called, "and stand on the mountain before the Eternal."

And lo, the Eternal passed by. There was a great and mighty wind, splitting mountains and shattering rocks by the power of the Eternal; but God was not in the wind. After the wind—an earthquake; but the Eternal was not in the earthquake. After the earthquake—fire; but the Eternal was not in the fire. And after the fire—a still, small voice. When Elijah heard it, he wrapped his mantle about his face and went out and stood at the entrance of the cave. Then a voice addressed him: "Why are you here, Elijah?" He answered, "I am moved by zeal for the Eternal, the God of Hosts; for the Israelites have forsaken Your covenant, torn down Your altars, and have put Your prophets to the sword. I alone am left, and they are out to take my life" [I Kings 19:5–14].

For the moment, forget about why Elijah was afraid for his life, forget about what came before this part of his story, and forget about what would happen next. Just concentrate on what happens in this sequence of extraordinary events: the angel; the bread and water; the journey of forty days and forty nights; the cave; the wind; the earthquake; the fire; and the still, small voice. Would one meal, or even two, be sustenance enough for a journey of forty days? Would it really have taken forty days for Elijah to walk from Beersheba to Mount Horeb (another name for Mount Sinai), a distance of perhaps 250 miles? Why does God ask Elijah to state the purpose of his visit twice? Does Elijah actually witness a storm, an earthquake, and a fire? Was the Horeb that Elijah visited involved in some volcanic episode? And so on. As long as we try to reconstruct this story in a factual, logical way it poses question after question.

Our preconception that the text is literal is at fault here. Over and again we have read this and other biblical stories at face value. But biblical stories are part of a tradition that considers all reality to possess layers of meaning. So, for example, this story not only has the dreamlike quality that we noted in the two prior episodes from Elijah's life, it is also possible to read the entire narrative as a dream based on what the narrative itself tells us. The opening statement here is "[Elijah] lay down and fell asleep under a broom bush." From that moment on, there is no reason to believe that anything being related is not a dream.

Thus we can assume that Elijah awoke twice and ate twice *in* his dream. We can assume that he made the symbolic journey to Sinai *in* his dream. We can assume that he spoke with God, witnessed the wind and earthquake and fire, and heard the murmuring voice, all *in* his dream. He had no need of a meal to provide him with sustenance for the forty days and forty nights journey back from Sinai because, in fact, he had been sleeping. When he wakes up to do what God orders him to do, the narrative does not say that he left Mount Horeb to travel back to Israel, it merely states, "He set out from there..." [I Kings 19:19]. We can as easily assume that this means from the broom bush as from Horeb, and the story makes perfect sense if we make this assumption.

Yet, if the whole story is a dream, why does the text not say so in so many words? This, too, exposes one of our preconceptions. Our modern sensibility is disturbed by not knowing the "truth" about this incident. Did Elijah visit Mount Sinai or not? Inquiring minds want to know! Did Elijah perform a miracle in resuscitating a child or not? Inquiring minds want to know! Did the ravens feed him or not? Inquiring minds want to know! And we want to know for certain because we are trapped by our need for logical explanations. It was not always so.

☽

Our biblical ancestors saw no difference between the reality of everyday life and the reality of dreams and vision. The one was as "real" as the other. Until relatively recently, Jews and Christians understood their lives in this way. But our attitudes toward waking and dreaming are strongly influenced by our belief in the centrality of the individual and our reliance on science.

Beginning as far back as the Renaissance, Western society began to adopt a view that expressed the centrality of human beings. The idea of the "Renaissance man" stressed the ability of a single individual to achieve dramatic knowledge in more than one sphere by dint of personal talent. Technological advances—the printing press and its concomitant, the broadside, in particular—assigned the opinions of individuals new importance. By the eighteenth century, individuals were asserted to have certain "unalienable rights." The beliefs and opinions of the peasant and the noble were assigned equal rank. At first, this was a tentative admission. The framers of the Declaration of Independence, for example, could not speak of the unalienable rights of human beings without saying that these rights were granted by "their Creator." Led by philosophers, however, the assumption steadily grew that the rights of individuals did not necessarily derive from a divine source, but from an implied social contract. In effect, modern Western thought removed God from the equation.

Throughout the Western Hemisphere, Western civilization was thought to be the highest form of human culture, and the reasoning individual was regarded as the very purpose of the universe. From a religious stance, we might say that we began to speak less of a God who was the Creator of human beings and more of human beings as creators of God—or, at least, as creators of the idea of God. It followed that if we are God's creators, rather than God's creatures, then our dreams, like our rights, must also be our own creations. Intimations of this understanding sometimes appear in writings much earlier than the eighteenth century, but it was the broad acceptance of the worth of the individual—forged in the revolutions in America and Europe, and in the world of the Enlightenment—that led us to believe that dreams emanate from our own psyches.

The other modern force impinging on our ability to identify with the Bible's attitude is our post-Enlightenment belief that the more scientific we become, the more the world may be brought under the control of science. This progression also seems natural to us: astrology gave way to astronomy, alchemy to chemistry, magic to physics. In medieval times, phenomena were being catalogued and categorized. By modern times, nearly all observable phenomena were also being quantified, analyzed, and manipulated. It only remained for Sigmund Freud to apply these scientific methods to dreams. His theories—along with the theories of Carl Jung and their respective followers—today enjoy widespread acceptance and influence.

One result of these two forces was the impression that dreams originate in the dreamer as an expression of something inherent in the particularity—the "personal consciousness"—of the dreamer. Another result was the impression that eventually dreams could be explained through the logic of science—through psychology, neurobiology, or genetics.

Literature regarding dreams changed accordingly. In keeping with modern views, two new streams of dream research appeared and developed. One of these streams treats dreams as self-inspired, as instruction from some deeper self to our waking self. As Roland Cahen notes:

> The dream, which reveals an underlying psychic current and the imperatives of a vital pattern engraved in the deepest layers of our being, is the expression of the individual's most profound aspirations and, as such, provides us with infinitely precious information.[3]

Here we see both preconceptions—the centrality of the individual and the promise of science—clearly juxtaposed. Books based on these assumptions utilize symbol and metaphor to explain "what we are saying to ourselves." This genre has proliferated widely in the last hundred years, and inevitably makes extensive use either of the works of Freud or Jung, or both.

If Freud or Jung had come to the conclusion that Elijah's visit to Sinai took place in a dream, they would have analyzed Elijah's dream as a reflection of the zeal of the prophet. No doubt, we would have read about how Elijah's angst led to his visions of fires and earthquakes and storms. The still, small voice might be portrayed as a metaphor for the deepest yearning of Elijah's faith to emerge from his subconscious world into his consciousness. No doubt, some commentaries would have stressed Elijah's repressed sexuality in terms of the conflicts of his drives for Eros and Thanatos—all of which would have been interesting from a scientific point of view, none of which would be relevant either to the probable purposes of the authors of the biblical account or to our ancient forebears themselves.

Alongside psychology, another modern stream seeks to explain dreams as bodily functions. Most proponents of this objectively scientific school feel that dreams need only be quantified, identified, analyzed, and typed. Elijah's need for food would have been stressed in this view. His ideation—that ravens brought him bread and meat or that angels cooked for him—might be portrayed as metaphors expressing the body's simple hunger.

Pure science—explorations of brain functions, neurology, REM (rapid eye movement) sleep, and the like—produce interesting and demonstrable theories, but studying the observable phenomena of dreams only hints at a more perplexing puzzle. The shell of an egg does not entirely define an egg. After all scientific probing, there remains the need to comprehend the *content* of our dreams or of Elijah's dreams. While the dream mechanism may be measurable since it is rooted in the physiology of the individual, the meaning of dreams may permit of no measurement whatever.

In the course of this book, we may take notice of scientific observations, but our major concern is with the content of biblical dreams and our innate abilities to apply this content to our lives. With this in mind, the question that comes into sharp relief for us is, "How much weight shall we give to the dreamer?"

$$)$$

We cannot escape the fact that we have been born into and reared according to an egocentric, scientific worldview. We tend to have a strong sense of self-worth. Between the twin mysteries of birth and death, we conceive of ourselves as beings concerned with making sense of reality. We ask, "If I am a unique individual, what is my *particular* purpose?" Such a question presupposes that there is a strong commitment to individuality.

To retain our self-confidence, we call on science to "explain away" any intrusion of the extraordinary into the ordinary. If we hear of someone making a miraculous recovery from an illness, or of someone seeing a loved one appear though that loved one has died, or of someone predicting in a dream or a vision an event that has not yet occurred, or even of Elijah reviving a child who is no longer breathing, we rely on science to eventually explain the seeming incongruity. We are conditioned to turn to science to examine every miracle for evidence of fraud. To the extent that science can offer some explanation or accounting, our self-confidence is strengthened.

In encountering dreams, however, we are ill-served by clinging to these preconceptions. We have to wonder: Are we human beings *actually* the center of the universe? Can scientific explanations *actually* account for everything in our experience? If an honest answer to either of these questions is no, we may lose the security that our modern point of view affords us, but we may gain insight or even spiritual

awakening. But how can we overcome the ingrained prejudices of our own modernity?

☽

Actually, we are forced to overcome our worldview every
time we are faced with an inexplicable incursion into our
well-organized logic. The simplest example is also the most
common: Although science maintains that time can be
measured to an atomic degree of precision, our experience
tells us that time is subject to a certain amount of elasticity. Most of us, for instance, have learned the commonplace
that water boils faster if you do not watch it boiling. Our experience of time also tells us that intense moments in our
lives seem to take far longer than ordinary moments. We
tacitly accept the scientific explanation that time is an absolute—only our *perception* of it is changed through experience. But we could as easily aver that the person who lives
life to the fullest, savoring every minute, has far more time
than the average person. Both of these statements are true,
depending only on the kind of truth we are seeking. Elijah's
imagined journey could well have lasted forty days and forty
nights and still have taken place entirely in one dream.

Or consider an example of the kind of inner consciousness that science does not easily explain. Perhaps you recall
a moment when you were conscious of being outside yourself, watching yourself. Most of us have had such an experience. This is a common mode in dreaming. In dreams, you
are accustomed to witnessing yourself in action. You do not
stop to object that such a vision of yourself is physically impossible. Dreams are supposed to be imagistic and subjec-
tive, so you allow yourself the luxury of not questioning this

slight aberration. You allow yourself to dream the dream that is dreaming you.

Seeing yourself in a dream may seem acceptable, but, in fact, you are also accustomed to seeing yourself in action during your waking moments! Imagine yourself holding this book open. With the slightest shift of focus, you can see the way in which you picked up the book, you can see the position in which you are sitting or reclining, and you can see yourself reading the book. Yet, to actually see these things, you would have to be outside yourself looking *at* yourself. Nevertheless, you "see" this way all the time. On the one hand, you are fully engaged in your everyday tasks. On the other hand (and at the same time), you are a witness—disengaged, sometimes outside yourself, watching. Even in waking reality, you allow yourself to dream the dream that is dreaming you.

A teaching story of the early Hasidim, the Jewish mystics of eastern Europe, tells of a *rebbe* who took his students to the circus. Together, they watched in awe as a man walked a tightrope high above. A student asked, "Why is that man risking his life in this way?" The *rebbe* answered, "I do not know why. But I know this: As long as that man is walking along that tightrope, he is concentrating his whole mind and soul to that single purpose. If, for one moment, he stopped to worry about the money that he is earning by walking the tightrope or thought about how he looks walking the tightrope, he would be lost, and would fall to his death. Only when he concentrates on the task at hand, the work that he has to do in walking the thin cord, only then can he hope to succeed."

We are like that tightrope walker. When we concentrate on the task at hand, our egos slip away. We forget ourselves in being ourselves. When we concentrate on ourselves again, the task at hand slips away. When it comes to dreams and visions, insisting on logic can only destroy the moment.

Our worldview also interferes by its insistence that the universe must operate according to the same logic for each and every individual. The events of our lives may be unique, it is thought, but every event must conform to logic.

Contrarily, the Bible believes that prophets are different from other people—their experiences are often removed from plain logic. Jonah can be thrown into the sea, swallowed by a great fish, spit out whole on the land days later, and proceed to prophesy to the city of Nineveh. None of the rest of us can do this. Does that mean that we are less than equal? Or does it mean that we have encountered a dreamlike experience that is meant to teach us something about fleeing from our responsibilities, about ignoring the messages that we receive from a God who is beyond scientific explanations? Obviously it is the latter. We could argue that the whole Book of Jonah is a fiction or that the whole life story of Elijah is metaphorical. Or we could choose, as the Jewish tradition has chosen, to accept these tales as spiritual truth, relying on the fact that truth itself may be beyond explanation.

So time may have an elasticity that does not depend on clocks, and logic may have an elasticity that allows proofs to be adduced in more than one way. To this, we must add a third elasticity: Contrary to what most of us have been taught, there is a sense in which every event may not have a cause. The Sufis of Persia—among the most irreverent mystics—offer a humorous example of how cause and effect are not inevitable:

> A sage was walking along the road when suddenly a
> man fell from a rooftop and landed on the sage's

neck. The man who fell was unhurt, but the sage had to be taken to the hospital. His students came to visit him, and asked, "What can we learn from what happened to you?"

The sage replied, "We learn from this that you must not rely on the inevitability of cause and effect. That man fell from the roof, but my neck was broken! Give up theoretical questions such as: 'If a man falls from a roof, will his neck be broken?'"[4]

Can it be that some events happen merely because they do? Is it possible that some events have causes and effects, while other things do not? This is difficult for most of us to admit. It means opening the possibility that our stable, steady model of cause and effect is only one of many possible models of reality. Here, too, we are nevertheless always ready to admit this possibility in a dream, in a fiction, in a vision. Then, why not view reality, at least partially, as a waking dream? In some sense, we should admit, Jonah could be swallowed by a fish. Exactly how, does not really matter. When we examine the biblical text our question is not how, but why.

True enough, in modern times there has been a swing of the pendulum from the divine to the human. Yet it still remains one pendulum, and the religious awareness of our biblical ancestors is at the other end. In our present model of reality, we conceive of human beings as the "Great Event," the "Central Intelligence." If the pendulum continues to swing in this direction, we will continue to use our scientific temperament to seek deeper and deeper for ultimate causes. The more we do so, the more we come to realize that what we actually seek is an intelligence much like our own that was the original "Great Cause." In fact, the more rigorously scientific we become, the more the pendulum will tend to gravitate back toward religious awareness. The scientists' present search for a unified theory is not so far from a spiritual search for God. The more we are faced with the imperfections of human beings, the more we must seek a cause that is greater than (and other than) human. This is, after all, the nature of the pendulum.

The spiritual path opens to us when we realize that human beings may be more than just by-products of genetics and environment. We are also what we dream by night and what we envision by day. As we concede that reality may be more elastic than we normally admit, we are likewise returned to the motto of the Bushmen: "There is a dream dreaming us." Their proverb may have seemed convoluted at first but it now appears more sensible. It may be, as the philosopher Arthur Schopenhauer stated it, that we and our universe are "a vast dream, dreamed by a single being, in such a way that all the dream characters dream too."[5]

☽

The first question can now be posed again: "Do dreams emanate entirely from our own consciousness?"

Despite our modern prejudices, we can seek a higher ground here. A vast river of experiences obviously runs within us, providing us dreams and visions that often seem to surpass our personal capacities. It is just possible that this river could have a deeper source. Is it too much to say that dreams—perhaps not all dreams, but the most significant ones—may have their origins beyond our own inner resources, beyond even the "collective unconscious" of all the imperfect beings in the world? If we find the courage, we can at least concede that our dreams may present portents and prophecies, oracles and teachings—intimations of something beyond human invention.

This is a mind-set that would be familiar to our biblical ancestors. It is not even so foreign to us today. Nonetheless, I expect that you may be among those who approach this with a great deal of skepticism, as I did in beginning my journey. How could it be otherwise, since we have inherited such a deep-seated dependence on our scientific and ego-centric models of reality? Things in our world are supposed to be organized in a simple order: Atoms are always composed of protons, neutrons, and electrons; all else in the universe is always composed of atoms. Are we willing to be discomfited?

Playwrights often call for a suspension of disbelief in order to allow their dramas to unfold. Certainly, the temptation is great for me to call on you to use your imagination in order to allow the drama of biblical dreams and visions to unfold. Yet I urge you to enter this spiritual path otherwise. Do not set aside your skepticism. Envision yourself instead as a wanderer in the woods. Here there is no set path; there is no logical way to proceed. Every tree is interesting, and each leaf is worthy of consideration. The darkness is interrupted by occasional clearings and by the light that reaches the forest floor through the natural breaks in the foliage above.

As wanderers we proceed. As dreamers we enter the forest. It may be that along the way we will discover a greater respect for the positions taken by our biblical ancestors—those whose consciousness of reality was less dependent on analysis and definition, and whose understanding of themselves and their religion was enriched by the world of dreams and visions as much as it was by the outer garments of cause and effect. Together, we may discover all the visions we need and all the dreams we require in the dreams and visions we already possess. Together with Elijah, we may actually be fed by ravens and visit Mount Sinai.

Dreamwork

USING THIS BOOK

🌙

And Moses said to him, Are you jealous for my sake? Would
God that all the Lord's people were prophets, and that the
Lord would put his spirit upon them! — Numbers 11:29

As you read about the dreams and visions in the Bible—and
as you share passages or thoughts about dreaming with
others—you will probably discover that you are remembering more of your own dreams upon awakening. This is a
common response to a heightened awareness of the gifts
that dreams offer.

Dream therapists suggest that the best way to capture
your dreams for later analysis is to make an immediate record of them. I do this most comfortably at a computer not
far from my bed. For me, recording dreams on a computer
has the advantage of rendering them legible. If your hand-
writing is better than mine, a notepad or diary beside the
bed will serve the same purpose.

It is most effective to record dreams as quickly as possible upon awakening. In a recent experiment, some members of a dream group were asked to dial up a weather report before recording their dreams. This group was able to recall far fewer dreams than the control group that began their morning by writing in dream journals. We experience many dreams each night, but we are typically able to recall only the last few of these. Yet the number of dreams we are able to recall seems to increase through the simple practice of recording them at once.

Dream therapists also suggest that giving each dream a title enhances your memory of it. I titled the dream I recorded in the first chapter, "With Moses on the Mountain." You can see that a title can further elucidate the dream. In addition, it provides a setting for the dream when you share it with others. The title is not usually a part of the dream; instead, it is the first reaction of our waking conscious to an extraordinary experience. Yet this imposition of common reality on uncommon reality begins the process of framing a useful commentary.

))

A recorded dream, whether it is a dream in the Bible or your own dream, is a text, a narrative, an inspired work of the imagination. Not every dream is necessarily of great significance. Nor is every event in our daily lives. Yet events and dreams alike deserve thought and analysis, especially in the aggregate. Dreams most often manifest themselves as visual imagery, but visions per se are not easily shared. By contrast, texts describing imagery can be shared, discussed, and analyzed.

This contrast should be kept in mind. Dreams are not narratives. Since they tend to be highly visual, some folk find it difficult to express dreams in narrative form. If you are artistically inclined, you can sketch your dreams and keep notebooks of the sketches. Like narratives, these sketches or story boards can also be given titles.

Sigmund Freud kept notebooks of his dreams for nearly fourteen years until, at the age of twenty-eight, feeling overwhelmed, he destroyed these notebooks. Looking back, he explained that "the stuff simply enveloped me as the sand does the Sphinx." Carl Jung, on the other hand, maintained his dream notebooks far longer, recording both nightly dreams and fantasies he had by day. In fact, he took his original dream notebook, transferred the dreams to a new notebook, and embellished the texts with drawings in the manner of an illuminated medieval manuscript. Both Freud and Jung used their dream notebooks to create significant segments of their life's work. Freud gave us enormously interesting commentaries on forty-seven of his dreams in *The Interpretation of Dreams*. And Jung performed intensive self-studies on his dreams and fantasies, summarizing many of his ideas in his later work.

In keeping a dream notebook, you need not contemplate anything as intense as the work of Freud or Jung. No matter the depth of the narratives or the detail of the sketches, your dreams have the unique virtue of being entirely your own. As the pages of your dreams accumulate, you may find patterns in your dreams that surprise, delight, or even impress you. You may also find clues in them to otherwise hidden aspects of your self.

You may also find, especially in the course of reading this book, that your own dreams form parallels and comparisons to the dreams and visions of the Bible, or that they provide you with new insights to the Bible texts.

$$\pmb{\mathbb{)}}$$

According to the Bible, God created man and woman in God's image. The religious philosopher Martin Buber commented that, unlike many of the passages of the Bible, this passage should be taken literally: It is in the image of the Creator that we are created. We are therefore most God-like when we enter actively into the process of creation. Creativity is the hallmark of the sacred, so from Buber's point of view the act of creating a notebook of dreams is a sacred act, one that brings us directly into the work of creation.

Moreover, Buber adds, God did not create a single individual in God's image. The verse in Genesis 1:26 reads, *And God said, "Let us make the human in our image, after our likeness."* Then verse 27 continues, *And God created the human in His image, in the image of God He created him: male and female He created them.* Verse 28 begins, *God blessed them....* In reading these three lines of text, the first thing we notice is the seemingly inconsistent shift from plural to singular and singular to plural. Many commentaries attempt to explain why God says, *Let us...* instead of *Let Me...,* but it seems to me that Buber's insight is revelatory.

Buber states that God's image is pluralistic. That is, the One God is seen in many different ways by many different peoples in many differing religious systems. It follows that no single human image could be said to encompass *all* of God's image. God actually created multiple images— "male and female He created *them*" and "God blessed *them.*" Buber implies that God's image is found in our plurality, just as God is found in the plurality of God images conceived by human beings. Buber comments that we can only understand the true image of God when we live in community with others.

In order to create a true image, Buber continues, God created us in community. In our very creation, God provides us with the potential for sharing, for reaching out to others, and for creating together with others. We are most like our Creator, not when we create alone, but when we join others in the act of creation. God says, "Let *us*...," as if to say that in the course of creating together, shaping together, and building together we are acting in the image of God. As individuals, when we record a dream, we are performing an act of creation. Thus there is an added holiness when we share our dreams with others, especially in the creativity we bring to interpreting our dreams and visions together.

The practice of sharing dreams as a part of spiritual questing is reported through many cultures. Hopi Indians encourage dreamers to store good dreams in the heart, while discussing ominous dreams with friends and relatives until the problems revealed in them can be solved or, at least, ameliorated. The Kagwahiv and the Quiché regularly share dreams at any time and in any social situation. Moroccans have a more circumspect social norm. They skillfully weave the telling of their dreams into otherwise mundane conversations. In addition, many Moroccans share their dreams with professional specialists who help in their interpretation.

The Senoi and the Raramuri Indians employ "dreamtelling" as a means of educating their young people. The Senoi consider all dreams to be reflections of and extensions of their everyday reality. The Raramuri discuss dreams in the morning but also during waking periods in the middle of the night. Anthropologists report instances of cultures employing dream sharing "at healing ceremonies, initiation rituals, public and secret storytelling sessions, gossip sessions, and during hunting, trading, and gardening trips."[1]

In our own culture, dream sharing is a feature of therapy and psychoanalysis. Dream workshops and other dream groups have also been gaining popularity.

I have often speculated that God created human beings *because* God loves stories. For me, each dream is a story worth sharing. The opportunities, even in our society, are plentiful. You may wish to share your dreams with others whom you trust. You may choose to share them with a therapist, with a loved one, with other members of a dream workshop, or with friends and colleagues. Moreover, you need not limit your dream notebook to your own dreams or to dreams alone. You can incorporate interesting interpretations of your dreams. You can record striking dreams from books or magazines. You can record dreams that others share with you. In a sense, this is what the Bible has done in choosing to record dreams that helped to shape the lives of our ancestors.

As you wend through this book, the dreams you have, the dreams you record, those you evoke from others in conversation, and those you choose to analyze and interpret may begin to take on new shapes and meanings for you. It is possible that you will emerge with a greater understanding of yourself based on the visions and dreams of the Bible, but it is certain that you will emerge with a greater understanding of yourself based on your own dreams and visions.

Are We on the Right Path?

ABRAHAM'S MIDLIFE CRISIS

))

When, in sleep, the mind is separated from the companionship of the body and is not in touch with it, it remembers the past, sees the present, foresees the future. — Cicero, On *Divination*, 1.63

Have we created God or has God created us? No matter who is answering, the answer must rely on faith. Human beings attempting to connect with God have placed faith in a wide variety of activities including sacrifice, magic, religion, logic, philosophy, psychology, and science. These activities are equally ineffective, since none provides any incontrovertible truth. Still, to achieve a modicum of certainty, each of us willingly subscribes to one or more. As we grow and change, we now and again shed faith in one in order to subscribe to another. Entering the forest as spiritual explorers, we can tentatively place some faith in a poetic outlook popular among many societies: that, just as we have characters in our dreams, so we are the characters in God's dream.

The Bible does not include mundane dreams, even though we know that not all dreams are remarkable. So we have no record of what Solomon dreamed after eating a disagreeable dinner. Likewise, we have no record of the nightmares that may have been suffered by Tamar after she was raped by her half-brother Amnon. Instead, the Bible presents us with a series of extraordinary dreams and visions. Whether oracular or inspiring, prescient or reflective, marvelous or terrifying, they seem to have one thing in common: The dreams in the Bible are intimations of the connection between the sacred and the mundane. They represent events through which God or God's message enters the human world.

Visions and dreams have been considered direct communication from the divine from time immemorial. Originating in the darkness of prehistory, this idea persisted among scholastics and mystics throughout the Middle Ages and continues to coexist today alongside other scientific and religious views. Textual archaeological evidence dates from nearly five thousand years ago. It comes from the earliest human writings we possess: clay tablets incised with cuneiform symbols. Most of the surviving clay tablets afford us glimpses of daily life in ancient times. They are financial records, legal records, and chronicles of royal courts. A cherished few of these tablets, however, offer us insight for our spiritual path. These are the myths and literature of the ancient world, stories originally passed from generation to generation, probably by word of mouth, until they reached the written form in which we have uncovered them.

Judging by the many sites in which we find similar or identical written fragments, the stories were widespread and well known. And, again judging by the number of copies we have unearthed, one of the most popular of these myths was the epic of Gilgamesh. The most complete version of this epic was found in the library of Ashurbanipal at Nineveh, but we possess many fragments from other sites, in such languages as Akkadian, Hittite, and Hurrian. In large part, the epic is what we today might call "secular." It deals with nature and love, combat and friendship, life and death. Scholars of Akkadian name it by its first words, "The one who saw everything...." We commonly know it best by the name of its hero, Gilgamesh.

In the epic of Gilgamesh, faith in dreams and in the interpretation of dreams play a central role. Gilgamesh relates his dreams to his "wise" mother, who is "versed in all knowledge." She reveals the meanings of his dreams, and the remainder of the story details how his dreams come to fruition.[1] At one point, Gilgamesh climbs a mountain, offers up a sacrifice, and prays, "Mountain, bring me a dream."[2] More dreams are recounted in the course of the epic, each of them at major turning points in the plot.

Based on this epic, we can offer some surmises on ancient beliefs and attitudes toward dreams. High places ("mountains") were considered especially suitable as locales for receiving dreams or visions. (Presumably, high places are closer to the abode of the gods in the heavens; or, perhaps, local gods were associated with the mountains themselves.) It seems that, to receive an extraordinary dream, the dreamer must first make preparations. As preparation and perhaps as tribute, Gilgamesh offers up a sacrifice before asking for his dream. The epic also indicates that there were individuals like Gilgamesh's "wise" mother who were especially adept at dream interpretation. Most of all, the epic affirms our intuition: On the path of the spiritual quest, not much has changed. Just as we do today, our ancestors searched their dreams for meaning. These are some of the underlying notions that would have been commonplaces by the time of Abraham.

Indeed, the ancient Sumerians, Akkadians, and Mesopotamians all regarded significant dreams as portents, visitations, or visions. By the time of Abraham, Isaac, and Jacob, the practice of seeking dreams and interpreting dreams as messages were as familiar as the mythic stories of gods and heroes.

Here, too—though the Bible does not explicitly make mention of it—there is good reason to believe that Abraham would have been acquainted with the basic myths of his homeland, including the epic of Gilgamesh. According to Jewish tradition, Abraham's father was a maker of idols—a profession that both occasioned and required extensive knowledge of religious literature. Abraham grew up in a time of oral traditions, so every likelihood existed that his parents and grandparents would have related the story of Gilgamesh to him. His early years were spent in Ur and in Haran, two Mesopotamian cities connected with the worship of the moon god—a worship that surely had a dream component. Abraham lived in the context of the culture of his time, just as we live in the context of our culture. Thus, it is safe to assume that Abraham may have studied the outstanding spiritual technology of his time: how to find meaning in visions and dreams. It is not surprising, therefore, that the Bible portrays dreams and visions and their interpretation in the same terms as they are portrayed in the epic of Gilgamesh.

Through the generations, commentators have explored the meaning of the dreams and visions recorded in the Bible. They often observed that it is not enough to ask, "What did these dreams mean to Abraham?" In any case, they and we could never escape contemporary culture to find the original answer to this question. Even as the question is asked, we are also asking, "What did these dreams and visions mean to those who decided to include them in the Bible?" "What did they mean to people in the intervening centuries up to our time?" "What can we learn from past interpretations?" And, finally, "What can they mean for us today?"

In our spiritual quest, these questions yield to two more pressing inquiries: "Can the dreams and visions in the Bible help us bridge the chasm that now exists between the secular and the sacred?" And, "Can they help us interpret our own lives and understand our own dreams?" With these questions before us, we are drawn personally into the biblical texts.

In a sense, we can still experience the dreams as Gilgamesh and Abraham did. We can approach each biblical dream as if it happened last night and was recorded this morning. Our eyes should be clear, naïve, even if we are not. Our ears should be perked, ready to listen as though we have never heard the dream before. Our feelings should be open, raw, prepared to be touched, as if for the very first time. Applying this sense of immediacy, we can attempt to read Abraham's dream vision as if for the first time.

☽

In Genesis 15, Abraham (still known by his Mesopotamian name, Abram) has a dream.[3] As with many of our own dreams, Abram's dream comes as the answer to a waking question. Abram has obeyed God's call and journeyed to a distant land. He has traversed it and settled in it. He believes that God has promised this land to him, yet, at the moment this dream takes place, Abram owns none of it. Abram believes that the land will belong to his descendants, yet at the moment this dream takes place, he has no children. On the positive side, the Bible states that Abram is rich in cattle, in gold, and in silver. He has many followers. The inhabitants of the land respect him—kings regularly converse with him. But his earlier vision—the call of God that brought him to this land—the vision to which he has remained faithful, is now a distant memory.

Like any of us, Abram questions. He questions himself in particular. Did he get it right? Did he come to the right place? Did God really promise him children? Did God really promise him the land? His intuition and his reality are dissonant. Despite the solidity of his faith, doubt nips at his heels like a troublesome dog. Here is the narrative:

> Some time afterward, the word of the Lord came to Abram in a vision. God said, "Fear not, Abram, I am a shield to you; your reward shall be very great."
>
> But Abram said, "O Lord God, what can You give me, seeing that I shall die childless, and the one in charge of my household is my wine steward, Eliezer!" Abram continued, "Since You have granted me no offspring, my steward shall be my heir."
>
> The word of the Lord came to him in reply, "That one shall not be your heir; none but your very

own issue shall be your heir." God took him outside and said, "Look toward heaven and count the stars, if you are able to count them." And God added, "So shall your offspring be." And because he put his trust in the Lord, God reckoned it to him for righteousness.

Then God said to him, "I am the Lord who brought you out from Ur of the Chaldeans to assign this land to you as a possession." And he said, "O Lord God, how shall I know that I am to possess it?" God answered, "Bring Me a three-year-old heifer, a three-year-old she-goat, a three-year-old ram, a turtledove, and a young bird." Abram brought God all these and cut them in two, placing each half opposite the other; but he did not cut up the [young] bird. Birds of prey came down upon the carcasses, and Abram drove them away.

As the sun was about to set, a deep sleep fell upon Abram, and a great dark dread descended upon him. And God said to Abram, "Know well that your offspring shall be strangers in a foreign land, and they shall be enslaved and oppressed four hundred years; but I will execute judgment on the nation they shall serve, and in the end they shall go free with great wealth.

"As for you, you shall go to your fathers in peace; you shall be buried at a ripe old age.

"And they shall return here in the fourth generation, for the iniquity of the Amorites is not yet complete."

When the sun set and it was very dark, there appeared a smoking oven, and a flaming torch which passed between those pieces. On that day the Lord made a covenant with Abram, saying, "To your off-spring I assign this land, from the river of Egypt to the great river, the river Euphrates ..." [Genesis 15:1–18].

Envision the scene: You are Abraham in your tent as the narrative begins. God takes you outside the tent. Try to imagine a dark landscape under a profusion of stars. Listen again to Abraham's dialogue with God. Imagine gathering the birds and animals for the sacrifice. Hear the threaten-ing noise of the birds of prey as they circle and dive around you; feel your arms flapping and your legs running and hear the noises that you make to drive them off. Sense the dread that Abraham felt as the deep sleep enveloped him and try to feel the depth of his concern—so much of his life's work was riding on the answer to his sacrifice. How does it feel to know that your descendants will be enslaved for four hun-dred years? How does it feel to know that they will surely be redeemed? Are you comforted in the knowledge that you will die at a ripe old age? And, last, try to grasp the emo-tions that fill your mind and heart as the darkness gathers, only to be pierced by the eerie appearance of the smoking oven and the flaming torch.

))

In the text we just read, God promises Abram that his prog-eny will be as numerous as the stars and that they shall in-herit the land. Abram "put his trust in the Lord" and God "reckoned it to him for righteousness." Despite this decla-ration of absolute belief, Abram asks, "O Lord God, how shall I know that I am to possess [the land]?" God then in-structs Abram to prepare a sacrifice, and Abram waits for the sacrifice to be accepted. It is while Abram is guarding the sacrifice that the dream seems to occur. Then, at sunset, God accepts the sacrifice.

This text is hardly a straightforward narrative of a historical experience. It is imagistic, dreamlike, from start to finish. No mention is made of Abram's location as the narrative begins. We assume he must be indoors, since it states that God takes him outside. How long does the vision take? Are we listening to a narrative that describes one continuous event? If so, how can it be dark enough for Abram to see countless stars, then be light enough for him to gather the birds and animals and make the sacrifice, then be time for the sun to set so that he can fall asleep, and then have the sun set and darkness fall again when the smoking oven and the flaming torch appear?

We think we know when the dream begins—when Abram falls asleep—but we do not know when it ends. It may be that the smoking oven and the flaming torch—even the second sunset—are still a part of the dream. Abram is told at once that the message is one of comfort ("Fear not..."), but the dream is accompanied by a visceral feeling of "a great dark dread." The beginning of the sacrifice is recorded, yet the sacrifice is never completed. Abram never does sacrifice the young bird, and, although we anticipate that it will later be sacrificed as God commanded, surprisingly it is never mentioned again. And in answer to a personal question ("O Lord God, how shall I know that I am to possess it?"), the message foretells the history of a nation; and the covenant made with Abram is made on behalf of that nation.

In Jewish tradition, this incident in Abraham's life is called "The Covenant of the Pieces" ("pieces," referring to the splitting of the animals). Surely, the message of the vi-

sion transcends Abram the individual. Yet the text specifically states that the vision is granted to allay Abram's
personal fears; and the prophecy is interrupted by a personal note of comfort specifically meant for Abram himself.

These are just a few of the incongruities. Even if the
text did not specify that a vision and a dream are operating
here, we would be forced to assume that in this narrative we
have entered an extraordinary, shadowy world.

Modern, psychoanalytic modes of interpretation are
the first to break down. Abram is not simply the victim of
his own *angst*. Both the vision and the prophecy go far beyond this. True, there are archetypes among the images in
the dream, but they are hardly central to the dream's im-
port. The revelation is direct, simple, and transparent—the
sunset, the flaming torch, the smoking oven, even the
sense of dread accompanying the vision, do not give the
dream its substance. The Abram who places absolute faith
in God—faith enough to later attempt to sacrifice a son
without question—is not concerned here with simple self-
doubt or personal anxiety.

The vision (except for its intervening statement concerning Abram's long life and peaceful death) is, in the
main, a typical ancient oracle, a prediction of the fate of
the Hebrew people. In fact, it employs a typical oracular
mode. Sacrificing animals as a means of seeking God's will
was a common practice in the ancient world. Divination,
cutting animals and birds in half to study their innards for
omens, was standard magical practice. Much of the tension
in the narrative is created when Abram reserves the young
bird, presumably to cut it open last—after God accepts the
sacrifice—to discover the ultimate sign that will indicate
whether God has spoken in favor of, or against, Abram's
dream. If this was done—and the text does not tell us

whether it was or not—the answer must have been positive, for the dream prophecy was accounted truthful enough to be recorded for all time.

☽

In his masterful Bible commentary, Nachmanides (c. 1194–1270) offers explanations for two of the dream's central premises. First, he notes that Abram never doubted God. God had already accounted Abram's complete faith as a mark of righteousness. Therefore, Abram was not merely seeking an oracular sign. Nachmanides believes that Abram's actual request was that he might know God's will with a true *inner* knowledge. If the early dream expert Artemidorus, a Roman scholar of the second century, had read this narrative, he would have classed this as a "worrying" or "asked-for" dream. It seems self-evident, both from the text and from Nachmanides' observation, that in this case it was not the vision that sought Abraham, but Abraham who sought the vision.

Next, Nachmanides observes that the "great dark dread" Abram experienced in his sleep was itself a symbol, a foreshadowing of the future oppression of the Jewish people. The dream deals with communal existence at the same time as it deals with Abram's personal fate. It even attempts to explain why the Hebrew tribe should have to wait four generations before possessing the land: "for the iniquity of the Amorites is not yet complete." (The Amorites were the most powerful tribe among the Canaanites, and God here foretells that their evil ways will catch up with them four generations hence—not one moment sooner and not one moment later.) The dream foretells what the

Hebrew tribe will be doing in the meantime.[4] According to Nachmanides, this is the "inner" knowledge that Abram has requested. The vision of the future of the nation is the plain and simple meaning of the dream.

So much is left open-ended that we could begin with this text and interpret outward to encompass very nearly the entire history of Abraham's people. Nachmanides points us in this direction. We unravel the thread as we attempt to follow his lead. If the "dread" that Abram feels is a physical manifestation in our primary ancestor for what would happen to his offspring, then what are the smoking oven and the flaming torch that pass between (and, so "cut") the two halves of the sacrifice? Could we say that these represent Abram's premonition of the sacrifice that would be required when the Romans destroyed nearly half the Jewish people after putting Jerusalem and the Temple to the torch? Or the sacrifice required during the Crusades when whole Jewish communities were slaughtered and put to the torch? Or the sacrifice required during the Holocaust when smoking ovens destroyed half of the entire Jewish nation?

Can all this have been foreseen in Abram's dream? But doesn't that really beg the question? We know so little about truth that even what we call fact is just theory waiting to be disproved. It is highly improbable that Abram could see four hundred years into the future, one thousand years into the future, or two thousand years into the future. Nevertheless, the path he chose, as dictated by his adherence to the call of the One God and as reinforced by the promises repeated in this dream, is the reason for what happened four hundred, one thousand, and two thousand years later. The entire history of Abram's people from the moment of this dream to the present was just a matter of putting one foot in front of another. Then, what we *can* say about this dream, which is what Abram knew, and what Nachmanides knew, is that there is an element of truth in it *for us*.

☽

There is yet more to be examined here. Where was Abram when this all took place? Look again at the text. Physically, Abram was somewhere indoors, perhaps in his tent ("God took him outside" [Genesis 15:5]). Mentally, Abram was in doubt, perhaps self-doubt, else why would the vision begin by saying, "Fear not, Abram, I am a shield to you; your reward shall be very great" [15:1]? But the location and the events do not quite jibe. God takes Abram outside to count the stars—but how can Abram see the stars when the sun has not yet set? Is the first part of the vision a daydream? Or has the dream already begun? Are the sunset, the dark dread, and the final dream all parts of some already occurring dream that the Bible has called a "vision"?

Or consider the possibility that the text means just what it says. When God took Abram outside, the day became night in order that God could show Abram the stars. Then the night rewound to evening, so that Abram would have time to prepare the sacrifice, fend off the birds of prey, and, before sunset, a deep sleep could overtake him.

God was known to cause such deep sleeps, we remember. Imagine if we had the dream that Adam dreamed when God caused a deep sleep to fall on Adam in order to create woman. As it is, the Abram narrative provides us with evidence that our ancestors connected deep sleep with dreams of significance, believing that intense dreaming and deep sleep are both gifts from God.

And what of the young bird whose sacrifice was commanded by God but withheld by Abram? Could this be a foreshadowing of the story of the binding of Isaac? This dream narrative begins with the words, *Acher hadevarim ha'aleh*, "Some time afterward ..." [15:1]. The narrative of the binding of Isaac begins by saying, *Va-yehi acher hadevarim ha'aleh*, "And it was some time afterward ..." [22:1]. The language is so close as to be uncanny. The next time that the biblical narrative begins by saying, *Va-yehi acher hadevarim ha'aleh*, "And it was some time afterward ..." [40:1], the story that follows is the story of Joseph interpreting the dreams of the cupbearer and the baker!

When next the narrative begins with these same words [48:1], Jacob is on his deathbed and tells Joseph about a time when God appeared to him in a vision. True, the words are a common idiom—they bring to mind the hackneyed opening, "Once upon a time ...." But it is precisely because they are such a recognizable idiom that they grab our attention. In each of the four instances in Genesis, they precede an extraordinary story—a covenantal moment. In three of the four, they precede a dream narrative. Could it be that in the case of Isaac in chapter 22, these words are used to refer our attention back to the dream of Abram in chapter 15, to let us know that the story of the binding of Isaac was foretold in that dream along with the story of the destiny of the nation as a whole? After all, at the moment of the sacrifice, Isaac is Abraham's only legal heir, actually representing the future of the Hebrew people. If Isaac had been sacrificed atop the mountain, the future of the people would have come to an abrupt end, or at least would have been far different—no Jacob, no twelve tribes, no Joseph, no descent into Egypt, and so on.

In the story of the dream that is before us, the narrative begins by saying, "Some time afterward, the word of the Lord came to Abram in a vision." In the story of the binding of Isaac, the narrative begins, "And it was some time afterward that God put Abraham to the test." Are not the vision and the binding of Isaac both tests of Abraham's faith? In both cases, Abraham is given instructions regarding a sacrifice and, in both cases, the sacrifice is never fully consummated. In both cases, the future of the nation is at stake and, in both cases, Abraham is said to have passed the test. In 15:6, we are told, "And because [Abram] put his trust in the Lord, God reckoned it to him for righteousness." In 22:12, in the story of the binding of Isaac, God says, "For now I know that you fear God ...." And, in both cases, the reward is identical. In 15:5, God says, "'Look toward heaven and count the stars if you are able to count them.' And God adds, 'So shall your offspring be.'" In 22:16, God says, "Because you have done this ... I will bestow My blessing upon you and make your descendants as numerous as the stars of heaven ...." Is it still too far-fetched to connect these two narratives? Both are visions—and both visions foretell the fate of a nation that will time and again face imminent death, only to escape at the last moment by the good grace of God.

In a sense, the New Testament story of Jesus is the story of Isaac in another iteration. Of both Isaac and Jesus it is said that God foretold their births. Jesus is represented as the sacrificial lamb even as Isaac was the intended sacrifice. Jesus carries the wooden cross on his back even as Isaac carries the wood for the sacrifice up the mountain. Jesus is placed on the cross and Isaac on the altar, and both survive—Isaac is spared by being replaced by a ram caught in the thicket, and Jesus is spared through resurrection—

but the effect is similar: In sparing their lives, the futures of their "nations" are assured. The recurrence of similar imagery is hardly coincidental, and this is well attested in the works of both Jewish and Christian theologians. Both stories are deeply spiritual in their inception, both are oracular, foreshadowing the experiences of nations.

$$\text{☽}$$

The belief that dreams can be instrumental in foretelling a nation's future has a long history. Throughout the ancient world, royal courts regularly employed cadres of dream interpreters. Following this tradition, the founder of Islam, Muhammad, made it a practice to begin each morning by asking his followers what they had dreamed the night before so that he might interpret their dreams for any communal significance.[5] And dreams were considered so important in medieval China that "it was obligatory for all officials of higher ranks when entering a walled city to pass the first night in the temple of the city god, in order to receive his instructions in a dream."[6]

In fact, dreams of religious significance could occur to anyone—rank in society was no guarantee of privilege in this regard. And these dreams could be made manifest no matter where the dreamer slept. Still, some sites were considered more sacred than others, set aside for religious purposes. And some of these sacred sites, often mountains or high places, were considered especially suitable for inducing the proper kind of dreaming. The Hebrew language preserves this ancient understanding. No matter where one's journey begins, the act of going to the Land of Israel is described in Hebrew as *aliyah*, "going up." Once in Israel, the act of going to Jerusalem is also described as "going up." And, once in Jerusalem, the act of going to the site of the Holy Temple is still considered *aliyah,* "going up." In the language, as in the culture, the site of the Temple in Jerusalem was and is considered the highest place on earth— this, despite the fact that Jews have always been aware of higher mountains, including Mount Sinai. At least one tradition holds that the binding of Isaac took place on what would later be the Temple Mount—that is, the highest spiritual place on earth. As we shall see, this sense of "the holy mountain" pervades many religious dreams.

We should also take into account the preparation of the dreamer to receive the dream. As we see even in the brief description of Abraham's dream, it is critical that the dreamer be ready. Abraham, like Gilgamesh, must offer his sacrifice first. Both of them literally ask for a vision. These are the parameters of what Artemidorus later called "worrying dreams" or "asked-for dreams." In the technical language of Middle Eastern scholars, they are known as "incubated" dreams. To incubate is "to form or consider slowly and protectively, as if hatching." Incubating a dream was a hallmark of ancient dream technology. To better understand Abraham's dream, and the dreams of the Bible in general, we need to examine how this spiritual technique was used.

)

The technology of dream induction was sometimes as simple as Gilgamesh's asking the mountain for a dream or Abraham's posing a question to God. But it could also be quite elaborate. It begins in the belief that dreams can be "incubated," or deliberately forced to serve our waking selves. Many methods were employed for inducing or "incubating" dreams. Fasting was common. Early and medieval Christians employed flagellation and spent extended periods as hermits to induce dreams and visions. Jewish mystics employed flagellation, fasting, and deep meditation. What these and other methods imply is that our ancestors conceived of a vast difference between "ordinary" dreaming and dreams that were induced. The latter were thought to be of deeper significance, to be answers emanating from a divine source.

No Western civilization embodied the belief in this difference more than the ancient Greeks, who developed an entire "art" of dreaming. The Greeks viewed dreams both as a means to answer their questions and as a means to obtain cures from sickness. The procedures employed at the temple at Epidaurus (dedicated to Asclepius, the god of healing) are instructive. As you enter into this description, imagine yourself as a Greek afflicted with some lingering illness that you wish the gods to cure (but try not to imagine this too vividly, please—imagination, as we have seen, should not be taken lightly). The faithful speak of a visit to Epidaurus as a sacred event, one that almost certainly can evoke a cure.

Like most Muslims making the pilgrimage to Mecca, the Greek pilgrim bound for Epidaurus generally undertook a long journey to reach his sacred site. The nearer the pilgrim came to the temple, the more pilgrims he or she encountered on the same path. Once arrived, the pilgrim would fast or eat very little (certain foods, including wine and meat, were thought to inhibit dreams). A period of abstinence from sexual intercourse was considered a beneficial way to prepare. And the temple had a motto engraved above the entry gate stating, "Purity means to think nothing but holy thoughts."[7] All this was just preparation for the ritual to come.

Near the entry to the temple itself, the pilgrim encountered stone tablets set up as pillars, one after another, each describing miraculous cures that had been effected for previous pilgrims. Once inside the temple grounds, the smell of incense and the incantations of the priests combined to produce a dizzying effect. Should all this not be sufficient inducement for the dream cure, there was the discipline called *Enkoimisis*. This consisted of sleeping in a "forbidden" dormitory, the *abaton*, and was permitted only after the pilgrim had an initial dream in which the god beckoned the pilgrim to enter this inner sanctum. In the *abaton*, the pilgrim bedded down for the night on the skin of a recently-sacrificed animal. Nonpoisonous snakes writhed on the floor all around. The temple priests chanted hypnotic prayers calling for healing dreams, then extinguished the torches. Here was a carefully construed example of "dream incubation."

The ancient Greeks inherited the culture of the Minoans, whose outposts existed throughout the Mediterranean world. It would therefore be difficult to conceive of any serious Greek activity, custom, or tradition that did not have a parallel, a progenitor, or a descendant among the other peoples of the Mediterranean. This is true of the practice of dream incubation as well. Perhaps it was not as developed in its aesthetics, but we find a close parallel (and possible progenitor) in the Gilgamesh epic. (The Egyptians also practiced dream incubation.) Our biblical ancestors would also have encountered techniques of dream incubation through their contacts with Phoenician merchants, who traded not just in alphabets but also in culture-blending between the Greek and Hebrew worlds. Moreover, direct contacts with the Mesopotamians continued through the biblical age. We can safely assume that the methods of dream control and dream incubation discussed by the ancient rabbis were influenced either by the Babylonians or the Greeks.[8] In the meanwhile, our description of the Greek practices of seeking dream-cures leads to some interesting observations.

Stelae (the upright stones or tablets with inscribed or sculptured surfaces, used as monuments or commemorative slabs) found at the Temple of Asclepius at Epidaurus tell the history of forty-three pilgrims. (It was said that there were as many as four hundred temples like the one at Epidaurus, and many stelae have been found at other sites.) In studying the Epidaurus stelae closely, researchers detected an instructive pattern. The earliest tablets tell of miraculous cures that took effect simultaneously with the dreams. Immediately following the dream, the pilgrim's symptoms and diseases disappeared entirely, so that the pilgrim was cured sometimes even upon awakening. Tablets dated from a slightly later period indicate that dreams provided recipes for remedies that took effect as soon as the pilgrims applied the remedies. Tablets from still later periods indicate that the dreams provided remedies that would cure infirmities only over the course of time. Scholars speculate that this decline in the apparent efficacy of the incubated dreams was consistent with a declining faith on the part of the pilgrims.[9]

Scholars also speculate on the close association between the serpents employed in the temple and Asclepius. A few scholars have ventured that the earliest cures sought at these temples may have been cures for sexual dysfunctions, such as impotence.[10] One researcher states, "If this is so, the sacred snake of Asclepius may take on additional symbolic meaning, as it does in psychoanalysis, as the male sex organ, in this case a part of the god."[11]

We should take such explanations with a grain of salt. It is hardly necessary to inject Freudian interpretations into the past. Nor is it healthy to base our interpretations solely on "modern" criteria based on the assumption that modern understandings are more nearly correct. In fact, disregarding this Freudian interpretation leaves us with a much more plausible understanding of the close relationship between the snake and the miraculous cures at the Temple of Asclepius, for the snake is singular in nature in being able to shed its old skin in exchange for a new one—an observation that could hardly escape people who associated more closely with snakes than modern city- dwellers tend to do. And what could be a better metaphor for a miraculous cure?

☽

Are modern psychological explanations for dreams inevitably flawed? Could we use the advances of psychology to gain deeper insights into our spiritual selves? The answers to both these questions are yes and no. Undoubtedly, psychology can offer us many insights into our inner selves and into our adjustment to the modern reality we have created as a society. But being a product of that reality, as we have seen, it suffers from the emphasis it places on the centrality of the individual. In its classic forms, at least, psychology removes the divine from the equation, reframing the spiritual quest as a quest for a healed inner spirit.

In his fascinating book *Man and His Symbols,* Carl G. Jung maintains that primitive folk were better integrated in body and psyche than their modern counterparts. In becoming more "civilized," he says, "we have increasingly divided our consciousness from the deeper instinctive strata of the human psyche." Nevertheless, we have retained our more primitive instincts in our unconscious, "even though they may express themselves only in the form of dream images."[12] In the same volume, Dr. M.-L. von Franz describes "The Process of Individuation," by which an individual's conscious and unconscious can come to terms with one another. His assumption, like Jung's, is that the modern individual stands in need of integration. We are not at peace with ourselves.

In portraying the schism between the conscious and unconscious, Jung and von Franz almost personalize these two aspects of self. It's as if there are two beings in each of us, vying with and contending against one another. Both need to be convinced to make peace: "to know, respect, and accommodate one another."[13] In effect, the psychologists create a new mythology of the inner workings of our minds. To apply this new mythology, we could say that the two parts of Abram's mind play the two parts in the dialogue. The unconscious comes to the fore in the role of God—pointing to the heavens, demanding the sacrifice, speaking of years of slavery to be followed by ultimate freedom, predicting a long life for Abram, and accepting the sacrifice through dreamlike symbols. The only problem with this application is that it requires us to put our faith in Jung and Freud's mythology. In the end, though it seems more rational, it is no more sophisticated than believing that Abram received a divine message.

Inevitably, modern metaphors (Freudian and Jungian interpretations, scientific interpretations, and so on) will continue to influence us. We live and think in the context of our culture. This need not be a disadvantage. In fact, this is the ultimate reason for exploring the texts of ancient dreams. If we *could* understand the dreams of the Bible entirely in their original context, there is a sense in which they would lose any usefulness to us. In the final analysis, we must filter each text through the lens of our modern perceptions to find meanings in them that make sense to us. I attempted to demonstrate this technique above, as I interpreted a part of Abram's vision to relate to the Holocaust, an event that could not form a reference point until the second half of the twentieth century. Such an interpretation serves us by bringing the *text* into our *context*, forcing us to recognize the immediacy of visions and dreams irrespective of their historical setting.

☽

It had been many years since Abraham first heard God's call, "Go forth from your native land and from your father's house to the land that I will show you" [Genesis 12:1]. According to the Bible, Abraham was seventy-five years old when he left Haran. Just after the vision of the flaming torch and the smoking oven in Genesis 15, the barren Sarah gave her maidservant, Hagar, to Abraham to bear him a child. When the child was born, Abraham was eighty-six years old. (Abraham died at the age of one hundred and seventy-five.) It had been a long time since Abraham heard God's promises in Haran, even since he heard God's promises when he arrived in Canaan (see Genesis 13). It had been a long journey, from Haran to Canaan to Egypt and back to Canaan, and still he had no children and none of the Promised Land belonged to him. This, essentially, was Abraham's mental condition when he incubated a dream, searched for an oracle, and sought a sign that he was still on the right path.

It is a moment of transition and transformation for Abraham. In modern terms, we might call it Abraham's midlife crisis. As such, it speaks to us powerfully. It is a moment that most of us encounter on our own spiritual journeys. And the Bible records this moment in a way that allows believers in every age to read their lives into it. We, too, can read ourselves into it. If you are too young to have encountered your midlife crisis, you can learn what to expect and how to cope with it when it comes to you. If you are passing through your midlife crisis, you can empathize with Abram and find solace in the fact that the crisis will pass and you will be stronger for it. If you have passed this point in your life, you can examine yourself to see if you grasped its spiritual meaning. If not, you can still compose the questions according to Abraham's questions and receive the solace that Abraham receives. As long as you are alive, it is not too late to cross this spiritual threshold.

Like Abraham, we sometimes set out on a long path certain that it is the right path, feeling "called" to pursue it. It may be a career you believe you must pursue. It may be a physical destination you believe you must visit. It may be a project that called out to you, demanding your time and effort. It may be a mission you feel you must accomplish to fulfill your purpose. At the moment it became your "calling," it felt sacred to you. When you took the first steps toward its achievement, you had the sense that completing it would prove that you and your life had been a blessing.

Many months—sometimes many years later—with the path still before you and the goal still seemingly distant, you encounter a time of uncertainty and self-doubt. Was this truly the right path? Were you truly "called" to pursue it? Or have you been on a fool's errand? This is the question that preceded Abraham's vision. This is the "great dark dread" that descends as we wonder—as Abraham wondered—if we will fulfill our life's goal. What vision, what sign, what oracle can we expect?

In such a moment of transition, the Bible implies, we may seek answers in dreams. Self-doubt may call forth a glimpse into the future, may become the means to "incubate" a vision or a dream. Moreover, the resultant dream may be more than merely an affirmative or negative answer. It may be that the dream we call forth from ourselves will give us hints of the path that lies ahead for us and for our progeny, just as Abraham's dream gave him hints of the entire future of the Jewish people. In the spiritual quest, the dream comes when the dreamer prepares for it, when the dreamer is open to its message, when the dreamer is ready to receive its answer.

A young scholar approached his master, saying, "I have learned so much. Can I ever expect to hear God's call?"

The master replied, "God is always calling. The real question is, When will you listen?"

Dream Types

ARE ALL DREAMS TRUE?

☽

The prophet who has a dream, let him tell a dream; and he
who has my word, let him speak my word faithfully.
— Jeremiah 23:28

Spiritual leaders, scholars, mystics, therapists and scientists all agree that dreams have had a profound influence on human development. Since long before written records, dreams have informed, enlightened, and inspired. They have helped human beings achieve self-awareness, perhaps even awareness of that which is beyond self. Dreams and visions, whatever their source, refresh our imaginations and awaken our creativity, especially at critical moments—in the passages that mark personal and social transformation. The content of human dreaming, however, seems to have changed very little through the centuries. Allowing for cultural variants, the dreams of Gilgamesh and Abraham are much like our dreams today.

The act of dreaming continues to lead to speculation about the origin of dreams, speculation about the physiology of dreams, speculation about the purposes of dreams, speculation about the meaning of dreams, and so on. It is easy to lose any sense of direction in this forest, even when we consider only our own dreams. In dream recall, our minds often play tricks on us. Vivid dream memories can suddenly fragment and dissolve. What was bright and clear in the moment of awakening becomes dim and murky but a moment later. Like archaeologists deciphering remnants of inscriptions on broken shards of pottery, we often find ourselves struggling to recover bits and pieces of lost visions. Dreams also change in the telling. Ordinary language resists bizarre images. Important details fade as we fumble to find words appropriate to describe them. And, in the end, dreams that astonished us as we experienced them may sound so plain in narrative form that they merely bring a shrug to the shoulders. On the contrary, a dream that seemed simple at first may come to haunt us in waking moments, stubbornly refusing to relinquish a deeper message that we sense but cannot quite grasp.

As modern folk, our first thought is to somehow categorize dreams. We want to separate important dreams from lesser ones. We want to bring some kind of organization to our most imagistic activity. This chapter analyzes past and present systems of categorization that have proved useful and prepares us for the Bible dreams to follow.

☽

In 1977, Rosalind D. Cartwright of the University of Illinois reported that people coping with serious life problems tended to experience richer and more complex dreams than those currently free of emotional stress.[1] This would indicate that our dreams are not *an other world* divorced from our daytime reality, but *another world* in which our daytime reality is reflected through shapes, sounds, and sensations. As one of life's inherent and irrepressible miracles, dreams seek new possibilities *for us*—sometimes providing breakthrough solutions. Dreams inform our waking reality. Cartwright's studies indicate that our dreams correspond closely with our waking state. The Kalahari Bushmen would no doubt agree, adding only that it is silly to think there is some big wall inside of us dividing sleeping moments from waking moments—they would merely say, all of life is a dream.

Some people instinctively resort to inner dream resources. Faced with an important decision, they may say, "Let me sleep on it." Troubled by a vexing problem, they may say, "Let's call it a night. Things will be clearer in the morning." These commonplace sayings may have had their parallels in ancient times. We can imagine a Greek saying, "I must consult the gods on that." Or we can imagine Abraham saying, "I must have God's word to guide me." None of these phrases speaks directly of dreams. All of these phrases are tantamount to the same thing. They imply that dreams and visions deliver messages to us *when we most need the messages*.

Dreams are, thus, a natural resource. If we ever truly appreciated how valuable a resource, Wall Street might trade them and the commodities markets might sell futures in them. Spiritual initiates, however, would find this suggestion somewhat ludicrous. Their inner awareness indicates that, even now, dreams and visions are the *only* things that Wall Street and the commodities markets ever offer to sell.

Unlike other resources, though, dreams are virtually inexhaustible. The more we encounter obstacles to growth and change, the more our dreams respond in suggestive and vivid ways. The more invested we become in a frustrating endeavor, the more insistent our dreams become on awakening us to alternative possibilities. With this in mind, the master's words ring in our ears: "God is always calling. The real question is, When will you listen?"

$$\smile$$

In an informal fashion, we organize our waking moments. Some time is devoted to earning a living. Some time is devoted to pleasure. We devote portions of time to education, exercise, family, friendship. We even set aside some time for maintenance—time spent at doctors' or dentists' offices, beauty parlors or barber shops, nail salons, grocery and clothing stores, and so on. When we need to accomplish some special goal—to learn a new computer program or a new sport—we purposely set more time aside to pay it special attention. We even tend to judge people by the way they spend their time. For example, we may admire people who have become wealthy or famous, but we admire them less or pity them more if we discover that their fame or wealth came at the expense of their families.

In the same way, our dream world includes many categories of experience. Some dreams reveal, some inspire, some inform, some invigorate, and some lead us to new levels of awareness. A bad day may be reflected in disturbing dreams, and anxiety may result in dreams that reflect our attempt to confront, or our inability to confront, difficulties. (Dreams that exhibit such simple relationships to waking reality lead many cognitive psychologists to believe that all dreams emanate entirely from events in our own experience or from images carried in our own psyches.[2] Yet, as we have noted, this does not easily accord with every dream.) Perhaps, we should judge people by their dreams, as we do by the way they spend their waking moments. Of course, before we could do that, we would need to provide a scale of relative values for dreams.

In his book *The Multiplicity of Dreams*, Harry Hunt describes two major streams of belief regarding dream categories. Freud and those who advance the Freudian tradition view dreams as the result of the conflict between the coherent organization we impose on reality and the more primitive, disruptive self that we restrain in our waking hours. Dreams arising from this conflict may either be attempts to reconcile these two aspects of our self through language and thought, or they may be little more than randomly conceived nonsense. Jung and his followers dismiss the idea that our dreams begin in some disruptive inner nature. Instead, Jungian researchers attest to an inner self that is symbolically aware. They claim that dreams arise as this more "imagistic" or "affective" aspect of our nature lays claim to our otherwise rational attention.

Initially, Hunt set out to reconcile these two streams of dream research. His researches took him beyond the patients of Freud and Jung, and beyond the writings of the two masters. He studied dreams from a diversity of sources —ancient literature, the literature of anthropologists, clinical case studies, the research literature of sleep laboratories, published and unpublished dream journals, his own dreams, and the dreams of his friends. He soon realized that certain patterns emerged so often that they could be loosely categorized. Hunt proposed six major categories: (1) *personal-mnemic* dreams, (2) *medical-somatic* dreams, (3) *prophetic* dreams, (4) *archetypal-spiritual* dreams, (5) *nightmares*, and (6) *lucid* dreams.

On the simplest level are *personal-mnemic* dreams. These arise from ordinary, everyday experiences and concerns in our lives. We can usually pinpoint, with a fair degree of certainty, the issues and events to which these dreams relate.

Comparable to these are *medical-somatic* dreams that arise from the dreamer's physiological or bodily condition. These are the dreams that may accompany a sour stomach or a fever. Nevertheless, such dreams may also contain metaphor, as when a person suffering from a sinus infection dreams of behaving in a superior way toward friends—being, as we call it colloquially, "stuck up."

More complex are *prophetic* dreams that, in Hunt's system, present the dreamer with images or portents of the future. These may concern events that will occur over a long course of time, as in the case of a woman with a three-year-old daughter who dreams of playing on the beach with her grandchildren. Or they may concern immediate future events, as in the case of a dream that foretells the imminent assassination of a president or the impending crash of an airliner.

On a similar plane, *archetypal-spiritual* dreams bring the dreamer into relationship with the symbolic, the numinous, and the extraordinary. These dreams are often marked by strong physical sensations. They may involve communicating with spirit guides—plants, human beings, gods or heavenly beings, animals, or even inanimate objects. Or they may involve encountering religious or archetypal symbols. They may even emulate archetypes or spiritual experiences, replacing older symbols with more modern ones. A dreamer may encounter a mandala while replacing a flat tire on his automobile. Likewise, a dream may contain an escalator that connects earth with heaven.

Strong physical and upsetting mental associations also tend to accompany *nightmares*. In a sense, nightmares are the dark counterparts to archetypal-spiritual dreams. In nightmares, we encounter the power of a nature that is not consistently kind. Dragons and demons, whirlpools that threaten to swallow the dreamer, fissures that suddenly open up at the dreamer's feet, the sensation of endlessly falling, whips that lash and chains that bind—these are as much a part of the dream experience as earthquakes and hurricanes, disease, hunger, and slavery are a part of waking reality. Nightmares are not necessarily evil or harmful. Terrifying experiences often force us to open our eyes to the possibility of new realities.

As the last category, Hunt points to *lucid* dreams— dreams in which the dreamer is aware or "awake" during dreaming. In lucid dreaming, the dreamer exercises a degree of control over the dream, its characters, and its events. Many lucid dreamers report learning to fly, describing flying in various ways from gliding to instantaneously transporting from one point to another in the dream landscape. Some lucid dreamers conduct conversations with other dreamers. Some describe directing their dream as if they were directing the action in a motion picture.

A word of caution is in order. Our spiritual quest does not stand to profit by a strict categorization or an ordering of dreams by rank. Nor does Hunt claim that most dreams fit his categories neatly. In waking reality, some folk consider time spent at work as pleasurable, others consider it toil, while still others consider it a mixture of pleasure and toil. In the same way, similar dreams may fit in different categories. The categories must be adjusted in light of the dreamer. Nevertheless, if you have been keeping a dream journal, you may find it enlightening to see how your dreams fit in Hunt's six categories.

A word of celebration is also in order. The message that sings out from Hunt's work is that all of us have all the inner resources we need to experience every category of human dreams in all their rich variety. If we only open ourselves to its myriad possibilities, dreaming can be an empowering experience.

$$\mathbb{D}$$

Having even a tentative list of categories is helpful as we set out to interpret Bible dreams. Abraham's vision in Genesis 15 seems to have elements of several of Hunt's dream types. It is *prophetic* in that it foresees the future of Abraham's nation. In its direct encounter with God, the strong physical reactions it brings about in Abraham, and its distortions of time and space, it might also be *archetypal-spiritual*. It may also be said to be *nightmaric* in some aspects. And, assuming that Abraham deliberately performed some of the actions in the course of the dream, it may also be a *lucid* dream. Though this dream fits in many categories at once, what is most useful about Hunt's categories is that they provide us with a language for speaking about dreams.

Hunt's studies further suggest that, despite the fact that all dream types are always available to us, different types do not occur with equal regularity.[3] Societal standards may have a hand in controlling the frequency of different dream types. In Hunt's words, "in each historical era and phase of culture a shift in relative importance" occurs among these types. It may be, for example, that in our modern view of reality we have shifted away from prophetic dreams, but our predisposition toward lucid dreaming—dreaming in a way that allows individuals greater control—may be enhanced.

Hunt concludes that both the followers of Freud and of Jung have correct theories regarding dreams, depending on the kind of dream being analyzed. Some dreams are most readily interpreted as narrative structures (as Freudians prefer), and others may best be viewed as imagery (as Jungians prefer). Both types, Hunt says, are normative. He maintains: "The dream is an imagistic experience occurring in a creature who structures its ongoing experience in the form of 'stories' to be told and understood."[4] Here we get another glimpse of the richness of dream experiences.

Abraham's dream is cast in narrative form. As we have seen, it employs phrases and words that suggest its connection to other biblical narratives as part of a larger, ongoing story. Since it may have gone through many recensions—first being told orally, then written, then edited innumerable times—it has become, in the course of time, much more than an imagistic experience. It has become an essential element in the narrative story of the patriarch.

As we tell and retell our dreams, they take on more and more of the cultural context in which we live. As we interpret our dreams, the dreams of others, fictional dreams, and historical dreams, we also tend to bring them into our cultural context. When we neglect to look outside our particular culture, our secular predisposition may become stifling. By comparing ancient and modern, literate and

preliterate, secular and spiritual perspectives, we open ourselves to a multitude of possibilities.

☽

With this in mind, we can compare modern dream theories
with their Greek and Roman dream forerunners. Greek historians reported that Posidonius, the Greek Stoic philosopher of the early first century B.C.E., wrote extensively on
many subjects, including dreams. Unfortunately, none of
his works survived. Fortunately, the Roman philosopher
Marcus Tullius Cicero (106–43 B.C.E.) chose to refute Posidonius' theories on dreaming. In doing so, he preserved the
views of Posidonius. This imaginary "dialogue on dreams"
provides us a fascinating glimpse into two different cultural
contexts in the merging worlds of Greece and Rome.

In Posidonius' view (as presented by Cicero), "the air is
full of immortal spirits on which the seal of truth appears as
if it had been imprinted." These are souls recently released
from human form through death. Freed from their mortal
bodies, they are at last able to develop their full potential.
Somehow, Posidonius claimed, these souls are able to converse with the gods while still maintaining their ability to
converse with living human beings through dreams. Posidonius was especially interested in accounting for the phenomenon he observed in which the dying are given special
insight into the future. Cicero reported:

> Posidonius thinks that there are three ways in
> which the gods cause dreams in men: first, because
> the mind foresees the future all by itself; second,
> because the air is full of immortal spirits on which
> the seal of truth appears as if it had been imprinted

on them; third, because the gods themselves talk with those who are asleep.[5]

Cicero objected to this theory on the grounds that not all dreams come true. If the source of dream inspiration is so imbued with "the seal of truth," how then shall we account for this?

Cicero then imagined how Posidonius and the Stoic philosophers might have responded to the problem he raises. They would argue that we do not often remember all the details of our dreams. If we did, they might say, we would see that all dreams are true. Moreover, even when we remember entire dreams, we are often unable to interpret them correctly. If we could, this would also prove that all dreams are true.

Cicero dismissed these claims as irrelevant. Since the gods are defined as loving and caring, he argued, if they had truly chosen dreams as the way of revealing truth to us, they would also have made it possible for us to know the meaning of our dreams.

To this, Cicero imagined the Stoics replying that not all dreams are equal in their value. Most of us have dreams that are nonsensical, incomplete, and even confusing. By contrast, the wise have dreams that are clear, consistent, and meaningful.[6]

Cicero cites the same position in the work of a Roman poet, and responds with a more agreeable position taken by a Greek philosopher:

> [Are] all dreams are true? "Some dreams are true," says Ennius, "but not necessarily all." But what kind of distinction is this, anyway? Which does he consider true, which false? And if the true ones are sent by a god, where do the false ones come from? For if they, too, are divine, what could be more in-

consistent than god? And what is sillier than to vex the minds of men with false, deceitful visions? If true visions are divine, and false ones are human, what kind of arbitrary distinction are you proposing? Does this mean that god makes this, nature that? Should one not rather assume that god made everything—but this, you deny—or nature made everything? But since you deny the former, one must necessarily admit the latter.... When the body is tired, it encourages vague visions of different kinds from residual impressions, as Aristotle says, of things that it did or thought while awake; when those get out of control, strange kinds of dreams result.[7]

Posidonius provided three categories of dreams, but Cicero countered that dreams are too unreliable to be categorized. The words of Ennius, "Some dreams are true, but not necessarily all," are logically inconsistent to Cicero. It makes more sense to concur with Aristotle that dreams are manifestations of the present condition of our bodies. This argument satisfied Cicero's rational stance.

Applying Hunt's categories—and our modern context—to this dialogue, we might say that Cicero concentrated on *personal-mnemic* and *medical-somatic* dreams, while Posidonius was more concerned with *prophetic, archetypal-spiritual, nightmaric,* and *lucid* dreams. The fact that we have dreams of the former types does not deny the fact that we also have dreams of the latter types. In the system proposed by Hunt, both Cicero and Posidonius are correct since they study different dream types.

It is equally important to note that the Roman Cicero was predisposed by his culture—the rational, practical, aggressive nature of the ancient Romans—to follow Aristotle's conclusion that dreams are formed in response to our physical self; while Posidonius spoke for the majority of Greeks—faithful mythmakers and fanciful story lovers—in positing that dreams somehow enter our world from a spiritual source. Both views were extant simultaneously, even as the theories of Jung and Freud are simultaneously available to us today. Hunt's categories allow us to see the truth of both sides of the coin at one and the same time.

We might ask ourselves which view—that of Cicero or that of Posidonius —makes the most sense to us today. You may wish to see which view is most compatible with the kinds of dreams you are recording in your dream journal. But the overarching principle is a recurrent theme: We need not relinquish our belief in science in order to study dreams in a less-than-scientific way.

$$\text{)}$$

A more spiritual study of dreams was undertaken in ancient times by Artemidorus, who lived in the second century C.E.[8] Artemidorus distinguished between two broad types of dreams: "theorematic" and "allegorical." "Theorematic" dreams are self-evident; they require no further elucidation. "Allegorical" dreams, on the other hand, always require interpretation.

After wandering far and wide in search of great dreamers and well-known dream interpreters, Artemidorus concluded that interpretation fails most often because we do not have a complete dream to interpret. He suggested that six questions should be asked of any dreamer before we interpret a dream. These six are listed in Georg Luck's *Arcana Mundi: Magic and the Occult in the Greek and Ro-*

man Worlds: "(1) Is it in accordance with nature? (2) with law? (3) with custom? (4) with art? (5) with the person's reputation and standing? (6) with time?" Luck explains:

> The distinction between "nature" and "law" seems to correspond roughly to the one between "unwritten" and "written" law, while "custom" somehow belongs to both areas. "Art" means the profession of the dreamer, whose "reputation" also plays a certain role in the interpretation. "Time" apparently designates the period in the dreamer's life....[9]

Basically, Artemidorus claims that, if we cannot answer these six questions adequately, we do not yet have enough of the dream to interpret it properly. If we only have the answers to three of the questions, for example, we may need to ask the dreamer for greater detail to answer the remaining questions. We should do this *before* offering any interpretation because it is usually futile, and sometimes dangerous, to interpret a dream with too little information regarding the dreamer. To get a sense of how these questions operate, we can attempt to apply them to Abraham's dream:

(1) Is it in accordance with nature? When Artemidorus asks whether a dream accords with nature, he means with the nature of the person having the dream. It is self-evident that a visionary like Abraham should have a rich and complex dream and, since Abraham has other experiences that closely repeat the message of the dream, the dream is certainly within his nature.

(2) Is it in accordance with law? The "law" here refers to societal norms. In Abraham's times, visions and dreams were common. The Bible reports prophetic dreams and visions occurring to Hebrews, Egyptians, Canaanites, and Mesopotamians. So Abraham was well "within the law";

that is, the dream fit within the established norms of Abraham's society.

(3) Is it in accordance with custom? The dream also makes sense with regard to the "customs" of Abraham's time. Seeking auguries and omens in sacrifices and dreams was standard ritual practice throughout the ancient world. In the vision, Abraham performs a typical divination ritual, veering from it only by not sacrificing the young bird. This seeming omission may require further interpretation, but the dream obviously fits with custom.

(4) Is it in accordance with art? If we were to think of Abraham only as a shepherd or a merchant, this dream would not fit with his "art" or profession. But, the Bible does not portray Abraham in such a simple manner. Though he may live as a merchant and shepherd, his single-minded devotion to God makes him, according to tradition, both the first prophet and the first priest of the Hebrews. His officiation in the dream sacrifices fit with his profession as priest. The vision he receives here also fits with his prophetic art.

(5) Is it in accordance with the person's reputation and standing? Abraham's reputation and standing are closely associated with the dream and its events. He is well known as a person who has been specially blessed by God. He has distinguished himself as a leader even among the kings of Canaan (see, for example, Genesis 14). The dream confers a prophecy that he will be the founder of a great nation. Here, too, we can see that Abraham is "fit" for such a dream.

(6) Is it in accordance with time? Artemidorus' last question finds echoes in the vision. There is a strong correlation between the moment at which Abraham calls forth this dream and the moment at which he needs it. He is

questioning the path that his entire life has taken. We can see that the dream comforts and reassures him at a critical moment.

Having answered all six questions, we have already taken a large step toward an interpretation of Abraham's dream. Artemidorus next turns to the issue of the type of dream we are interpreting. If the six answers make the meaning of the dream self-evident, so that it requires no further interpretation, then we could say the dream is "theorematic." But Abraham's dream contains complex symbols and compound messages. The six questions barely scratch the surface of this dream. Artemidorus would certainly have typed it as "allegorical."

Faced with an allegorical dream, the six criteria only provide a starting point for interpretation. They tell us that we have enough of the dream to interpret it in terms of the dreamer. When Pharaoh tells his dreams to Joseph, Joseph interprets them in a way that makes sense to Pharaoh. If the same dreams had come to a simple farmer living along the Nile, Joseph would not have made a prediction regarding all of Egypt. Artemidorus' questions thus help us to focus on the centrality of the dreamer to any interpretation of a dream.

When you apply Artemidorus' questions to your own dreams or to the dreams of others, you focus your interpretation in the way you might focus a camera. When you forget to focus the camera, you sometimes get a lovely picture of the background, but the subject is entirely blurred. Or you may accidentally set the focus so close that you get a great picture of your thumb at the edge of the lens, but the background and the subject are entirely blurred.

☽

In interpreting your own dreams, you can choose any or all of the above systems and approaches. It matters little whether the categories or questions are ancient or modern. Compare Artemidorus and Rosalind D. Cartwright, for example. Cartwright tells us that people with current life problems and people in transition tend to experience richer and more complex dreams than people free of emotional stress. Artemidorus tells us virtually the same thing when he writes:

> The dreams people have when they worry about some business or other, or when they are moved by some irrational urge or desire, you may consider "worrying dreams." We also call them "asked-for dreams," because one asks a god to send a dream concerning some business at hand.... You must pray to the god about the things that worry you, but the way in which you phrase your request beforehand you must leave to the god or to your soul.[10]

Even the definition of a dream has not changed greatly. Hunt defines a dream as "an imagistic experience occurring in a creature who structures its ongoing experience in the form of 'stories' to be told and understood." Artemidorus defines a dream as "a motion or formation of the soul with many aspects, hinting at good or bad things to come." But he adds:

> Let me tell you that dreams which are not remembered completely cannot be interpreted, no matter whether the dreamer has forgotten the middle or the end. For if you want to make sense of a dream

you must explore the point to which the vision leads: only what is remembered from beginning to end can be interpreted.[11]

In other words, both agree that a dream must be a complete "story"—beginning, middle, and end—before it can be interpreted.

This seems to be a touchstone: A dream is a story. We not only narrate our dreams as complete tales, we even attempt to narrate our entire experience of reality in the same way. As Joseph Campbell taught, each of us is the hero or heroine of the story of our lives—each of us is, according to the title of his seminal work, *The Hero with a Thousand Faces.*

> Throughout the inhabited world, in all times and under every circumstance, the myths of man have flourished; and they have been the living inspiration of whatever else may have appeared out of the activities of the human body and mind. It would not be too much to say that myth is the secret opening through which the inexhaustible energies of the cosmos pour into human cultural manifestation. Religions, philosophies, arts, the social forms of primitive and historic man, prime discoveries in science and technology, the very dreams that blister sleep, boil up from the basic, magic ring of myth.... Freud, Jung, and their followers have demonstrated irrefutably that the logic, the heroes, and the deeds of myth survive into modern times. In the absence of an effective general mythology, each of us has his private, unrecognized, rudimentary, yet secretly potent pantheon of dreams.[12]

☾

The quest continues. We are now a bit more familiar with the abstract territory of our dreams. We are a bit better equipped to determine the kinds of dreams we are experiencing. We are more sophisticated in our techniques to analyze and interpret them. We understand our need to view dreams as stories. But from what source do our dreams emanate? Does extraordinary imagery come from our inner selves? Is it a product of our imagination? Or should we— no matter how rational we are in our ordinary lives—view our dreams as a living connection with a true dimension of the sacred? Here, again, the spiritual enigma rears up like an unruly steed: Who is the creator? Have we created God, or has God created us? The quest continues. There is more evidence to be uncovered in the dreams and visions of the Bible.

The Stairway
to Heaven

THE SAGES INTERPRET
JACOB'S DREAM

)

Can you hear the wind blow, and did you know, your stairway
lies on the whispering wind. — Led Zeppelin[1]

The dreams in the Bible are integral to the biblical narrative just as our dreams are integral to our lives. Dreams enrich our inner selves, bringing us messages of consolation,
helping us past difficult moments, putting us in touch with
our past and our future, and enabling us to overcome our
fears. From biblical times to our own times, the spiritual
path has remained virtually unchanged. In the words of psy-
choanalyst Dr. Erich Fromm, "The dreams of someone living today in New York or in Paris are the same as the
dreams reported from people living some thousand years
ago in Athens or in Jerusalem."[2] It stands to reason that if

the dreams are similar, the concerns and the hopes must also be similar.

Societies, however, differ in their attitudes toward dreams and dream interpretation. We can assume a vast distinction between our ancestors hearing the text, "And Jacob dreamed…," and our hearing Dr. Martin Luther King's stirring text, "I have a dream.…" Both texts may include prophetic statements, both may be inspired narratives, yet the social context inevitably draws forth vastly different expectations.

The visions and dreams included in the Bible were extraordinary in the sense that they held messages not only for the dreamers themselves but also for the entire spiritual community. Placed in written form long after the event, the stories in the Book of Genesis—including the dreams— were first handed down for generations by word of mouth. Other stories must also have survived, even though they were not accepted into the canon. For example, there is an ancient tradition that Abraham's father was a maker of idols, but there is no trace of this in Genesis. This tradition and hundreds like it almost certainly predate the canonization of the Bible, yet they were not included in the final redaction of Genesis. The decisions of what should be included in the Bible seem to have depended on which stories were considered so integral that they could be understood as "God-given."

☽

In this chapter, we pursue the spiritual quest by becoming eyewitnesses as several generations of Jewish teachers interpret Genesis 28:10–22, well known as "Jacob's Ladder."

These teachers were spiritual leaders collectively known as "sages" or "rabbis." Allied with, or inheritors to, a Jewish political and educational movement known as the Pharisees, they originated in the time of the Second Temple and gained prominence in the time of the Hasmoneans (165–63 B.C.E.). Taken as a whole, their teachings and accomplishments were so persuasive that they influenced the subsequent course of Judaism, Christianity, and Islam.

The sages established their first schools and academies in the Holy Land toward the beginning of the Common Era. By contrast, the patriarchs—Abraham, Isaac, and Jacob—are normally dated in the first half of the second millennium before the Common Era. Thus the culture and society of the sages diverged both from that of the Bible and, of course, from our own. Their manner of biblical interpretation is far different from what we might encounter in modern times. Nevertheless, through their studies of legend and law, the sages raised biblical interpretation to an art. They accomplished this by bringing to their work an aesthetic charged with spiritual awareness.

Their discussion on Jacob's dream is found in the vast literature known as *midrash,* or "investigation." Specifically, it is found in the compilation known as *Bereisheet Rabbah* (*Genesis Rabbah*), one of the earliest and largest collections of midrash. In its present form, *Genesis Rabbah* contains nearly one hundred sections, each consisting of chains of freewheeling biblical interpretation. *Genesis Rabbah* reached its final form not later than the sixth century C.E. It may have been called *Rabbah,* which means "Greater," because it was based on an earlier, smaller version compiled in the third century.[3] (Other midrashic books continued to take shape well into the eleventh century.)

The interpretations given by the sages are intensive, in line with their belief that every jot and tittle of the Five Books of Moses was significant. In fact, the phrase "jot and tittle" comes from two Hebrew characters, *yod* and *tet*— one a vowel letter and the other a decorated consonant— implying that every letter and every decoration in the sacred text was infused with meaning. Pharisaic mystics averred that, in the world to come, even the white space between the letters of the text would be interpreted. And, it is essential to note, the sages never took the Bible literally. They considered it "God-given," but man-made.

In interpreting Jacob's dream, the sages were interested in how its meaning might shape the future of the people. They had little regard for the dream's placement within the biblical narrative. And they had little to say about what the dream meant to Jacob. They were intent on creating interpretations for the dream that would be "true" *for them*. For us, the encounter between the Bible's most famous dream and the interpretations placed on it by the sages provides new clues for how the interpretation of dreams may ultimately shape destinies.

$$\smile$$

We know Jacob as the son of Isaac and Rebecca, the twin brother of Esau, and the grandson of Abraham and Sarah. Jacob is considered the Bible's ideal dreamer and has even been called the Bible's ideal man.[4] Jacob's "ladder" dream occurs at a dramatic turning point in his life—the moment at which Jacob leaves home.

The enmity between the twin brothers, Esau and Jacob, is persistent. While they were still in their mother Rebecca's womb, they caused her such agony that she "went to inquire of the Eternal" [Genesis 25:22]. This implies that she posed a question at some holy place, seeking an answer through oracle, by augury, or in a dream. The answer she received indicated that she had two nations in her womb, that the two nations would be "separated; one people would be stronger than the other," and that the older would serve the younger [25:23]. When they were born, Esau emerged first, but Jacob's hand gripped tightly to Esau's heel. The Bible tells us that the name Jacob means, "he [who] grasps the heel" [25:26].

Esau was ruddy and hirsute, with rough hands and rougher habits. The name Esau probably meant "hairy." (He was also known as Edom, a wordplay for "red.") Esau became a hunter, a roamer, a man of action. He displeased his parents when he took two Canaanite women as wives. Despite this, Esau was ever his father's favorite son.

Jacob was gentle and studious—his hands were soft and so, too, his muscles must have been. Jacob was portrayed as a trickster, one who lived by his wits. In contrast to Esau, Jacob stayed close to home. Jacob was ever the apple of his mother's eye.

Thus the scene was set for trouble. The twins were natural-born enemies. The fact that a different parent favored each added the kind of tension we associate with melodrama. And with each twin representing a nation, all the elements were in place for an epic tragedy.

Sometime prior to his dream, Jacob "tricked" Esau into selling him the birthright, the *bechorah*—the entitlement of the older son to the physical belongings of their father, Isaac, including the right to inherit the Promised Land.[5] Just before the dream episode, Jacob (with his mother's help) tricked Isaac into bestowing his blessing on

Jacob, the younger son.[6] According to the ancient Near Eastern custom, the father's blessing, the *berachah,* was reserved for the next leader of the Children of Israel. Once granted, it could not be renounced.

When Esau learned that the blessing had been stolen, he swore to kill Jacob. It was only out of respect for his father that Esau decided to postpone his revenge until after Isaac died.[7] Both Isaac and Rebecca recognized Esau's wrath. Both advised Jacob that he should save his life by fleeing to the ancestral homeland, Haran, where he could also seek a wife.

As Jacob prepared to flee Canaan, he paused at "a certain place," later identified as Bethel. The choice of Bethel as the place hardly seems coincidental. Abraham worshiped twice at Bethel, building an altar there; and we must assume that his grandson knew this. Jacob chose to sleep in this sacred spot, no doubt indicating that he intended to "incubate" a dream. So, just as Abraham had, Jacob would act as a partner to God in seeking his own revelation. Ultimately, the dream repeated for Jacob the promises made earlier to Abraham and Isaac. Like the vision of Abraham in Genesis 15, this dream served both as a confirmation and as the answer to an implied, but unrecorded, question.

Reconstructing Jacob's concerns from the content of the dream is not difficult. Jacob gained his present position through trickery. He secured his worldly fortune through conning Esau into selling his birthright. He secured his position as the next leader of the Hebrews by deceiving Isaac into conferring his blessing. Among another people or in another age, this might have been enough, but not in the biblical world. Though the omen Rebecca received had been positive, the real test had not yet been passed: God

had not yet spoken to Jacob. Would God concur in this tri-
umph of the younger over the older brother?

As often in the Bible, the story is said to serve another
purpose as well. It purports to explain how Bethel got its
name and why Israelites were accustomed to journeying
there to worship God. Yet, as we shall later see, the single
sentence explaining these things reads suspiciously like a
later insertion into the uninterrupted flow of the dream.
For now, we have learned enough of the characters and the
setting to present the dream text, Genesis 28:10–22:[8]

> And Jacob left Beersheba bound for Haran. And he
> encountered *[vay-yifgah]* a certain place *[ba-makom]*;
> and he slept there because the sun had set. Of the
> stones of the place, he took one for his pillow; and
> he rested in that place.
>
> And he dreamed, and there was a staircase
> *[sulam]* implanted on the earth, with its top reach-
> ing heaven, and there were god-like beings *[mala-
> chei-elohim]* ascending and descending on it. And
> there was the Eternal, standing beside him, saying,
> "I am the Eternal, God of your father Abraham and
> God of Isaac. To you and to your children in perpe-
> tuity, I give the land that you are lying on. And your
> descendants shall be like the dust of the earth; and
> you all will spread out westward, eastward, to the
> north, and to the south. Through you and your de-
> scendants, all the nations of the earth shall be
> blessed.
>
> "And I will be with you, to guard you, in every
> journey you take; and I will bring you back to this
> ground, for I will not desert you, until I have done
> for you that which I have spoken to you."

Then Jacob awoke from his sleep *[mi-shnato]*; and he said, "Surely this is the place of the Eternal; and I did not know it!" And he was overawed, and he said, "How awesome this place is! This can be none other than God's house *[beit elohim]*; and this is the gateway of heaven!"

Early that morning, Jacob arose. He took the stone which he had used as a pillow, and set it up as a place-marker, and poured oil on its top [anointing it]. And he named that place, Beth-El, "The House of God," though before the city's name had been Luz.

And Jacob vowed a vow, saying, "If God will be with me, will guard me in this path I walk; [if God] will give me food to eat and clothing to wear, [if] I peacefully return to the house of my ancestor [Abraham]—then the Eternal shall be my God. And this stone which I have placed as a marker shall be God's house *[beit elohim]*; and all that You give me, I will give a tenth to You."

As the dream begins, Jacob is bound for Haran—on his way to leave the Promised Land for the first time in his life. He is leaving a seminomadic existence, bound for a sophisticated city of great renown. Of course, for Jacob, Haran was physically distant, but not psychologically distant. After all, his grandfather, Abraham, once lived there. It does not stretch the imagination to assume that Abraham would have told his grandson stories about "the old country."[9]

What wonders would Abraham have described to his grandson? Rivers crowded with the commerce of trading vessels; vast and fertile floodplains—nothing like that could be seen in Canaan! Great walled cities with populations of thirty, forty, or even fifty thousand souls—nothing like that could be seen in Canaan! Immense palaces, their entrances flanked by colossal statues of human-headed winged bulls—nothing like that could be seen in Canaan! And, certainly, the greatest of all ancient Mesopotamian wonders, the ziggurats—nothing even remotely comparable to them existed in Canaan! Jacob's dream reflects some sort of preparation like this. What he sees in the dream—even what he hears—is an image reminiscent of the Mesopotamian culture and civilization to which he is bound.

In the dream Jacob sees a *sulam*. The Hebrew word *sulam* does not mean "ladder"—despite the familiarity of that translation. It could mean "ramp," but most scholars agree that in this narrative it actually means "staircase." The dream immediately makes more sense when we think of this as a staircase connecting earth to heaven. In fact, we readily recognize this particular staircase as the central feature of the ziggurat.

Ziggurats were the Mesopotamian equivalent of the Egyptian pyramids. Unlike the pyramids that were built to serve as tombs, however, ziggurats were built as platforms for temples. In Mesopotamia, that flat and fertile plain, as in the flat landscape of Egypt, people often sought to create "high places" by constructing man-made mountains. At one Mesopotamian site, excavations have uncovered a progression of temples and ziggurats built one on top of another extending back through history for 3,500 years.

The Egyptian pyramids impress with their form, their mass, and their shape. The Mesopotamian ziggurats were actually platforms whose tops were meant to be reached. Their outstanding feature was a dramatic staircase extending upward from the earth, reaching level after level, to the altar or temple at the top. Reconstructions of the ziggurats and archaeological evidence also lead us to believe that there may have been elaborate gateways at the uppermost landing of each flight of the stairs. These would have added to the majesty of the sacred ceremonies, when a procession of priests climbed the staircase to the last landing. From the last landing, only the highest priest was allowed to ascend to the small temple atop the ziggurat.

Surely, Abraham would have described these marvelous structures—perhaps including the ritual ascensions—to his children and grandchildren. He might also have featured his memories of an actual ziggurat as he related the semisatirical story of the Tower of Babel, explaining how the pride of the builders caused them to erect a ziggurat too high for its own good, and how the people of the earth came to speak in a babble of tongues. Jacob's dream "staircase" is not a mysterious symbol, then. It is the ancestral memory of a ziggurat staircase implanted firmly in the earth with its top reaching toward the heavens.

Just as we might, Jacob pauses to anticipate what lies ahead by dreaming of this staircase—a wonder he has never seen, but one he has imagined all his life. It is as if a person whose grandparents came from New York to Iowa was preparing to make a journey to New York. Among the many things that the grandparents would have described would be the Empire State Building. What dream might the traveler expect on the night before beginning his journey to New York? What sight might the traveler envision while riding toward the city from which his grandparents had come? Yet it is one thing to imagine something while awake and quite another to actually "see" that thing in a dream or in a vision.

This, then, helps us better understand the symbolism of the *sulam,* the staircase, which plays an important part in the dream. What remains is to eavesdrop as the sages interpret the dream.

))

The sages walk along covered colonnades crowded with stalls that offer everything from trinkets and jewelry to food and clothing. Sepphoris is a typical Roman city, laid out on a grand scale in the Galilee of the land then known as Palestine. The disciples of the sages walk beside them, forming small groups that jostle the shoppers as they struggle to stay together along the crowded sidewalk. When the sun reaches its height, the day may become blazingly hot; but in the mornings and evenings, the air is refreshing and cool. The sages are bound for the academy of Rabbi Judah. As head of the Sanhedrin, Judah carried the title *HaNasi*, "the Prince." Known throughout Palestine as the greatest scholar of the time, Rabbi Judah had originally situated his academy in the city of Bet Shearim. Only recently, his physicians had advised him to move his academy and the Sanhedrin to Sepphoris, where the air was more salubrious.

Entering the academy, the sages arrange themselves by a kind of seniority. The most learned sit on benches at the front of the semicircle. Immediately behind them sit the brightest of their students. Behind these are the novices. Everyone is free to speak, but the students rarely enter the discussion, and novices are well-advised to spend their time listening. The Torah portion for this week is *Vay-yetze*, "And he left...." It begins with the story of Jacob's dream. For the sages, the name *Jacob* in the dream is synonymous with the name that Jacob later received, *Israel*; and the name *Israel* is synonymous with the *Children of Israel*, the

Jewish people. The sages, led by Rabbi Judah the Prince and Rabbi Phineas, commence their discourse by quoting the first verse of the dream:[10]

❋ And Jacob left Beersheba bound for Haran.

The sages pose the question: "Why should the Bible bother to mention this fact?" Wasn't it self-evident? Surely, Jacob was not the only one who left Beersheba. So many caravans leave Beersheba!

From the front row, two of the elders recall an answer to the question given by their teachers: "When a righteous man lives in a town, he is its luster, its majesty, and its glory; when he leaves the town, its luster, its majesty, and its glory depart." They compare this to the words of the Book of Ruth regarding Naomi, *She left the place where she was* [Ruth 1:7]: Was Naomi then the only one who left that place? So many caravans left there! The rabbis complete their answer by repeating the lesson, "When a righteous woman lives in a town, she is its luster, its majesty, and its glory; when she leaves the town, its luster, its majesty, and its glory depart."

Another sage points out that there is a difference between the case of Naomi and that of Jacob. In the case of Naomi, she was apparently the only righteous woman in her city. But when Jacob departed, Isaac remained. Does the answer suffice in view of the fact that Isaac is also righteous? The response again comes from a remembered tradition: "The merit of one righteous man cannot be compared to that of two righteous men." Thus, no matter how many righteous people dwell in a particular town, whenever any one righteous person departs, his absence diminishes the town.

To the sages, every sentence, every word, of a narrative is open to interpretation. Have they stretched the meaning of this sentence? Perhaps. But they have seized an opportunity to express two communal values they hold dear. The reputation of cities depends on the righteous folk—male or female— who live in them. And there can never be enough righteous folk in a city. They may even have had in mind the recent movement of the sages themselves from Bet Shearim to Sepphoris.

From the outset, then, we sense their social context at work. As they might explain it: When an individual interprets a dream, the interpretation should be truthful for the dreamer; but when a community interprets a dream, the interpretation must make sense for the community. Their primary concern in interpreting Jacob's dream is what meaning it has for their community.

The next verse is cited:

✳ **And he encountered [*vay-yifgah*] a certain place [*bamakom*]...**

One of the sages comments that, although the word *bamakom* can mean "*to* the place" in the sense of any place, the sages also use this term as one of God's names. God is often referred to as "the Place." Why is this so?

Several explanations are offered. Most of the interpreters agree that God is the Place of the world since the world is wholly contained in God, while God cannot be contained within the world. One of the sages offers a metaphor to clarify the relation of God to the world: "God is like a warrior riding a horse with his robes flowing over the horse's flanks on both sides. The horse is subsidiary to the rider, but the rider is not subsidiary to the horse."

Another rabbi suggests an interpretation for the entire verse. The verb *vay-yifgah* ("to encounter") can be understood here in the sense of "prayer," since prayer is a means to encounter God ("the Place"). This connection of the dream to prayer leads to an aside regarding prayer. The sages apply the dream verse to explain why the Jewish community prays three times daily.

> *The rabbis taught that the custom of praying three times daily arose through the model of the patriarchs. Abraham instituted the morning prayers. In Genesis we read:* And Abraham got up early in the morning to the place where he had stood before the Eternal *[19:27]. According to the sages, "standing" refers to prayer. Isaac instituted the afternoon prayers, as it is written:* And Isaac went out to meditate in the fields toward evening *[25:63]. Here, "meditation" connotes prayer. Jacob instituted the evening prayers, as it is written:* And [Jacob] encountered God.

Turning back to the dream, another sage notes that the verb *vay-yifgah* ("to encounter") can also be understood as "to come up against." So we can interpret **And he encountered *[vay-yifgah]* a certain place *[ba-makom]*...** to mean that Jacob was not yet ready to stop, but when he "came up against" this "certain place," the world stood like a wall before him. Jacob simply could not continue his journey. He had encountered something that literally brought him up short. Can the text tell us what he encountered?

The sage continues: It was the sunset that Jacob encountered! **He slept there because the sun *had* set.** Jacob was surprised by this sunset. It came too soon to be natural;

otherwise it would not be mentioned. The Bible is pointing out that God caused the sun to set prematurely this particular evening in order to create an opportunity to speak with Jacob privately. On this occasion, the sage says, the sun set two hours ahead of its normal time.

But another sage offers a different explanation. He refers to Joseph's dream in Genesis 37:9ff., where the sun and moon bow to Joseph. Here, the sun refers to Jacob, his father, and the moon refers to Rachel, his mother. If Jacob represents the sun in Joseph's dream, it follows that in Jacob's dream Jacob also represents the sun. The verse should then be read, "Jacob slept there, because the sun [Jacob] had set."[11]

In either case, the inference here is that the sun set early on this occasion. So the sages ask, "When did God restore the two hours which Jacob lost when God caused the sun to set prematurely?" And the answer is given, "Upon Jacob's return to the land of Canaan, as it is written: *And the sun rose for him*" [Genesis 32:32].

We can hardly resist interpolating something "modern" in the conversation. Jacob was traveling east. As we travel east, we lose time. In the course of his journey, we can assume that Jacob actually lost time. In essence, this would also explain how Jacob could regain the time he lost when, twenty years later, he returned to Canaan. Whether or not travelers of this period were aware of the time differences occasioned by travel, it is interesting that the sages pick up on this issue of the loss and gain of hours. There is a certain beauty in conceiving of the time as "lost" in making the journey and "regained" in returning.

One of the sages carries this idea a step forward, relying on the poetic sense of "loss and gain," instead of the literal sense of losing and regaining hours. He imagines God saying to Jacob, "You are a token for your children. Like you, when they go down into Egypt I will cause the day to darken prematurely. But on their return the sun of righteousness shall shine upon them prematurely."

This sage has no interest in the time differential from a geographic point of view. His interest is in finding a spiritual truth. He is speaking of what was lost when the community became enslaved and what was gained when the community was subsequently freed from slavery. He may also be making a veiled political point, which would be more recognizable to his colleagues. Whether times were good or bad, the rabbis considered Roman rule to be a new form of slavery. The sage implies that God, too, views Jacob as a cipher for the entire community of Israel—not only the community at the time of Jacob or enslaved in the land of Egypt, but the community suffering at Roman hands at this very moment.

✻ Of the stones of the place, he took one for his pillow...

One of the sages comments: Jacob took twelve stones ("the stones," *plural*) but they became one ("one for his pillow," *singular*). On that occasion, Jacob thought, "God has decreed that twelve tribes shall spring forth. Since neither Abraham nor Isaac has produced them, perhaps I shall. If these twelve stones cleave to one another as one, then I know I will produce the twelve tribes." When the twelve stones became one stone, Jacob knew he was destined to produce the twelve tribes.

Another sage takes up the same theme, interpreting it differently: Jacob took three stones, thinking, "God has communed with Abraham and with Isaac. If these three stones cleave together as one, I will be certain that God will also commune with me." The sages refer to the connection of the dream to prayer, saying that this explanation fits with the central daily prayer of Jews to "the God of Abraham, the God of Isaac, and the God of Jacob."

Another rabbi adds: Since "stones" is plural, it may mean the least number of stones that would cause the word to be plural. Thus Jacob took two stones, thinking, "From Abraham came Ishmael who became a great nation; and from Isaac came Esau who is destined to become a great nation. If these two stones cleave together, I will know that I too am destined to bear a nation."

Which of these is the "true" interpretation of the several stones that became one pillow? The midrash preserves all of these explanations, indicating that all are "true." The rule seems to be that, in the expression of spiritual truths, there is no necessity for a single truth to be the only possibility. The sages felt free to interpret "truth" on a case-by-case basis, leaving alternative "truths" side-by-side to serve the varying needs of their generation and future generations. This fluid approach derives from one of their most beloved principles. As they stated it: "Both these and those are the words of the living God."[12] As we might restate it today: God's world is a world in process. The process would be frozen if we were to accept any final word on any given subject. Every verse of Torah—indeed, every phrase and, as we have noted, every jot or tittle—is an encounter between heaven and earth. Endless messages can be adduced, all of them "true" in some sense.

This is a powerful statement regarding the meaning of truth in the time of the sages. Truth is not an absolute, they postulate, every truth remains open to interpretation. In such a fluid condition, every human situation—waking and dreaming—is dreamlike. The sages believe that the past and the future, the inner and the outer life, all things and their opposites are with us all the time. If they can find two contradictory ways of interpreting the same verse, or even the same incident in a lifetime, they are satisfied that both may be true. Why? Because God is "the living God," always in process. What seems good today may turn out to be evil tomorrow; what seems evil to us may ultimately have a good purpose in God's sight. Since there can be no absolute truth in our lives, all of us live as if in a dream all the time. "Both these and those are the words of the living God."

✺ And he rested in that place. And he dreamed...

One sage remarks, "If you take dreams literally, they have no influence whatever." He explains by telling a story. A man brought his dream to a rabbi. In the dream, the man was told to fetch his father's wealth from Cappadocia. The rabbi asked if the man's father had ever been to Cappadocia. When the man answered, "No," the rabbi said, "In Greek, *Cappadocia* could be separated into two words, 'twenty' and 'boards.' Go and count twenty boards in the flooring of your house and you will find the money." The man said, "There are not twenty boards there." The rabbi said, "Count to the wall and then back again until you reach twenty, and you will find it." The man returned home, followed the rabbi's advice, and found the treasure. Of course, if the man had taken his dream literally, he would have traveled to Cappadocia in vain.

Another sage observes, "No dream is without its interpretation." He immediately offers a well-articulated interpretation of Jacob's entire dream:

And there was a staircase *[sulam]* symbolizes the stairs in the Holy Temple that led up to the altar. **Implanted on the earth** refers to the altar itself, as it says, *An altar of earth you shall make for Me* [Exodus 20:21]. **With its top reaching heaven** refers to the sacrifices, their aroma rising to heaven. **And there were god-like beings** *[malachei-elohim]* refers to the High Priests. **Ascending and descending on it**—and the priests were going up and down the stairs. **And there was the Eternal, standing beside him** just as it is written, *I saw the Eternal standing beside the altar* [Amos 9:1].

The sages reply: We can also interpret the dream to refer to Mount Sinai, thus:

And he dreamed, and there was a staircase *[sulam]* symbolizes the Mountain of Sinai. **Implanted on the earth,** for the Children of Israel stood on the earth at the base of that mountain. **With its top reaching heaven,** as it is written, *And the mountain burned with fire unto the heart of heaven* [Deuteronomy 4:11]. **And there were god-like beings** *[malachei-elohim]* refers to Moses and Aaron. **Ascending**—*And Moses went up to God* [Exodus 19:3]. **And descending**—*And Moses went down from the mountain* [Exodus 19:14]. **And there was the Eternal, standing beside him**—*And the Eternal came down upon Mount Sinai* [Exodus 19:20].

This gives rise to a disagreement between two sages. One rabbi holds that the angels were **ascending and descending** *on it* [meaning, "on the staircase"], while the other claims that the angels were **ascending and descending** *on him* [meaning, "on Jacob"]. The Hebrew for both readings is identical. It is easy to understand the first explanation ("on the staircase"). The second must be understood metaphorically: To say that the angels were ascending and descending on Jacob means that some were praising him, while others were degrading him, leaping on him, maligning him. But why would some of the angels degrade Jacob when God has said, *Israel [Jacob] in whom I will be glorified* [Isaiah 49:3]? It is precisely for this reason! In heaven, these angels heard it said that Jacob's features were "engraved on high," yet when they went down to earth, they found him sleeping. They were rueful that a person glorified by God should sleep as if unaware of the glory bestowed on him by God. So these angels disparaged Jacob.

The sage may be driving home a political point here. The angels rebuke the Children of Israel (symbolized by Jacob) because they "sleep" when they should be rousing themselves to action. They allow the Romans to rule over them. If only they were aware of the glory that is already "engraved on high" (ordained for them by God), they would awake and throw off the Roman yoke! It is entirely possible that his interpretation was nowhere near as subtle as it seems to us today. It may have been immediately understood by all present.

The mention of angels occasions an aside regarding guardian angels. One of the sages teaches that inside the Holy Land, a person is escorted by two angels. But when a person leaves the Holy Land, those angels do not leave.

Thus **ascending** refers to the angels who had always escorted Jacob in the Holy Land and were now ascending to heaven [to wait until he returned to the Holy Land], while **descending** refers to the angels who came down to escort Jacob on his journey outside the Holy Land.

Returning to the dream, another sage offers a different interpretation. Jacob's dream, he says, could refer to the Exile, when the Babylonians forced the Jews to leave the Holy Land.

And Jacob left, just as the Children of Israel would be forced to leave the Holy Land. **Bound for Haran**, just as the Children of Israel would be afflicted in Babylon. **Because the sun had set**, since the glory of Israel had been lost. **Of the stones of the place, he took**—for the stones of the Holy Temple were rubble in the streets. **And he rested in that place**—*Let us lie down in our shame, and let our confusion cover us* [Jeremiah 3:25]. **And he dreamed**, which hints at Nebuchadnezzar's dream of the four great powers that represent Israel's four exiles. **And there was a staircase [sulam],** no doubt the same symbol Nebuchadnezzar saw. [*Semel*, the Hebrew for "symbol," is used here as a wordplay on the word *sulam*. In Hebrew, the last two letters of *sulam* are transposed to form *semel*. So the sage transforms the "staircase" into the "symbol" seen by Nebuchadnezzar.] **And there was the Eternal, standing beside him**, standing beside Daniel, as it is written, *Servants of God Most High, come forth and draw near* [Daniel 3:26].

Speaking of the Babylonian Exile, one of the other sages recalls a legend from those years. It is a legend of Daniel, especially appropriate since Daniel was one of the great dream interpreters of the Bible. The sage interprets a part of Jacob's dream to refer to this legend:

And there were god-like beings *[malachei-elohim]* refers to Daniel. **Ascending and descending on it** [on the
Dragon]. For Nebuchadnezzar had a great dragon, which
swallowed up everything thrown to it. Nebuchadnezzar
bragged to Daniel, "How awesome is the dragon's might! It
swallows up everything!" Daniel replied, "Give me permis-
sion and I will make the dragon weak." Nebuchadnezzar
agreed, and what did Daniel do? He took hay and hid nails
in it and threw it to the dragon. The dragon ate it and it lac-
erated the dragon's bowels. That is the meaning of the
verse, *And I will bring out of his mouth all that he has swallowed up* [Jeremiah 51:44]. **And there was the Eternal,
standing beside him**—as it is written, *O Daniel, servant of
the living God* [Daniel 6:21].

> *It is left to the reader to interpret this parable. Daniel
> seems to represent the Children of Israel who were
> "swallowed up" by Nebuchadnezzar, just as he
> swallowed up many other peoples. Nebuchadnez-
> zar could brag that the dragon (which stands for As-
> syria) could swallow up anything it chose, but
> Daniel shows that the dragon's strength is also its
> weakness. In the end, the tenacity of the Israelites'
> spirit was as sharp as the nails in the hay. The im-
> plication is that God used the Assyrian exile of the
> Jews to bring Nebuchadnezzar's empire to its knees,
> destroying it from within.*
>
> *Of course, the Exile and the Daniel story come
> long after the time of Jacob, so the interpretation as-
> sumes that Jacob's dream was prophetic for the
> community. This is also true when the sages read
> the Holy Temple or Sinai into the dream's interpre-
> tation. Here, again, the sages assert their spiritual
> prerogative: Time and space are entirely irrelevant*

when our interest is in spiritual truth. Many true interpretations are possible. The onion does not cease to be an onion just because its first layer is peeled away, nor does it cease to be an onion as successive layers are removed—every layer of an onion is still onion. Similarly, every interpretation of the dream leaves the dream essentially unchanged.

✸ And there was the Eternal, standing beside him...

The sages explore an anomaly. "Standing beside him" assumes that Jacob was standing, yet we know that Jacob was lying down, sleeping. How is this possible? Rabbi Jose ben Zimra quotes, *My soul thirsts for You, my flesh longs* [literally, "stands"] *for You, in a dry and weary land, where no water is* [Psalms 63:2]. One sage says this can be compared with mushrooms that "stand up" or "long" for the rain. So, too, Jacob stands up for and longs for the Eternal.

Another sage offers a variant reading: **beside him** could be read as "on him" or "on it." The sages disagree on how the text would make sense if either of these changes were incorporated. One claims that "on it" would mean that God stood on the staircase. Another maintains that "on him" would mean that God stood "on" Jacob. There is no difficulty in understanding how God could stand on the staircase; but "on Jacob" must again be understood as a metaphor: perhaps God stood "over" Jacob, in the sense of protecting him.

The idea of "standing over" reminds one sage of a homiletic lesson. He teaches, "The wicked stand over their gods [to protect them], as it says, *And Pharaoh dreamed, and behold, he stood over the river* [Genesis 41:1][13]; but this verse teaches us that the God of the righteous stands over the righteous [to protect them]."

Another sage returns to the dream, saying, "Why mince words? God stood *on* Jacob. After all, the patriarchs are the Chariot of God on earth, spreading God's teachings far and wide." In the sense that God depends on the patriarchs to spread God's truth, God could literally be said to stand "on" them.

This sage asks the assembly to admit their prejudice: The truth of God is represented on earth by those who represent God (namely, by the Pharisaic sages themselves). He finds this truth in the very same verse that demonstrated how God protects those who represent God on earth. In this way, "truth" is extended at one and the same time in more than one direction. And the sages, as a community, are reminded of the holiness of their role as spiritual educators.

❋ **To you and to your children in perpetuity, I give the land that you are lying on.**

One sage remembers a tradition that God folded up the entire Land of Israel as one might fold a journal and put it under Jacob's head, as if to say, "Whatever you are lying on belongs to you." Another sage says, "No, it goes deeper than that. My teacher used to interpret this verse to mean that God placed a condition on Jacob's inheriting the land: Jacob would inherit the Promised Land, 'provided you [Jacob] are buried here.' That is what God meant by **the land that you are lying on.**"

It is expected that the listeners will recall another, later story from Genesis. Finding himself in Egypt at the end of his life, Jacob asked his son Joseph to promise to carry Jacob's corpse back to the Prom-

ised Land and to bury him there. Again, the sages use their interpretation to bring a political message to their generation: Just as the Holy Land belongs to the Jews, the Jews belong to the Holy Land, even in death. This, it is said, is the "condition" under which the land was inherited. They read this truth from the end of Jacob's life into this dream that occurs at the beginning of it.

✼ **And your descendants shall be like the dust of the earth...**

The sages ponder this comparison. How can God's Chosen People be like dust? Three interpretations are offered:

As the dust of the earth can be blessed only through water, so will the Children of Israel be blessed only for the sake of the Torah—the study of which slakes the thirst for knowledge.

As the dust of the earth wears out all utensils even of metal, yet itself remains forever, so will the Children of Israel outlive all other nations and exist forever.

As the dust of the earth is trodden upon, so will the Children of Israel be downtrodden beneath the powerful. They will be downtrodden; nevertheless, even this will be to their benefit, for their sufferings will purify them of guilt.

The sages merely set the three interpretations side by side. They feel no need to determine which of these is the "true" interpretation. All three bear marks of spiritual truth. Other interpretations could as easily be drawn out of the verse, and they too would be "true."

✼ **And I will be with you, to guard you, in every journey you take; and I will bring you back to this ground, for I**

**will not desert you, until I have done for you that which I
have spoken to you.**

The sages comment: God fulfilled Jacob's wishes—all but
one—even before Jacob expressed them. Jacob later prayed,
If God will be with me...; but God had already assured him
by stating, **And I will be with you.** Jacob later prayed, **[If
God] will guard me**; but God had already assured him by
saying, **With you, to guard you.** Jacob later prayed, **...In
this path I walk**; but God had already assured him by saying, **In every journey you take.** Jacob later prayed, **[If] I
peacefully return to the house of my ancestor [Abra-
ham]**; but God had already assured him by saying, **And I
will bring you back.** The majority of the sages agree, however, that God had provided no assurance in advance in regard to Jacob's request for food and clothing.

One sage disagrees. He says, "God even answered this
request. Behold, God said, **I will not desert you,** as it is
written, *Yet I have not seen the righteous deserted, nor his
offspring begging bread* [Psalms 38:25]."

> *This sage quotes a proof text from the Scriptures.
> The proof is drawn from the Book of Psalms which
> was composed much later than Genesis. In Psalms,
> the verse in no way refers to Jacob's dream. In the
> world of the sages, this is not considered incongru-
> ous. The sages accept spiritual truth contained in
> any proof text that fulfills the test of eloquence, so
> long as it comes from the Bible. As far as they are
> concerned, "There is no chronological order in the
> Bible."[14]*

✻ **Then Jacob awoke from his sleep [mi-shnato]...**

One of the elder sages interprets this verse by observing,
"The word *mishnato* can also mean 'his *mishnah*' or 'his

studies.' In other words, Jacob arose from his dream—his studies."

> *Tying together the words for "study" and "sleep," this sage points to another dimension of Pharisaic interpretation. A dream is like a text one studies—it must be explored, rehearsed, and plumbed for its message. Actually, the word* mishnato *cannot carry both meanings in this verse. In the dream, the word clearly means "from his sleep," where the prefatory, mi-, is a prefix meaning "from." It is an elegant play on words, however, since when we remove the entire word from the dream it means exactly what the sage says: "his studies." And the sage neatly calls Jacob's dream "his studies." He is saying that if the community of Israel wishes to awaken from its sleep, it may do so only through study.*

✻ **And he was overawed, and he said, "How awesome this place is!"**

The sages pose a question: In what way was this particular place *awesome*? They remember that, according to an old tradition, Jacob's staircase stood in Beersheba (south of Jerusalem), yet its center was over the Temple (in Jerusalem). They add: It is for this reason that the story begins, **And Jacob left Beersheba...** (where the staircase had its foundation).

One sage takes up this theme, amending it: "The staircase stood on the Temple site (in Jerusalem), while its head was over Beth-El (north of Jerusalem). How do we know this? It states, **'How awesome this place is!'**—*this place* could only refer to Beth-El [the 'place' where Jacob dreamed his dream]."

Of course, it is impossible to take either of these interpretations literally. The point here is not how large the staircase was. The staircase connects things symbolically—Beersheba (where the patriarchs lived and Jacob's journey began) with the Temple (the center of the world); the Temple (the center of the world) with Beth-El (the place where Jacob encountered God). But how could the second be "true" in a spiritual sense. Haven't we already learned that the Temple is the highest point in the spiritual geography of the Bible? How could the staircase extend from the Temple at the bottom to Beth-El at the top, if the Temple is higher (more sacred) than Beth-El?

Perhaps, the second sage is making spiritual sense, speaking about where God may be found. Normally, according to the Bible, the Temple was God's dwelling on earth. This is the place where the Children of Israel would find God in worship. But any high place may become more sacred if God chooses to appear to an individual there. Thus, Mount Sinai was a higher place than the Temple Mount in the moment Moses encountered the burning bush. And Beth-El was a higher place than the Temple Mount in the moment when Jacob encountered God in his dream. The sage infers that Jacob expressed this truth by saying, "Surely this is the place of the Eternal; and I did not know it!"

❋ **"This can be none other than God's house *[beit elohim]*; and this is the gateway of heaven!"**

One sage observes: "Here God assured Jacob that this was so, moreover, that the gateway would be opened for many righteous men like Jacob." Another interpretation is also offered:

This teaches that God showed Jacob the Temple built, destroyed, and rebuilt again. Jacob said, **How awesome this place**—this refers to the First Temple. **This can be none other**—the negative word hints at the destruction of the First Temple. **God's house** *[beit elohim]***; and ... the gateway of heaven!**—refers to the Second Temple, rebuilt, and then firmly established in the time of the Messiah.

✳ And Jacob vowed a vow, saying...

The sages focus on a redundant word in the verse. It would be enough to state, **And Jacob vowed a vow.** Why does the text add, **saying**? Perhaps, Jacob was **saying** to future generations that they too should vow in times of distress. In the Bible, Jacob was the first to utter a vow; therefore when anyone vows, the vow should refer to Jacob. One sage offers a biblical proof text: *How he swore to the Eternal, and vowed to the Mighty One of Jacob* [Psalms 132:2]. It does not say, "the Mighty One of Abraham or Isaac," but *the Mighty One of Jacob.*

Another sage proposes a more subtle difficulty. Perhaps the story is not presented in the proper order. Doesn't Jacob's vow belong *before* God's promises. The story would seem more logical if Jacob said, **If God will be with me...,** before God said, **And, behold, I will be with you....**

Another sage disagrees, claiming that the text is in proper order. Jacob's vow must be read as conditional. God is with Jacob *now*, but what if Jacob should later sin? Would God forsake him? So the meaning is, "If God fulfilled all the conditions which God set forth, then Jacob would fulfill his vow."

As moderns we may wonder, Doesn't that make Jacob's vow rather self-serving? Isn't Jacob laying down the rules here—forcing God's hand? That seems oddly out of place for one of the patriarchs. On the other hand, the Bible never commands blind faith. Abraham argued with God. Jacob tricked Isaac into giving him God's blessing. These are not the acts of people with blind faith. This is a knotty problem—surely the sages will not let it go unanswered. In fact, although the question is never posed in a direct way, one of the sages provides an indirect answer in his interpretation of the next verse.

✳ If God will be with me, and will keep me in this path...

The sage says, **in this path** means "away from slander." How do we know this? The word "bend" in Hebrew shares the same root (*drk*) as the word "path." And in Jeremiah, we find the word "bend" referring to slander in the verse, *And they bend their tongue, their bow of falsehood* [9:2]. What Jacob means by **in this path** is, if God will protect him from the sin of engaging in slander.

Further, Jacob says, **[if God] will give me food to eat...** and that implies protection from the sin of adultery. How so? In Genesis, we find the verses, *Neither has God kept back any thing from me..., save the bread...* [39:9; 39:6]. This is a delicate way of saying that God would not withhold any woman from Jacob, even a married woman. But Jacob seeks protection from this mortal sin.

Further, Jacob says, **[if] I peacefully return to the house of my ancestor...** and that implies protection from bloodshed, for it is Jacob's own brother, Esau, who would bar him from returning peacefully home, by shedding his blood.

Further, Jacob says, **then the Eternal shall be my God...** and that implies protection from idolatry.

The sages agree that the words "in this **way**" can be taken to mean protection from all of these—slander, adultery, bloodshed, and idolatry.

> *The community must choose a path. In Jacob's dream, the sages say, the path is God's "way." As long as people in the community walk in God's way, avoiding slander, adultery, bloodshed, and idolatry, God will protect them from these sins. In fact, the sages had a formula that expressed precisely this teaching: "Do God's will as if it were your will; thus, God will do your will as God's will."*[15]

))

The sages have presented us with abundant interpretations of the stairway dream. They have given us insights into their beliefs and their politics. They have used their interpretations to teach spiritual values. Above all else, and despite all their peregrinations, they reserved their interpretations of the dream to truths that made sense *for them*.

We have witnessed a style of interpretation that sounds strange to our modern ears. Even with the italicized commentary I added, you may have found it somewhat confusing to follow the sages' train of thought. In the coming chapters, we will witness still other styles of dream interpretation. Each of them opens us to new possibilities for interpreting our own dreams.

Return to the metaphor of the forest. The forest is hardly a logical environment. Still, the more we wander—the more we turn aside to examine anything interesting—the more we sense a possible mastery of this magic environment. Like the sages, we need to keep turning and re-turning this dream, looking for new truths in it, until the dream finally speaks to our existence, to our time, *to us*.

Paths of Interpretation

THE ART OF SEEKING MEANING

☽

I sleep, but my heart is awake... — Song of Songs, 5:2

Every dream is a kind of small miracle because, no matter how we interpret it, its interpretation *always* adds meaning to our lives. "The dream is a story you were telling yourself while asleep," says Rosalind D. Cartwright.[1] Dreams are the subtexts of our stories, our personal proscenium arch—the theater of our inner lives. We are the heroes and heroines in our dream stories, just as we are of our waking stories. Even as we interpret dreams in our waking state, our dreams interpret our waking state as we sleep.

This is not to conjecture that you live two lives. You are the same person, the same psyche, the same spirit, the same soul—say it any way you please—both waking and dreaming. In a visceral sense, without undue awareness, you treat your waking life as a dream and interpret it, too.

Almost all of us do this, for example, when we remember the loved ones we have lost. Looking back, we might ask ourselves, "How would they best like to be remembered?" Or, "What value did they place at the center of their lives?" Or, "What did they teach us by the way they lived?" What we are really asking is, "How shall we interpret the meaning of their lives *for us*?"

And we constantly ask ourselves, "What is the meaning of this life of mine?" Of course, it is always possible to assign our lives meanings from an assortment of widely available selections. Broadly speaking, every religion offers values and symbols on a ready-to-wear basis. You can shop around. What are some of the available selections? Suffering, accepting your destiny, love, helping others, waiting for a messiah, blind obedience, submission, sacrifice, waiting for another life, living for today as if there were no tomorrow, and so on.

Or choose from meanings readily available in fields other than religion: Politics infers that meaning is found in the exercise of power. Economics infers that meaning is in the accumulation and distribution of wealth. Mystics find meaning in enlightenment, in losing this life—which is to say, this ego or persona—and merging with some higher consciousness or being. Science avers that the question of meaning is meaningless—we happen by chance and through natural selection, our lives are shaped by genetics and environment, our fates are governed by actuarial tables and by the laws of statistics. And the list of endeavors is endless. Meanings are conferred by the creative arts, by the theater, by psychology, by families, even by social status.

Please do not mistake these snippets of description for sarcasm. I am perfectly aware that they are only characterizations. No choice I have listed is without merit. Every faith, every science, every endeavor offers a complex set of values and symbols. All of them bring a certain eloquence and aesthetic to the lives of those who pursue them. And all of them provide meanings for the lives of their adherents. The point I wish to make is simply that the person who puts complete faith in any *one* of them tends to lose perspective.

To accept any meaning as the single, incontrovertible truth is to lose sight of the vast range of our personal potential. Contemporary spiritual seekers are rediscovering the importance not of meaning but of *the search for meaning*. It is the process of seeking meaning that seems to have the power to bring peace and healing to our inner and outer selves. The dreams we experience by night, the visions we experience by day, the myths we create with our lives— these are present for everyone, but not everyone becomes present for them.

Open yourself to the possibility that dreams may not be self-induced hallucinations and you become a spiritual seeker. Open yourself to the possibility that you are creating a meaning with your life and you become a spiritual being. You can ask ultimate questions. "How will my loved ones remember me?" "What sign or symbol can I leave behind that will strengthen their covenant with life?" In turn, these questions open you to seeking meanings in yourself: "What are the values and symbols I live by?" And, "Are these the values and symbols I want to live by?"

☽

To use interpretation to seek meaning, we require an appropriate context. None of the available choices—such as loss of self, submission, acceptance, suffering, or love—is an absolutely "appropriate context." This is not surprising. Any context is like a camera lens. It "sees," but only according to its particular design. A zoom lens is excellent for viewing what is normally distant. A wide-range lens brings us more perspective and less detail. A macro lens brings the microscopic world into view. Still, no single camera lens is absolutely appropriate for all purposes. To view things in new ways, we must continually change conceptual lenses. Each time we do, we encounter a dream, a story, a text, or a life in a new context.

We generally begin with our normal lens. It is shaped and polished by the hopes, aspirations, imaginations, fears, terrors, and joys of our "real" world. There is nothing wrong with this lens. In fact, it's a wonderful gift. Though modern culture stresses secular thinking, it leaves room for that which is unresolved. Our preference for rational thought has hardly diminished our capacity for abstract emotions, symbols, and values. Using our normal lens, most dreams can be interpreted in a way that makes sense to us.

We can, however, enrich our interpretations by accessing a myriad of "foreign" lenses. There are two distinct techniques for doing this. One technique of accessing other lenses is by attempting to *apply* them—this is analogous to taking a photograph through a new lens. Another way of accessing them is by studying outstanding *examples* of dream interpretation—this is analogous to studying a photograph taken by someone else.

When we apply a new lens, we utilize dream theories set forth by individuals or groups in cultures other than our own. For example, we could study the dialogue between Cicero and Posidonius, then ask how a particular dream might have been interpreted by each of them. In fact, earlier, when we applied the questions of Artemidorus and the categories of Hunt to Abraham's dream vision, we were doing just this.

The process of applying a lens often frees us of enough of our normal presuppositions to make the new interpretations interesting and challenging. Still, when we use the application technique, what we are really doing is making intelligent guesses.

From time to time, we are lucky enough to encounter a dream that has a record of interpretation. Looking back at a "photograph" of a dream taken in another place or time, we can witness a dream interpretation almost entirely in a system other than our own. Jacob's staircase dream has been interpreted in many different cultural contexts. In turning to the sages, we abandoned our modern context to learn a new one by example. Learning by example requires less guesswork using the application technique. And there is much more likelihood that what we encounter will be different from anything we could easily imagine.

When we examine an interpretation by example, we "go with the flow," so to speak. We are forced to allow the example to speak to us. This may be bewildering at first, particularly since we cannot truly escape our normal ways of thinking even as we examine the example.

☽

No matter how we approach interpretation—through our normal lens, by application, or by example—it is difficult, almost impossible, for us to set aside our critical faculties. For this reason, I did not ask you to suspend your disbelief as you entered the forest to begin your spiritual seeking. Here are my exact words:

Playwrights often call for a suspension of disbelief in order to allow their dramas to unfold. Certainly, the temptation is great for me to call on you to use your imagination in order to allow the drama of biblical dreams and visions to unfold. Yet I urge you to enter this spiritual path otherwise. Do not set aside your skepticism. Envision yourself instead as a wanderer in the woods.

In fact, you could not *possibly* set aside your critical faculty (your "disbelief," your "skepticism," your "scientific point of view," your "egocentric beliefs"). So, instead, I asked that you attempt to be both critical *and* accepting. This is possible for all of us.

In our everyday experience, we are used to what we call "mixed emotions." We can be happy and sad at the same time—just ask the mother of the bride. We can be distant and close at the same time—just ask the absentminded professor. We can love and hate at the same time—just ask the betrayed lover.

When we ask a dream to open up for us, we must also learn to be both critical and naïve at one and the same time. This is what the philosopher Paul Ricoeur proposed in his book *The Symbolism of Evil*. Ricoeur believes that we lose something very precious if we only cling to the immediacy of what we believe to be true. We may not be able to experience again the actual dream, or even to recover the meaning that it originally had for the dreamer. Nevertheless, he argues,

> …if we can no longer live the great symbolisms of the sacred in accordance with the original belief in them, we can, we modern men, aim at a second naïveté in and through criticism. In short, it is by *interpreting* that we can *hear* again.[2]

He is issuing a provocative challenge and pointing to a fascinating opportunity. If we can invoke "a second naïveté," then through interpretation we can truly hope to "hear again" the great symbolisms of the sacred. Since philosophers choose their words carefully, it is important to pay special attention to Ricoeur's language. He speaks of "hearing again," not of "seeing again" or "revisiting." This distinction will become clearer to us as we proceed.

By presenting the example of the sages' interpretation in the last chapter, I tried to ease you into Ricoeur's approach. I set a scene, allowing your critical faculties to center on a concrete time and place. But I noted that the "discussion" actually took place only in an abstract sense, over the course of centuries. I simplified the interpretation of the sages, but I tried to leave it confusing enough to force you to approach it with what Ricoeur calls, "a second naïveté." At the same time, I added "commentary" (the sections entirely in italics) to make things more concrete, allowing you to continue to use your critical faculties. In this way, I hoped that you would be able to "hear again" the sages and their sacred symbolism. For me, this was a delicate balancing act. It is up to you to judge whether it was successful.

☽

We had two purposes in examining the sages' discourse on Jacob's dream: (1) It is an example of dream interpretation in a context entirely outside our own. (2) It is a demonstration of how dream interpretation was approached through the course of many centuries. In fact, the sages applied the same interpretive skills not only to dreams but also to the entire Bible, to the life of their community, and to events in their private lives. Actually, they developed more tools for interpretation than we find in this particular text. Still, we can begin to apply their technique by looking at those tools we have discovered by example.

Over and again, the sages manipulate the *language* of the dream in order to uncover new meanings in it. Sometimes words have more than one definition. Whenever this is the case, the sages suggest a new reading. For instance, to interpret the verse, *And there was the Eternal, standing beside him...*, one sage offers an alternative reading, saying "beside him" could be read as "on him" or "on it." The sages then consider the possibilities that are presented when the text is read in this new way.

Likewise, they feel free to investigate the relative placement of the words. Notice how one sage claims that Jacob's vow should come before God's promises, even though the dream placed Jacob's vow afterward. This juggling of placement also leads to new possibilities for interpretation.

We stand in awe as we watch the sages wend through the story of the dream. They are playing with the text. We cannot help but admire the way in which highly educated people "play." Their interpretation is a massive release of imaginative thinking. Even its arrangement is playful. The sages seem to use free association (the ultimate form of playfulness) with the closing word or idea of one piece of interpretation leading to an altogether new place. For example, the mention of prayer in the interpretation of a verse leads one sage to combine this verse with others to explain why the community prays three times daily. The mention of the Exile in Assyria leads to the tale of the dragon that represented Assyria. In the same way, one question leads to another question; one answer leads to another answer; one discourse gives rise to another.

The sages exhibit a remarkable ability to extrapolate new metaphors from the metaphors of the dream. Take, for instance, the verse "Of the stones of the place, he took one for his pillow...." Once one of the sages notices the transition from the plural, "stones," to the singular, "one," other sages take up this metaphor to find new metaphors. The stones are taken to represent the twelve tribes, then the three patriarchs, then the twin brothers and their nations. Each metaphor gives rise to its own interpretation. Even more elaborate, the entire dream is interpreted as a metaphor for the Holy Temple, then for Mount Sinai, then for the Babylonian Exile, and so on. It is only if we hold the preconceived notion that a dream is a metaphor with a single meaning to be unraveled that we find only one meaning. The sages begin by believing that a dream is a metaphor with many meanings, so they find many metaphors and many meanings.

In the same way, the sages stubbornly resist the temptation to demand a single, complete "truth." The finest interpretation for them, it seems, is one that can be expounded into yet another interpretation. The only "truth" for them is that a multiplicity of truths might emerge from the text—in fact, even from a single word in the text. Opposing interpretations are allowed to coexist, as in the case of the stones becoming one pillow. Even incomplete interpretations are deemed worthy of consideration, as in the instance of the legend of Nebuchadnezzar's dragon.

Here they operate according to their own well-rehearsed principle: If two things that seem to be at odds with one another both make sense, then both are correct. In their words, "Both *these* and *those* are the words of the living

God." Our critical thinking leads us to believe that we can somehow resolve the symbols and events of a dream into a single truth. Here, we need to evoke Ricoeur's notion of a "second naïveté" to help us accept that interpreting a dream is like passing a ray of light through a prism. As light enters a prism it seems to reflect a single truth. As it leaves, it presents us with a rainbow of possibilities—all of which are authentic and, more important, all of which are present in the original single ray.

The sages pay little attention to the way the dream is organized. While they proceed verse by verse, some verses receive extensive treatment while others are entirely ignored. They quote biblical verses as "proofs" irrespective of when the verses were composed or the context in which they occur. The sages offer interpretations based on events that happened long after Jacob's death. They place interpretations given by sages generations before them side by side with their own interpretations (as if all the sages somehow existed in the same place at the same time). Their reasoning is elegant: Since God is alive ("the living God") through all generations, the words of all generations should be equally alive to the spiritual mind.

We are accustomed to thinking that interpreting a dream means understanding all of it in a deductive or inductive manner—"making sense of it," as we would say. This is not the sages' method. They do not demand that there be a single "truth" to explain the entire dream. But, more than that, as they move from verse to verse, they even seek multiple truths in each verse. They circle the verses with endless associations and teachings, winding around and around each verse, until they "encompass" the dream.

Still, there is no summary or conclusion. The sages make no attempt to "end" their interpretation. Instead, they purposely leave it open, incomplete. After all, another sage may come along and interpret the text in a new way, uncovering a new truth that should be added to those already unearthed. As the sages say, "The student who studies his lesson only one hundred times cannot be compared to the student who has studied it one hundred and one times."[3]

)

In the last chapter, I often noted that the sages were interpreting Jacob's dream to discover what it meant *for their community* and *for them*. They showed little concern with explaining what the dream originally meant for Jacob. In fact, they seem to have viewed Jacob mainly as a symbol for the Children of Israel. Were they conscious of this fact? Surely, they were. Moreover, they had reason to believe that it was the right way to proceed. The following story from the Talmud, telling of an encounter between Moses and the eminent sage Rabbi Akiba, illumines their belief:

> When Moses ascended on high he found the Holy One, the Blessed, engaged in adding decorations to the letters of the Torah.[4] Moses said, "O Ruler of the Universe, Your words are already sacred. Do they also require decoration?" God answered, "At the end of many generations, a sage will arise—Akiba the son of Joseph by name—who will expound upon each tittle heaps and heaps of laws." Moses said, "Permit me to see this sage." God answered, "Turn around."
>
> Moses turned and found himself in the academy where Akiba was interpreting the Torah. He

went and sat down in the eighth row of students, to listen to Akiba's teachings. Moses was disappointed when he found that he could not understand Akiba's interpretations. But when they came to a certain subject, the students asked Akiba, "How do you know this is so?" and Akiba replied, "It was a ruling given to Moses at Mount Sinai." Hearing this, Moses was comforted.

Returning to the Holy One, the Blessed, Moses said, "O Ruler of the Universe, You have a sage with the wisdom of this Akiba, and yet You give the Torah by me!" God replied, "Be silent, for this is My decision."[5]

The sages recognized that their interpretations would be meaningless for their biblical ancestors. By the same token, if Akiba were to visit a modern dream group, our interpretations might seem meaningless to him. Yet we are all connected by a chain of tradition that began with Adam and Eve and continues through the human family to the end of time. So we know what we know based on what was known before us. As Akiba said, his interpretation was a ruling given to Moses at Mount Sinai, even though Moses did not understand Akiba's interpretation. Moses knew the words, but Akiba could fathom the decorations, which is to say, the nuances of the words. Here, the decorations stand for the metaphors behind the text. Which is to say, Akiba could "read between the lines."

To better understand what this means in practical terms, consider Exodus 21:23-25, the *lex talionis*, "the law of retaliation." The Torah states:

Yet if there is a serious injury, you are to take a life for a life, an eye for an eye, a tooth for a tooth, a

hand for a hand, a foot for a foot, a burn for a burn,
a wound for a wound, a bruise for a bruise.

In biblical times, this command may have been a step
forward. It actually served to limit the extent of revenge
that could be sought; to prohibit the endless blood feuds of
Montagues and Capulets, Hatfields and McCoys. By the
time of the sages, however, the *lex talionis* seemed somewhat primitive. Moses might have been satisfied accepting
the law literally; but Akiba never could. Here is the discussion of the sages concerning the interpretation of this law:

> Does the Sacred Writ not say, *An eye for an eye*?
> Why not take this literally to mean putting out the
> eye [of the one who takes an eye from another]?—
> Put such a thought out of your mind! ...
>
> It was taught: Rabbi Dostai son of Judah says:
> *eye for eye* means monetary compensation. You say
> "monetary compensation," but perhaps it is not so,
> but actual retaliation is meant? What then will you
> say where the eye of one was big and the eye of the
> other little, for how can I apply the principle of an
> eye for an eye in this case? If, however, you say that
> in such a case monetary compensation will have to
> be taken, did not the Torah state, *You shall have
> one manner of law...*, implying that the [compen-
> sation must be the same no matter the size of the
> eye]?

Rabbi Dostai interpreted the law of retaliation as a
metaphor. It was impossible, he claimed, to take it literally,
since eyes differ, teeth differ, feet differ, and so on. For him,
it was no longer a question of what the law meant to Moses,
but rather how the law could be interpreted to make sense
for the sages' community.

In the same way, we are able to use the texts and interpretations of those who came before us as a starting point for interpretations that will make sense *for us*. What we can never do, and what we should not attempt to do, is to assume that any interpretation remains true and unchanging throughout the generations. Each generation must attempt to "hear it again."

☽

Having said this, we can ask whether the way the sages interpreted dreams can have meaning *for us*. I believe that we have already encountered the answer in the sages' own words in the last chapter. Here is the passage, in a translation utterly faithful to the original:

> **And he dreamed ...** Rabbi Abbahu said, "Dreams have no influence whatsoever."
>
> A certain man went to Rabbi Yose bar Halafta and said to him: "I was told in a dream, 'Go and bring [the fruits of] your father's labor from Cappadocia.'" "Did your father ever visit Cappadocia?" he asked him. On his answering "No," Yose advised him: "Go and count twenty boards in the flooring of your house and you will find it." "But there are not twenty boards there," he replied. "If so, count from the beginning to the end and back again, and you will find it." The man went, did so, and found it. And how did Rabbi Yose bar Halafta deduce this? From the word *Cappadocia*.
>
> Bar Qappara taught: "There is no dream without its interpretation."[6]

Rabbi Abbahu said, "Dreams have no influence whatsoever." But the story he told shows that dreams do have meaning. What Abbahu was really saying was that a dream taken literally should be disregarded. The man understood the literal meaning of his dream, just as Moses may have understood the literal meaning of the text of the Torah. But Rabbi Yose looked beyond the words to interpret the dream, just as Akiba looked beyond the literal text of the Torah to interpret its meaning.

The sages applied this rule to interpreting all sacred texts. The important thing in interpreting dreams, the sages tell us, is not what is seen or said in the dream, but what the one who interprets it hears. This is true because, as Bar Qappara taught, "There is no dream without its interpretation."

Ordinarily, we think of "explaining" the things we see in a dream. The sages warn us that this is folly. Jacob saw a staircase in his dream. We should not search for the meaning of a staircase by trying to re-create the image of a staircase in our minds. Instead, we should analyze the language used to describe the staircase—the phrases that the words form, the sentences that the phrases form, and the ideas that the paragraphs form. Then we may find that what we hear provides us with many visual images of many possible staircases.

When as children we hear this narrative for the first time, we probably hear that Jacob saw a "ladder." We fixate on the image of angels going hand over hand and foot over foot up and down the rungs of a ladder. The process of visualization in us is strong. This image remains with us as we mature, despite the fact that it is only one possibility. If we now hear that Jacob's "ladder" was a staircase, we immediately shift the visual image in our imaginations, but we still

do not comprehend the meaning any better. It is only when
we free ourselves from any single visual image that we make
way for the words to represent a series of visual images such
as the sages presented to us—the staircase might represent Mount Sinai, or it might represent the stairs leading to
the altar in the Temple, it might have begun in Beersheba
with its top over the Temple, or it might have begun at the
Temple with its top over Beth-El, and so on.

The sages tell us, and Paul Ricoeur concurs, the interpretation of a vision or a dream is not found by "seeing it
again," but by "hearing it again." And what is true of visions
and dreams, is equally true of the stories of our lives.

To Awaken Transformed

JACOB'S DREAM OF SEPARATION AND DIVORCE

☽

From the beginning, we must infer, man was a dreaming animal .... It was the dream that opened man's eyes to new possibilities in his waking life. — Lewis Mumford[1]

The sages were attempting to transform a political nation into a spiritual nation. We wish to create a spiritual consciousness out of a secular consciousness. There are many parallels.

The sages did not necessarily bend their interpretation of Jacob's dream to their needs. In most cases, they were only seeking messages that had meaning for them. The result was that, after some time had passed, the interpretation required commentary and explanation to recapture its meaning. So, while the sages anticipated that future generations would continue and refine their process, actually new generations would read their interpretation as a literary achievement, while finding it necessary to approach the narrative of the dream directly and with a "second naïveté."

To create an interpretation that makes sense *for us*, we need to repeat this process. Our critical faculties can guide us, while our capacity for wonder and astonishment allows us to "hear it again" as if for the first time.

Most of the briefer dream narratives in the Bible yield a similar message: God protects the righteous (note the dreams of Abimelech in Genesis 20 and Laban in Genesis 31; and the dreams in Jeremiah 31). Other dreams and visions give clues as to how the sages called on God's help in interpretation (note the dreams of Joseph in Genesis 37, of the cupbearer and the baker in Genesis 40, of Pharaoh in Genesis 41, and the dreams throughout the Book of Daniel). Longer dreams and visions in which God "appears" tend to presage or initiate transformational moments. They mark momentous passages in the lives of the dreamers (and, by extension, of the people). This was the case with the vision of Abram we have already examined and with Jacob's dream of the staircase.

To recapture the meaning of this moment of transformation in Jacob's life, we need to investigate the symbols of the dream. In the passage of time, however, we may find that we lack some essential underpinning necessary for understanding a word or symbol, or we may no longer be able to make sense of a particular phrase or symbol. When this happens, we will fall back on Paul Ricoeur's advice and "play" with the narrative to develop "truths" that *we* can accept. In the end, we hope that our interpretation will achieve the power to transform us through its message. If it is successful, as in the case of the interpretation offered by the sages, future generations will view it as a literary achievement even as they repeat the process. What follows, then, is a "modern" interpretation of Jacob's staircase dream.

☽

❋ *Genesis 28 [10]* **And Jacob left Beersheba bound for Haran.**

The English translation misses a nuance of biblical Hebrew—in the Bible, the verb normally appears before the subject. We hear the action before we meet the actor. The verb that commences this dream narrative is *vay-yetze*, "and [he] left." Even before we know that Jacob is the one who left, the verb bespeaks separation.

We possess two glimpses of Jacob's early years: In Genesis 25:27, we read that, "Jacob was a quiet person, staying among the tents." And a few verses later, in 29, Jacob is "cooking some stew." From these slight details, we surmise that Jacob was a homebody. So it comes as no surprise to us that leaving Beersheba, leaving home, would be disturbing to a youth like Jacob.

Based on other passages, it seems that Jacob's anxiety derives from more than just leaving home. For one thing, Haran is not only physically far away from the Promised Land; it also is spiritually distant. For Jacob, the issue of separation has as much to do with leaving the Promised Land as leaving the comfort of the hearth.

The Promised Land was of vital importance for the patriarchs. At God's command, Abraham journeyed from Haran to the Promised Land. During a famine, Abraham removed his family to Egypt [Genesis 12:10]. As soon as possible, however, they returned to Canaan, where they pursued a seminomadic existence. Isaac lived his entire life without leaving the Promised Land. In a time of famine, God instructed Isaac, "Do not go down to Egypt; stay in the land which I point out to you" [26:2] And Isaac put down roots in a way his father never had: "Isaac sowed in that land and reaped a hundredfold the same year. The Eternal blessed him, and the man grew richer and richer until he was very wealthy" [26:12]. Times had changed. Abraham the great traveler had given way to Abraham the semi-nomad; and Isaac traded the seminomadic life for farming.

By acquiring the birthright and the blessing of his father, Jacob probably expected to stay close to home and to become the chieftain of a sedentary tribe. Like Isaac, he would be a wealthy farmer. Instead—as a result of the way he acquired the birthright and the blessing—he was forced to separate from home, land, wealth, and the people he expected to lead. Worse still, Jacob knew that God had forbidden his father to leave the land even in difficult times; and now—with Esau having vowed to kill him—Jacob was being forced to leave it. Being "bound for Haran" was tantamount to going into exile. In leaving the Promised Land, Jacob would not only be separated from his family, but he would be entirely estranged—physically and emotionally. For all these reasons, Jacob's heart burned with a question, "Is it wise for me to leave this Land?"

✸ *[11a]* **And he encountered *[vay-yifgah]* a certain place *[ba-makom]*; and he slept there because the sun had set.**

The opening verb in this verse, *vay-yifgah*, does not necessarily mean "encountered." While this is an acceptable translation, I adopted it mainly to clarify several points raised by the sages in their interpretation. The Hebrew for *vay-yifgah* more plainly means "and he came."

The Hebrew for "a certain place" is a single word with the preposition ("to") and the definite article ("the") prefixed to it. It literally reads "to the place." The definite article makes it clear that this was a specific place, *"the"* place—very possibly a place already familiar to Jacob. To convey this meaning in English, many translations add the word "certain," rendering it "a certain place."

This "place" is mentioned specifically throughout the dream narrative. Notice in verse 11b, "Of the stones of *the place*"; in verse 16, "Surely this is *the place* of the Eternal; and I did not know it!"; in verse 17, "How awesome *this place* is!"; and in verse 19, "And he named *that place*." In Hebrew, all of these references employ the same term. Thus "the place" must be of great importance to the message of the dream. The possible meaning emerges as we continue.

Jacob came to this certain place and slept there. In the next verse, we are told that Jacob rested. Did he "sleep" before he took the pillow-stone and lay down to "rest?"

Or, is it possible that the redundant use of "slept" and "rested," and the choice of a stone, indicated a ritual familiar to our ancestors? The Bible does not specifically state that Jacob's intention was to incubate a dream, to seek counsel at the place, yet all the indicators point in this direction—his taking the time to stop in the midst of fleeing for his life, his going to a certain place, and the strange sequence of "sleep, choice of stone, rest."

It would seem that the "place" was special because Canaanites regularly used it to incubate dreams.[2] If so, there were probably dream interpreters in residence. Interpreters made their living by explaining or confirming dreams, and they would naturally be drawn to a place where

incubated dreaming was common. The process was traditional throughout the ancient world. We recall that Gilgamesh went to a high place and prayed for the mountain to
bring him a dream. Afterward, he told the dream to his
mother so that she could interpret it for him. At the temple
at Epidaurus, priest-interpreters were present to help pilgrims make sense of their dreams. The court of Pharaoh
employed large numbers of dream interpreters. And so on.
It may be that Canaanite dream interpreters were on hand
in this place to help dreamers resolve the meaning of their
incubated dreams. That may be what made the place so special.

Dream interpreters might proceed in a number of
ways, depending on skill, training, and also on the content
of the dream. To determine whether a dream was true, the
interpreter might split open a bird or animal and search its
entrails for signs and portents. If the dream required further elucidation, the interpreter might act as an oracle. For
a complex dream, a skilled interpreter might attempt a de-
tailed analysis and explication.

Jacob seems to have expected to find guidance in this
place. From the narrative, it seems that Jacob did not expect a direct encounter with his particular God here. Since
people of various backgrounds probably frequented "the
place," it may be, that Jacob expected his guidance to
come from one of the local gods. This would explain the
profound astonishment he expressed in verse 17. We will
have more to say of that later.

✼ *[11b]* **Of the stones of the place, he took one for his pillow; and he rested in that place.**

This verse might also be translated more literally as, "He
took from the stones of that place; he put it under his

head." The problem of the transition from plural to singular bothered the sages and has continually vexed translators. What is clear, no matter how it is translated, is that Jacob chose one from many stones to serve as a pillow. The stones were obviously there for this purpose. Most likely, they were kept there as "dream pillows," to encourage dream incubation.

Much of this is guesswork. The skeptic might say that Jacob slept there merely "because the sun had set." He chose this specific place because it was a good place to sleep, and not necessarily because it was a good place to dream. This would be a sufficient explanation except that Jacob came from a wealthy family, and a family rich in flocks at that. Why should he choose to rest his head on a stone instead of a sheepskin, for example? Stones were certainly not intended to offer travelers comfort while they slept. They make excellent altars; as pillows, they leave a lot to be desired. That, and the fact that there were many candidate stones in that place, indicates that the place was used for dream incubation and the stones played an important part in the ritual.

"He rested" can also be read as "he lay down." There is not much difference, except that we should perceive of Jacob as lying full length on the earth. This reminds us of Adam's position in the first moment of creation—formed of earth, lying on earth, waiting for the breath of God to be blown into his nostrils to transform him into a living being. Since Jacob's position is suggestive, we may be intended to recall the ancient fertility myth embedded in the creation of Adam.

> ... And no shrub of the field had yet appeared on the earth and no plant of the field had yet sprung up, for the Eternal God had not sent rain to the

earth and there was no man to work the ground but
mist came up from the earth and watered the
whole surface of the ground—the Eternal God
formed the man from the dust of the ground...
[Genesis 2:5–7].

The word for "man" is *adam* (the same word as the
name Adam). And the word for "ground" is *adamah* (the
word *adam* with a feminine ending). The passage seems to
depict an ancient fertility formula. For the earth to be fertile—that is, to yield its shrubs and plants—it was necessary for God to send rain and necessary for man to work the
ground. There was a necessary relationship between *adam*
and *adamah* (which, with its feminine form, hints at the
idea of an "earth mother") just as there was a necessary relationship between God and *adam*. The last leg of this triangular relationship was moisture (rain and dew, which are
often referred to as God's "blessing" upon the earth),
which directly connected God and *adamah*. Before the creation of *adam*, God had not yet sent rain. Only through the
cooperation of God and *adamah*—*adamah* in providing the
moisture and God in breathing the spirit into *adam*—could
the relationship be set in motion.

Parts of this triangular relationship are reflected in our
dream story. The staircase is firmly planted in the earth;
God promises Jacob the land he is lying on; God promises
that Jacob's children shall be as plentiful as the dust of
earth; and God promises to bring Jacob back to the same
ground. In part, the answer to the separation trauma that
Jacob is suffering lies in the proper maintenance of this set
of necessary relationships among the man, the ground, and
the god.

❋ *[12]* **And he dreamed, and there was a staircase *[sulam]* implanted on the earth, with its top reaching heaven, and there were god-like beings *[malachei-elohim]* ascending and descending on it.**

The staircase, with its "god-like beings," is indisputably the central image in Jacob's dream, symbolizing the connection between earth and heaven. Jacob envisions a real, solid, reliable staircase—one firmly grounded, "with its top reaching heaven." Angels are simultaneously ascending and descending on it. Jacob has chosen a stone on which to rest his head, and he has chosen a staircase of stone on which to rest his hopes for the future. The image of permanence and reliability, of communication and connection, stands in stark contrast to his insecurities.

"God-like beings" is a more literal translation of the words *malachei-elohim*. The usual translation is "angels" or "angels of the Eternal." To stress that the staircase resembles a Mesopotamian ziggurat, I used the more literal translation. "God-like beings" could easily refer to the priests of the ziggurat climbing up and down in their elaborate rituals. Nevertheless, the term, *malachei-elohim,* is used throughout the Bible to mean "angels."

Belief in the existence of angels requires a leap of faith. Some of us believe in angels of one kind or another, while others assume that angels are merely an evocative metaphor. Perceptions regarding angels have undergone so many changes in the course of time that theologians have created a separate field of study called Angelology. In our limited space, the best we can do is to step aside and discuss angels for a moment. If you prefer, you can continue with the interpretation of Jacob's dream by skipping the next section.

A Brief Discourse on Angels

The term for angel in the Hebrew Bible is *malach*, meaning "messenger." The same term is used for a human messenger as for a messenger of God. At times, the Bible adds to *malach* the word *shamayim*, "heaven." The result should be translated as "a messenger (or messengers) from heaven," but it is often translated as "angel" (or "angels"). The Bible employs other terms that sometimes are translated as "angel." Thus we encounter *b'nei el* or *b'nei elohim* (literally meaning "children of gods" or "children of God"), *cherubim* (apparently winged beings, whom the sages said were "half-man, half-fire and half-water"), and *seraphim* (who are not well described but manage to perform numerous little functions for God).

Most of the prophets do not mention angels at all. Their communication with God was assumed to be direct. Ezekiel, however, describes the image of God as seated on a throne surrounded by four beings he calls *hayyot* ("beasts") in chapter 1 but later calls *cherubim* in chapters 8–11. His vision of "beasts with wings" leads some translators to offer the word "sphinx" for *cherub*. Zechariah's prophecy is filled with angels, but they seem to be mainly literary devices. Zechariah may be employing angels ironically, as a social comment on the contemporary "soap-opera" mentality of the people he was addressing.

The books of the Writings contain few references to angels, except for the Book of Daniel, which was heavily influenced by Babylonia and is chockablock with Babylonian angels. This is the only book in the Bible in which angels are named. For example, Daniel specifically identifies Michael (sometimes also identified with Ares) and Gabriel. The angel Michael is thereafter called "the champion of Israel."

The books of the Apocrypha mention angels in many places. Most of these writings were infrequently cited in Jewish literature. The Book of Enoch, however, includes a depiction of angels that entered mainstream Jewish thought, the image of four angels that stand on the four sides of God. They are called the *malachei ha-panim*, "angels of the Countenance." In Enoch, the four are identified as Michael, Gabriel, Raphael, and Phanuel (with Gabriel and Raphael changing places in various versions of the list, all contained in Enoch). In the Book of Adam and Eve, the four are listed as Michael, Gabriel, Uriel, and Raphael. In the Dead Sea Scrolls they are listed as Michael, Gabriel, Suriel, and Raphael.

According to other traditions, the "angels of the Countenance" are four of the seven "archangels." The seven archangels are Uriel (leader of the angelic host and guardian of the underworld), Raphael (guardian of human souls), Raguel (who "takes revenge on the world of lights"), Michael (who watches over Israel), Sariel (an angel without portfolio, it seems, at least at this juncture), Gabriel (who rules paradise), and Jeremiel (who guards the spirits of the underworld). The archangels have entry to the presence of God, and their function is said to be carrying out tasks that directly affect world history.

Only three archangels—Michael, Gabriel, and Raphael—are mentioned in the Talmud, but a few centuries later the list had expanded to seven, each of whom was associated with a planet. The names of the archangels in lists dating from the sixth century on varied. The usual list included Michael, Gabriel, and Raphael; along with Aniel, Kafziel, Zadkiel, and Samael. Either Hasdiel or Barkiel or both would sometimes replace any of the last four names. And there was also extant by this time a longer list of archangels that identified them each with a constellation of the zodiac.

In the time of the sages, Jewish popular belief held that angels actually existed. By contrast, the sages taught that angels were only symbolic. For example, they spoke of "seventy" angels who protect the "seventy" nations. According to one legend, Gabriel called all the nations together and let each choose its own guardian angel. The number *seventy* does not seem to have been meant literally, but only as a way of saying "the many" nations. In any case, the legendary seventy are called the *malachei hashareit*, "ministering angels." The sages also referred to another category of angels, the *tzofei shamayim*, "heavenly guardians." These angels watched over individuals. They were considered superior to common angels, but not as holy as archangels. The idea that human beings had one or more guardian angels was popular throughout the Semitic world.

It was also popular belief that there were evil or "fallen" angels. But the Talmud generally views these as entirely metaphorical. Satan (Samael) is called the personification of wickedness. At the same time, in the Talmud (Baba Batra 16a), it is also said, "Satan, the Evil Urge, and the Angel of Death are all one," implying that all three are a force within the individual that must be overcome. Likewise, the sages refer to the fact that good angels accompany the righteous, while evil angels accompany the wicked—this, too, is metaphorical.

The sages spoke poetically of angels being created by God each day to sing God's praises and do whatever tasks were required. At the end of the day, the angels descended into a river of fire. However, some sages claimed that two angels, Michael (champion of Israel) and Gabriel (who waited to announce the coming of the messiah), did not disappear at the end of each day.

In one place it was said that God's face was hidden from angels, even from Michael and Gabriel. In another instance, it was maintained that though angels were created on the second (or fifth) day of creation, they continued to be created from that time on, since every pronouncement of God results in the creation of an angel. Angels were sometimes divided into angels of peace (those near to God) and angels of anger and destruction (those remote from God). The Talmud says that the four archangels are Gabriel, Michael, Raphael, and Uriel, but any of Sandalfon, Zagzagael, or Suriel sometimes stand in for one or more of these. At times Metatron is at one hand, at other times at the other hand, of God ("hand," too, should be understood figuratively).

In the Talmud, the sages clearly state that Jews did not have names for the angels until they returned from the first Babylonian exile. The midrash proposes that some righteous people could become angels, either on their death or even before (this is obviously metaphorical); that angels are not necessarily superior to humans; and that angels form the "heavenly tribunal" or "court" when God judges (if one angel comes to accuse a person, another angel comes to defend that person). The sages also preserved a tradition that Samael once impregnated Eve (presumably to separate the paternity of Cain from Adam). This, too, seems more symbolic than dogmatic.

In the Middle Ages, Jewish mystics introduced the idea that human beings could not pray to God directly, since God is too holy, so we pray through intercessors—the righteous and the angels. The sages of the Talmud had earlier rejected this idea and, though it became central to Christianity and later to Islam, it continued to be rejected in almost all mainstream Jewish thought.

The most widely-known Jewish mystical work, the Zohar, dating probably from the thirteenth century, separates angels with masculine qualities from angels with feminine qualities. Masculine angels reside in heaven, close to God, while feminine angels wander through the world with the *Shechinah*, God's feminine aspect. The Zohar portrays the angels dividing into four groups around God's throne. Uriel's group stands in front, Raphael's group in back, Michael's group on the right, and Gabriel's group on the left.

An influential community of mystic teachers flourished in Safed in the sixteenth century. They were masters of imagery, and often exercised their poetic skills portraying angels. For example, they taught that the angel Sandalfon collects all the prayers offered each day and weaves them into a crown for God. Metatron bestows heavenly blessings on those who pray the eighteen central blessings of Jewish prayer each day. And so on. None of these teachings indicate that they took the idea of angels literally (though a few of them did claim that they were visited by, or instructed by, angels).

Jewish philosophers of the Middle Ages also gave serious consideration to the subject of angels. Maimonides translated the word *malachim* as "intelligences," adding that angels never had or could have any corporeality. Abrabanel concurred. Kimchi wrote, "True penitence does not require intercession by the righteous; feigned penitence will not be helped by either the dead or the righteous, by human beings or by angels." And most of these philosophers opposed the use of the popular prayer that included the phrase *malachei rahamim machnisei rahamim*, "angels of mercy, intercessors for mercy" on the grounds no intercessors should be exhorted on behalf of human beings.

All in all, the Jews from biblical times onward generally recognized the existence of angels as metaphorical. A spectacular tradition held that each angel is as large as one-third of the world. You can draw your own conclusions.

✳ *[12b]* ... **And there were god-like beings *[malachei-elohim]* ascending and descending on it.**

Throughout most of the Bible, angels are "messengers." Angels were not given names in the time of Jacob because, in early Semitic thinking, angels had no independent existence. God's message and God's messenger were one and the same. When the message was delivered, the messenger vanished. The Psalmist captures this evanescence in images of wind and fire: "[God] makes the winds His angels, the fiery flames His servants" (Psalms 104:4). With this in mind, what we have on Jacob's staircase, then, is a sophisticated form of ancient e-mail: "messages" that travel upward and downward.

If the beings on the staircase were angels and if angels are created in heaven by God, logically they should be going down first and then up. How could they possibly originate at the bottom of the staircase? One explanation, often offered in homily, is that we must send "messages" upward to receive a response from God. For Jacob, who incubated his dream by formulating a question and then "sleeping on it," this notion would ring true. To receive reassurance, he had to seek it out. We could say, "It is up to us to initiate the connection. The winds carry our prayers to the heavens; the winds bring us the messages of heaven."

Of course, it is possible that we should be examining the angels' motivation rather than their direction of travel. In an intriguing exchange, the sages asked, "Why were the angels going up and down the staircase?" For no other reason, they replied, then to take turns looking closely at Jacob. They were curious. They went "up to look at his face, and down to stare at him while he slept." What does it mean to say that they went "up to look at his face?" If he was asleep down below, how could his face be up above? Only symbolically.

For example, the mystics believe that what happens on earth has an effect on what happens in heaven—and vice versa. According to the mystics, from the time of this dream on, whenever the heavenly chariot appeared, the face of God seen in the chariot was actually the face of Jacob (Israel).[3] To recast this in modern terms, since we are created in God's image, we are the reflections of God on earth. This cuts both ways. The reflection and the image are so intertwined that Jacob can actually be said to be the image of God in heaven or the image of God when the heavenly chariot appears.

❋ *[13]* **And there was the Eternal, standing beside him, saying, "I am the Eternal, God of your father Abraham and God of Isaac. To you and to your children in perpetuity, I give the land that you are lying on."**

Jacob is still dreaming of the staircase. Suddenly, God is standing beside Jacob. God's placement with regard to Jacob is instructive. God does not appear in a chariot or on a throne. These would emphasize the separation and estrangement of humanity from God. Ancient Mesopotamian and Egyptian texts emphasized that human beings were created to serve the gods. The Bible rejects this view. God stands beside, and not above, Jacob.[4]

Likewise, God does not face Jacob as a teacher might face a pupil. This is another relationship often depicted in ancient times. For example, on the stele that records the laws of Hammurabi, the carving at the top shows Hammurabi receiving the laws from his god. The god sits on a throne. Hammurabi stands before him. Hammurabi's god is the instructor, the king is the god's student, and normal human beings are the servants of the king. This view of the king as a demigod, an intercessor for normal human beings, is also rejected by the Bible.

More in keeping with the spirit of the Bible is a Hittite sculpture in live rock at Yazilikaya unearthed by archaeologists. In this sculpture, a Hittite god stands beside a Hittite king, with his left arm around the king's shoulder. They are obviously not equal. The god is larger than the king, indicating a relationship of protection and guidance. Both face forward. With his extended right arm, the god points in a forward direction.[5] This attitude (minus the arm around the shoulder) is closer to the image that the dream conveys of God standing beside Jacob. In standing beside Jacob, God is portrayed as avuncular.

What we might expect at this moment simply does not happen. Jacob does not turn to look at God. For us, this is problematical. We live in an age and society that is highly visual. We believe what we *see* more than we rely on what we *hear*. And when we discuss a dream, we are accustomed to interpreting visual imagery. By contrast, the Bible stems from an oral tradition. For centuries, stories, teachings, genealogies, even laws, were memorized and passed down from one generation to the next by word of mouth. Even visions were handed down as poetry or word-pictures. They were considered to be correct only when expressed in language, when you could "hear" that the explanation fit "the picture."

In Jacob's dream, there is no visual description of God. God stands beside Jacob, yet Jacob does not turn to see God; instead, Jacob listens to God's words. Twenty years later, God appears in another of Jacob's dreams and tells Jacob to look at the goats of Laban's flock. Jacob looks at the goats but does not turn to see God; instead, Jacob listens as God instructs him to leave Laban and return to Canaan. In Jacob's vision, we *see* the goats; but we *hear* the voice of God [Genesis 31:11–13]. Three days later, God visits Laban in a dream. Laban is not surprised. Even Laban seems accustomed to such visitations. Again, there is no physical description of God. What is urgent is God's message: "Deal with Jacob with equanimity" [31:24]. Later, Pharaoh has dreams he does not understand. Joseph is called from prison to explain them. Joseph says, "I am not the interpreter. God will give you an answer to put your mind at ease" [41:16]. After reminding Pharaoh that in dreams it is God who is *speaking,* Joseph interprets the dream. When Pharaoh places Joseph in charge of Egypt, he says, "Where else shall we find such a one as this, a man in whom the spirit of God resides?" [41:38]. While our biblical ancestors speak of "seeing" God in a vision, what is actually described in the Bible is God's message which was heard.

❋ *[13b]* **"To you and to your children in perpetuity, I give the land that you are lying on. *[14a]* And your descendants shall be like the dust of the earth; and you all will spread out westward, eastward, to the north, and to the south...."**

God's promise to Jacob differs from the promises given to Abraham and Isaac. To them, God said, "Look toward heaven and count the stars, if you are able to count them ... so shall your offspring be" [Genesis 15:5].[6] There, the question seemed to be, "How numerous?" The answer was, "More numerous than the stars." In this case, the question seems to be, "How shall they be connected?" The answer is, "Through the land." God compares Jacob's descendants to dust that spreads out in all directions. Like dust, they are literally "of the land." It does not matter in which direction they may spread, for they can never lose their connection to the land.

Why would Jacob be worried about his connection to the land? There are two possible concerns, both made manifest in the dream. First, as we noted, Jacob is separating from his homeland—the land that God promised to Abraham, the land that Isaac inherited and never left. The land is all-important—it is the Promised Land. And Jacob has only recently made the land his—through deceiving both his father and his brother. He has reason to worry. He must be thinking to himself, "I have gained the land through trickery, must I now lose it by being forced to leave it?" Another way of understanding this relates to the issue of necessary relationships in Creation. Having joined himself to the land, allied himself to his earth mother, *adamah*, would he now be ripped again from her womb, separated and estranged? Here, God reassures him. No matter what direction Jacob and his descendants might take in life, their relationship to the land will remain intact.

The second concern is also existential. Can a wanderer be truly "implanted in the earth?" Or, to ask this in a more modern vein, "Can we feel safe and secure if we are not grounded in a profession, a home, a family, a piece of real estate?" Again, we realize that Jacob is undergoing a separation—divorcing from his immediate family, divorcing from the home which he cleaved to in his youth, divorcing from the only profession he knew (tending the household), and divorcing, too, from the one thing he wanted to possess more than any other, the Promised Land.

Except for death itself, divorce is the most serious separation we can face in life. It is therefore instructive to examine the psychology of divorce as an instance of separation. During the first transitional phase following a divorce, we feel outside of society, outside of "normal reality." We become groundless, detached, disconnected, alone. We feel stripped of resources, unable to meet our needs, unable to cope with even common circumstances. This is a fair description of Jacob's condition as he sets out for Haran. His is the customary experience of separation, of leaving home. In many ways, it is analogous to divorce. Treasured things seem to be slipping away. Jacob feels threatened and abandoned. God reassures him. Life holds a constant for Jacob. He will never be truly wayward, truly groundless, because he will never be divorced from the land. In the course of the dream, the Promised Land is redefined. It is no longer a single place. The dust of the earth is everywhere, constantly moving and shifting, yet it remains as reliable as the sun and the moon. Existentially, then, the Promised Land is inside Jacob, as much a part of him as he is a part of the land.

✱ *[14b]* **"Through you and your descendants, all the nations of the earth shall be blessed."**

This verse reiterates the idea that our actions on earth have their reflection in heaven. We encountered this notion in the interpretations of the sages, but it is also an element in the covenants made with the patriarchs. On calling Abraham to leave Haran, God promised: "I will bless those who bless you, and whoever curses you I will curse; and all peoples on earth will be blessed through you" [Genesis 12:3]. After the binding of Isaac, God reassured Abraham: "Through your offspring all nations on earth shall be blessed" [22:18]. When God renewed the covenant with Isaac, the statement was repeated almost verbatim, "Through your offspring all nations on earth will be blessed" [26:5].

But how do other nations benefit from the presence of the descendants of the patriarchs? In one source, the sages gave three suggestions: (1) Idolaters would be drawn to the true faith through contact with God's people. (2) Since God's righteous existed in the world, rain and dew (God's blessing upon the earth) would appear in their proper season. (3) When the nations were in need of guidance and counsel they would turn to God's people.[7] Based on experience, however, we can make another suggestion.

The old aphorism states, "We are God's hands on earth." In other words, the more good we do, the more of God's goodness we bring into the world. This is an apt interpretation of the verse. The dream delivers its message—that we will bring blessing to others—but it is clearly up to us to put our visions into action. As descendants of Jacob and inheritors of the covenant, we are commanded to walk in God's ways. As our good works bear fruit, all the nations of the world benefit from our presence in it. This is precisely the reverse of the sense of separation. Insecure as he is, Jacob nevertheless yearns to bring his blessing to the world.

✻ *[15]* "**And I will be with you, to guard you, in every journey you take; and I will bring you back to this ground, for I will not desert you, until I have done for you that which I have spoken to you.**"

God vows to be the guarantor of this promise. "Surely," God says to Jacob, "I will guard you in every journey you take." It remains for Jacob to make the journeys, to do the wandering, ultimately to realize his own potential. In the same way, those who recover from the first pains of divorce or estrangement, do so by overcoming their own helplessness, by realizing they are not entirely alone, by joining themselves back to society, by grounding themselves again in the world.

Jacob will return to this ground, to this very place. Here, too, the dust of the earth is a powerful symbol representing both what is incessantly shifting, moving, journeying, and changing and what is constant and everlasting. As there must be a process of separation for Jacob, there will also be a process of reintegration—of returning to the same place. The same guarantee is given to Moses at the burning bush:

> And God said, I will be with you. And this will be the sign to you that it is I who have sent you: When you have brought the people out of Egypt, you will worship God on this mountain [Exodus 3:12].

Moses was equally hesitant to leave his comfortable life in Midian. As with Jacob, God promised to accompany Moses on his journey. And, as with Jacob, the token that the journey was successful would lay in the return to the place it began. Separation is painful, but without suffering separation, redemption is impossible to achieve. This forceful message has ramifications for us far beyond its placement in Jacob's dream.

✻ *[16]* **Then Jacob awoke from his sleep *[mi-shnato]*; and he said, "Surely this is the place of the Eternal; and I did not know it!" *[17]* And he was overawed, and he said, "How awesome this place is! This can be none other than God's house *[beit elohim]*; and this is the gateway of heaven!" *[18a]* Early that morning, Jacob arose.**

The verb *vay-yikatz,* in 28:16, is used for "sudden awakening." In verse 28:18a, we read, "Early that morning, Jacob arose." The verb there, *vay-yishkem,* is used for "rising up early." Should we read these two verses to mean that Jacob's awakening is referred to twice or that he had two awakenings? The sages held the theory that the Bible never repeats a thing except to make a point. Considering the sparse language of the narrative, this was a reasonable assumption. Let us assume that they were correct and "play" with what that might mean in this case.

As we read the two passages, the first seems to be a spiritual awakening and the second seems to be a physical awakening. In the case of the second, the rising of the sun would naturally awaken a person sleeping outdoors, thus "early in the morning." In the case of the first, we note that Jacob takes no action on awakening. His awakening is one of astonishment, which he remarks. So the passages might indicate that, still dreaming or momentarily disturbed in his sleep, Jacob has a profound spiritual revelation.

Departing from the sages, another possible explanation exists. Jacob may first awaken *in* his dream, only to arise later with the sun. This possibility is suggested in modern dream work. Dr. Stephen LaBerge has conducted numerous studies in what he calls, *lucid dreaming*.[8] In lucid dreams, the dreamer becomes aware of being "awake" or active even while continuing to dream. Reports of lucid dreams are so common that Harry Hunt considers them one of his six major categories of dreaming.[9] The following two examples of lucid dreaming may provide some insight to how this relates to Jacob's two awakenings:

> It was snowing gently. I was alone on the rooftop of the world, climbing K2. As I made my way upward through the steeply drifting snow, I was astonished to notice my arms were bare: I was wearing a short-sleeved shirt, hardly proper dress for climbing the second-highest mountain in the world! I realized at

once that the explanation was that I was dreaming! I was so delighted that I jumped off the mountain and began to fly away, but the dream faded and I awoke.[10]

I was standing in a field in an open area when my wife pointed in the direction of the sunset. I looked at it and thought, "How odd: I've never seen colors like that before." Then it dawned on me: "I must be dreaming!" Never had I experienced such clarity and perception....[11]

Jacob's two awakenings may be explained by this premise. Jacob experienced a lucid dream. He awakened *in* his dream to be astonished by what he had witnessed. For him, "the place" had been transformed. He was like the dust, always in relationship to the earth, "everywhere" was the same as "anywhere" for him. Any place God appeared, even Beth-El, was a "holy mountain," a ziggurat. Seizing on his new awareness, Jacob described the staircase again in language that suggests the architectural structure of the ziggurat. "How awesome this place is!"—the staircase is firmly implanted on a massive foundation of earth and stone. "This can be none other than God's house"—the temple at the top of the ziggurat is shaped like a house, and only the highest priests can enter it to commune with God. "And this is the gateway of heaven!"—the massive stone gateways that stand guarding the landings on the staircase of the ziggurat become the gates through which the righteous must pass on their way to heaven. This humble place where he lay down to sleep had been transmuted into all of these *for him*. It also holds new meaning *for us*. Our dreams hold the potential to awaken us to new ways of perceiving our world, to the very place where we lie down.

We should not minimize the importance of this awakening. In a sense, it is the climax of the dream drama; all
that follows it is denouement. Jacob has awakened to a new
conception of his condition. This awakening can be taken
to be a realization. The hints are in the text. Not only does
he suddenly perceive this place as the "God's house," but
he knows that the dream has given him a "gateway" to
heaven. Symbolically, gates are indicators of passage from
one condition to another. Jacob has perceived the gateway
that will enable him to move beyond his sense of estrangement, to get past his homesickness, and to achieve a true
realization that he is not alone. God is with him. When he
arises in the next verse, he is prepared to signify this new realization in a number of concrete ways.

❀ **[18] Early that morning, Jacob arose. He took the
stone which he had used as a pillow, and set it up as a
place-marker, and poured oil on its top [anointing it].
[19] And he named that place, Beth-El, "The House of
God," though before the city's name had been Luz.**

Jacob awakened with the sun. He turned the pillow-stone
upright to create a *matzevah*, a marker indicating that this
was a sacred place. Its upright stance was no coincidence.
It symbolized the communion that had occurred in this
place between Jacob and God. In this sense, it was like a
sacrificial altar. (In fact, such place-markers were commonly found in association with altars.)

Jacob's dream echoes the sacrificial system. The Hebrew word for "sacrifice" is *korban,* derived from the root,
karav, "to draw closer." Like the older fertility myth still
buried under the biblical text—and in some ways a part of
it—the sacrificial system was a means of connecting us
with earth and heaven. The burnt-offering was called an

olah, literally, "that which goes up." In the days of the Temple in Jerusalem, such offerings were continual,[12] with a burnt-offering made at least twice each day. Though the ritual included other types of offerings, most were burned in whole or in part, and in regard to the vast majority of them we are told that they were offered to produce a *reah niho'ah*, "a pleasing odor," for God. The *minhah*, or "meal offering," for example, was made of fine flour mixed with oil and frankincense. It was burned for the sake of the pleasing smell that rose to heaven.[13] For the priests and the people, the sacrifices were acts of submission, expiation, and devotion. Sacrifices were not meant to "feed" God. On the stone altar, fire rendered the sacrifice into smoke—symbolically and viscerally, the stuff of life and earth was transformed into the stuff of heaven. Faithfully they offered their devotions, asking for God, in turn, to send the rain and dew—the stuff of heaven that could transform the stuff of earth into life. In the words of the Psalmist, "Take my prayer as an offering of incense, my upraised hands as an evening sacrifice" [141:2].

Having turned the stone upright, Jacob transformed the stone by anointing it. Anointing—the act of pouring oil on an object or person—was ritually performed to sanctify a sacrificial altar and to "crown" a new king.[14] The anointed stone was intended to remind Jacob and his descendants of the dream, so its location was significant. A later editor clarified the exact location by noting that it was the town long known as Luz. This editor either believed that people would better recognize the place by a more familiar name or, more likely, this insertion indicates that Jacob's use of the term *Beth-El* ("The House of God") was figurative, not necessarily referring to the already existing town of Bethel.

All of Jacob's actions on awakening were ritual com-
memoration well attested in archaeological sources. Jacob's "certain place" was transformed into a sacred space
for Jacob and his seed. All that remained was for Jacob to
pledge to keep the covenant he had received.

✱ *[20]* **And Jacob vowed a vow, saying, "If God will be
with me, will guard me in this path I walk; [if God] will
give me food to eat and clothing to wear,** *[21]* **[if] I peacefully return to the house of my ancestor [Abraham]—
then the Eternal shall be my God.** *[22]* **And this stone
which I have placed as a marker, shall be God's house
[beit elohim]; and all that You give me, I will give a tenth
to You."**

Jacob's oath seems strangely at odds with his transformation. He is now aware that he is separate but not alone. He
has unexpectedly received God's confirmation as the next
patriarch, God's promise of protection, and God's promise
of salvation. How could Jacob be so ungrateful, or so uncertain, as to say, "Sure, but let's make all this conditional. After all, what if You, God, default on *Your* promise?" Why did
Jacob begin his vow with "if?"

From the translation, it surely seems that this is Jacob's meaning. On the other hand, if this were the case, the
verse might have started with, "And Jacob stipulated a condition," rather than, "And Jacob vowed a vow." Now as
then, a vow is a commitment. It is left to us to find some
way of interpreting Jacob's statement as a promise. Having
no resources other than the dream story itself, we must
again "play" with the text to "hear it again" in a new way.

Jacob incubated his dream with a question. From what
we know of Jacob's life, we hear the implied question as,
"Will I lose everything by leaving the Promised Land?" He

needed guidance, because everything he knew and loved told him that leaving at this juncture might mean leaving forever. The dream answers Jacob's question, but goes far beyond what he expected. It resolves not only the issue of estrangement, but also that of redemption. In the sense that human beings are connected to the earth no matter where they roam, Jacob is of the Promised Land no matter where his life's journey may take him, and Jacob's descendants will live by the same truth even when they are scattered to the four corners of the earth. In turn, the earth is always connected to heaven, as symbolized by the staircase, the "gateway" to heaven.

In another sense, as human beings we are like the staircase. In our creation, we are part earth and part heaven, we are dependent on both, and both are dependent on us. The person whose entire being is centered on earthly matters seems brutish, bestial, common, churlish, or at best mundane. The person whose entire being is centered on heaven seems indifferent, uncaring, distant, childish, or at best aloof. The ideal person keeps both feet on the ground while walking in God's ways.

This does not imply that humans can be perfect. Only that we are created with the potential to seek our own kind of salvation, our individual "gateway." Even our greatest successes in life are made with the conditional understanding that we must go on from there. This is the realization that eventually emerges from every experience involving separation.

The angels, from the first, were instructed to praise God by saying, "Blessed is the Lord, the God of Israel." When Adam was created, the angels asked God, "Is this the man whose God we proclaim You to be?" God said, "No. This one is a thief, for he stole the forbidden fruit." When Noah was created, the angels asked again. God said, "No, this one is a drunkard." [After the Flood, Noah planted a vineyard, harvested the grapes, made wine, and drank to excess.] At the birth of Abraham, the angels again asked, "Is this the man whose God we proclaim You to be?" And God answered, "No. This one was once an idolater." At the birth of Isaac, the angels came again with the same question, and God's reply was: "No. This one loves Esau, whom I deplore." But when Jacob was born and the angels asked again, God replied, "Yes. This is the one."[15]

Adam was created to be the common ancestor of us all. Noah was chosen to enable humanity to survive the Flood. Abraham was created to become the progenitor of the Hebrew people. Isaac was chosen to suffer pain and sacrifice on behalf of his people. Jacob was chosen to be identified with God, to become the forebear of the Tribes of Jacob, and eventually to carry the name Israel. By implication, each of us comes into the world with some unique purpose. Never mind that everyone created before us also had a special mission. Never mind that everyone created before us also had faults. Never mind that we have faults, suffer setbacks, and endure failures. We are each unique in some way, chosen in some respect, closer to God in some aspect of our self than any other individual ever created.

Human existence is conditional, temporal, and evanescent. But it is not without purpose or potential. As long as the breath of life is in us, we can dream dreams and see visions. A Jewish teaching held that we must wear a garment with two pockets in order to carry two sayings at all times. Feeling proud, we can reach into one pocket and find a note reading, "I am but dust and ashes." Feeling disheartened, we can reach into the other and find, "For my sake the world was created." Our awareness is a gift from heaven, but our feet must remain firmly planted on the earth.

The salvation that Jacob seeks, then, is not awaiting us in some other world. He can find redemption in this world. How can Jacob be certain that he will overcome the vicissitudes of his separation? Only by returning to this place. True, he will not be the same Jacob who left, but he will know that he has returned from exile, that he has been redeemed. So God's promise is conditional, too, "*until* I have done for you that which I have spoken to you." Jacob is making this manifest—both must do their part, God and Jacob. Thus, we should read *if* in the sense of *as*. As God protects Jacob and guards him, *as* God provides him with food and clothing, *as* God returns him peacefully to his home, Jacob will be faithful and will set aside a portion of everything that he receives to be an offering at this place-marker, the house of God.

))

From the evidence, it seems that both Abraham and Jacob incubated their dreams. They sought divine answers to moments of uncertainty and distress by initiating the dream process in a ritual way. In effect, they sent a question upward. In response, they received the inspiration and guidance they were seeking. Both the process and the dream were significant.

I would argue that this path is available to us today; that divine guidance and inspiration are always available, though we are not always prepared to receive them. The interpretation of biblical dreams is an exercise in preparedness. These dreams speak to situations that reverberate in our lives. Abraham's vision seems to have been prompted by what we today would call a midlife crisis. Whether this would have been the biblical perception of the dream is irrelevant. Whether this is absolutely true is also irrelevant. Since it is an interpretation that speaks to us, it is true *for us*. Jacob's dream seems to have been a dream of separation, what is classically known as *estrangement*. The answer, however, is more than comfort and reassurance. Jacob's dream gives us the biblical meaning of *salvation* or, as Jewish sources prefer, *redemption*.

"Salvation" and "redemption" are religious terms, their definitions differing from one context to another. As moderns, we often equate them with words like "completion," "integration," or "wholeness." We might also speak of them as "spiritual healing" or "health." Jacob's dream illumines a more ancient concept of salvation. To see how it might have been otherwise, compare it to a dream experienced by the third-century Christian martyr Perpetua of Carthage. In prison, awaiting martyrdom, perhaps recalling the biblical image of Jacob's staircase, Perpetua also dreamed of a connection between earth and heaven:

> I saw a ladder of tremendous height, made of bronze, reaching all the way to the heavens, but it was so narrow that only one person could climb up at a time. To the side of the ladder were attached all sorts of metal weapons: swords, spears, hooks, daggers, spikes; so that if anyone tried to climb up carelessly or without paying attention, he would be mangled and his flesh would adhere to the weapons. At the foot of the ladder lay a dragon of enormous size, and it would attack those who tried to climb up and terrify and so discourage them from

trying. "He will not harm me," I said, "in the name of Christ." Slowly, as though he were afraid of me, the dragon stuck his head out from underneath the ladder. Using it as my first step, I trod on his head and went up. Then I saw an immense garden, and in it a gray-haired man sat in shepherd's clothes. Tall he was, and milking sheep. He called me over to him and gave me a mouthful of the curds he was drawing; and I took it into my cupped hands and ate it. And all those who stood around said, "Amen!" At the sound of this word I woke up, with the taste of something sweet still in my mouth.[16]

The central symbols are familiar. Yet, Perpetua's dream is entirely distinct from Jacob's. In Perpetua's dream, the connection between heaven and earth is narrow—only one person at a time may reach salvation. In Jacob's dream, the staircase is populated by angels, and salvation does not depend upon reaching its top. In Perpetua's dream, it is not her humanity which saves her, but partaking of the life-giving milk of heaven. Jacob is interested in this life, his faith is joined to the land, to the dust of this earth. In her dilemma, Perpetua gains the ladder by calling on "the name of Christ," by meeting a Christ-like figure in heaven (the "shepherd"), by relying upon heaven for the sweetness of salvation. By contrast, Jacob's dream seems mundane—he is motivated by his need for God's protection in this world, even vowing to share a tenth of all he gains through his human efforts. Perpetua seeks to leave this world and overcome her estrangement through an ultimate connection with God in heaven, even to eating "the food of the gods." Jacob seeks to overcome his estrangement to God here on earth, even asking God for such worldly blessings as ordinary "food to eat and clothing to wear." Perpetua's vision of redemption centers on what she does in her dream. Jacob's vision centers on what he hears in his dream.

The two dreams represent very different notions of the existential condition of human beings in the world. Perpetua's dragon may represent original sin or the evil in the lower world—these are the things that separate or estrange human beings from God. She overcomes the dragon by her unconditional faith and receives the gift of heaven from her shepherd—her faith gains her the reward of salvation. There is no dragon and no representation of evil in Jacob's dream. The staircase is, nonetheless, an expression of Jacob's longing to be connected to God. Like Perpetua, Jacob feels estranged—but for very different reasons. Jacob's connection to God depends on what Jacob does in this world and how God blesses him in this world. For Jacob, human potential is the key to salvation. This is the biblical understanding of salvation.

Of course, this is only one interpretation of Jacob's staircase dream. The narrative continues to exist outside this and every interpretation. It continues to open possibilities for new truths to be discovered. It cannot in itself be exhausted no matter how many readings are suggested. Like all dreams, once recorded in language, it continues to be elusive in content. We can turn to it again and again, revive it with a new naïveté, imbue it with new meanings, and make it relevant to the necessities of our own time and place. Nonetheless, this reading is "true," which is to say, it delivers a message that speaks *to us*.

))

Jacob awakens from his dream transformed. So much has changed. Through our act of interpretation, we can also awake transformed. Shall we remain our old uncertain selves once we realize that our individuality is absolutely assured? Can we possibly be our old doubting selves once we know that estrangement and divorce can surely be overcome? Can we possibly be our old fragmented selves once we realize that heaven and earth are inextricably connected? Can we possibly be our old disassociated selves once we know that God is constantly with us, speaking into our ears, guiding us, protecting us, and ensuring us that we will return from whence we came?

Salvation for us as individuals rests on these essentials: You are both earthly and divine—at the center of creation, the image of God on earth. Everything that happened in the history of the universe up to the moment you were created was designed for no other purpose than to prepare for your creation. Everything that will happen in the history of the universe from this time forth depends on how you fulfill the purpose for which you were created. In essence, you are the stairway connecting time past with time to come. Your influence will last forever. You are the "high place" of humanity. You are Jacob. You are Israel. You are the dreamer.

Preparing for Dreams and Visions

MODERN AND ANCIENT TECHNIQUES

☽

I do not know whether I was then a man dreaming I was a butterfly, or whether I am now a butterfly dreaming I am a man. — Chuang-tzu

Visions occur no matter where the visionary stands; dreams are manifested no matter where the dreamer sleeps. Ironically, when you reach a transformational moment in your life, when you face a vexing problem, when you come up against seemingly irresolvable difficulties, that is when dreams become most accessible to you. Nevertheless, all depends on preparation.

The two biblical dreams we have examined at length both came as answers to questions. The Bible tends to record the dreams and visions, the answers, but not the questions. In the case of Rebecca, however, the question is made explicit. When Rebecca was troubled by the struggle between the twins in her womb, she asked, "Why is this happening to me? So she went to inquire of the Eternal." The Hebrew word for "went" means "going from some physical place to another." She went to a particular place for her answer. The verb for "inquire" comes from the root that means "interpret." It is clear that Rebecca went to a sacred site to receive an interpretation of some sort—an omen, an augury, a sign, or a dream. The Bible does not include the details of the process. Instead, the result is recorded as the word of God: "And the Eternal said to her...."[1] More often, the eliciting question is not recorded at all, but we apprehend from the context that God's word is gleaned through some form of oracle or interpretation.

For the modern reader, this method—recording God's messages without describing the process by which they were obtained—leaves many issues unresolved. Is there a right or "better" method for asking a question we wish a dream to answer? Can we expect dream answers to any questions we pose? Do we need to find a "sacred place" before we can expect an answer to dreams? Do we have to be prepared in some ritual way? It is obvious that merely having a question to pose is not sufficient; we must devise a method for "invoking" an answer.

))

Despite myriad studies of ancient texts, few Bible scholars have concentrated directly on biblical dreams. One who has is A. Leo Oppenheim, professor of Assyriology at the Oriental Institute of the University of Chicago. Oppenheim studied Mesopotamian, Egyptian, and biblical sources, noting a number of brief references that seemed to indicate that people of the ancient Near East used incubation to invoke significant dreams. In Oppenheim's opinion, dreams bearing messages from the gods could most easily be explained as literary renditions of dreams actually experienced at incubation sites.[2]

As we have seen, incubation sites were often "high places" of religious significance. Though the term "high place" may sometimes be metaphorical, there is some evidence to suggest that it was originally a literal usage. Gilgamesh climbs a mountain, offers up a sacrifice, and prays, "Mountain, bring me a dream." At one time, the mountain may have been explicitly identified, as Mount Sinai or Mount Horeb or Beth-El are in the biblical tradition. Literal "high places" often bear a special significance for the spiritual quest.

For the Pitjendara tribe of central Australia, for example, the enormous hill of stone called Ayers Rock, which rises 1,100 feet from the red plain that stretches for 100 miles around it, is the center of their lives and the source of their dreams and aspirations.[3] For the Hebrew tribes, the Temple at Shiloh and the altar at Beth-El—two "high places" of the Holy Land—served similar purposes. This notion was pervasive in the ancient world. As Cyrus Gordon points out:

> One of the most intimate bonds between religion among the Greeks and among the peoples of Western Asia is the prominence of mountains as the abode of the gods. Olympus is for the Greeks what Saphon is for the Canaanites: the sacred mountain abode of the pantheon. Actually, the sacred mountain is not fixed in any of the widespread traditions.

The Mountain of God can be Sinai, Jerusalem, Gerizim (or Ebal), Carmel, etc., depending on the time, place and milieu in the Bible. To the peninsular Greeks, Zeus was the god of Olympus (though it is well to remember that the Greek world had many different Mount Olympuses); to the Cretans, he was the god of Cretan Ida; to the Trojans, he was the god of Trojan Ida (Iliad 24: 290-291).[4]

Since mountains and high places were "the abode of the gods," they also served as sacred points of connection, points at which humans could beseech the spirits. Greeks traveled from afar to receive instruction from the Oracle of Delphi on the slopes of Mount Parnassus. Moses first encountered God's message in the vision of the burning bush on the sides of Mount Sinai. As Karen Armstrong, author of *A History of God*, says of Jacob's staircase dream:

> We cannot but be reminded of Marduk's ziggurat: on its summit, suspended as it were between heaven and earth, a man could meet his gods. At the top of his own ladder *[sic]*, Jacob dreamed that he saw El. ... The story of this early epiphany shows that the High God of Canaan was beginning to acquire a more universal implication. ... [Jacob] was filled with the wonder that often inspired pagans when they encountered the sacred power of the divine: "How awe-inspiring this place is! This is nothing less than a house of God (*beth El*); this is the gate of heaven." He had instinctively expressed himself in the religious language of his time and culture: Babylon itself, the abode of the gods, was called "Gate of the gods" (*Bab-ili*).[5]

God could not be found in every high place. Moreover, there were many places where a god might conceivably be found that were not high at all. Hindu pilgrims seek religious awareness in the waters of the Ganges River. In the mountainous homeland of the Norse, the gods were said to dwell on the Plain of Ida. These could be classed as figurative "high places." More concretely, certain high places—actual mountains like Sinai and artificial mountains like the ziggurat—served as sacred intersections. These mountains were climbed not "because they were there" but because something sacred could be reached by the climbing.

In Egypt, tombs generally included a ladder to heaven. The soul of the awakened dead was supposed to climb the ladder to reach the ever-circling barge of Re. The Pyramid Texts, the most ancient of all known mythological texts, dating from the third millennium B.C.E., tell us: "The deceased goes to his mother Nut [the Sky]; he climbs upon her in this her name of 'Ladder.'"[6] The Northern Aranda tribe of Australia marks a particular site at ground level, hardening it with blood from their sexual organs and arms, inscribing targetlike circles in it with closely-packed down. This was the site at which their first ancestor rose at the dawn of the world. Often, the sacred site is depicted as an axis (the *axis mundi*), represented as a stairway, a ladder, a pole, or a tree. To this day, Christians annually set up a sacred pole in the form of the Christmas tree, which symbolically reaches from roots in the earth to the star at its top. Likewise, the cross of the crucifixion represents the same "world tree" in death. The Buddha reached enlightenment beneath the *Bodhi*-tree, the tree of "Waking to Omniscience."

Nearly every synagogue is considered a sacred site and is marked by the presence of a sacred tree, the seven-

branched *menorah,* or candelabrum. Jews refer to the Torah as "the Tree of Life." Jewish mystics even depict the Torah as a sacred site. For them, it was a literal Tree of Life,
with its roots in heaven.

> Rabbi Judah discoursed…, "Happy is the portion of
> Israel," he said, " in whom the Holy One, the
> Blessed, delights and to whom God gave the Torah
> of truth, the Tree of Life, whoever takes hold of
> which achieves life in this world and in the world to
> come. Now the Tree of Life extends from above down-
> ward, and it is the sun which illumines all. Its radi-
> ance commences at the top and extends through the
> whole trunk in a straight line.[7]

A place on the ground, a sanctuary dedicated to the
Eternal, a tree in bloom or a cross that is a tree stripped of
leaves, a pyramid or tomb, a ziggurat with its temple above,
a mountain, or a stone turned upright to become a place-
marker—all of these were symbolic of the site where heaven
and earth intersect. All of these mark a sacred point. Black
Elk was the last Keeper of the Sacred Pipe of the Oglala
Sioux. He had a vision while standing on Harney Peak in the
Black Hills. Then, he added to his vision the comment, "But
anywhere is the center of the world."[8]

Do you wish to incubate a dream? You may dream beneath a tree, make a sacred place for yourself under the
stars, climb a hill and rest your head on a stone, or set aside
a place within your home that you use only for incubating
dreams. You may choose to prepare this place in some elaborate way or not. There are an infinite number of ways for
making a site sacred, as many ways as there are individuals
with imagination in the world. Any site you elect becomes
your "high place." As Black Elk said, anywhere *is* "the center of the world."

)

Not only the place, but also the dreamer must be prepared. Abraham, like Gilgamesh, offers his sacrifice first. Both literally ask for a vision. We may assume that Jacob did likewise. In the words of Artemidorus, the resultant dreams were "worrying" or "asked-for" dreams. In the technical language of biblical scholars, they were "incubated."

Oppenheim studied several dream-omen texts of the Near East. In addition to *message* dreams, he suggested that *mantic* and *symbolic* dreams were also incubated. Mantic dreams were consulted for signs or omens (*omina*) that would indicate what the future would bring. The Abraham dream includes several references to commonly used omens: patterns of stars occurring in the night sky, patterns or spots found on the livers of dissected birds, and patterns or signs delivered in dreams. Interpreting dream omens meant deciphering why human beings turned into various animals, found themselves in certain locations, or dressed in various kinds of clothing.[9]

Symbolic dreams were generally considered dangerous. They involved unusual, sometimes evil, interactions between human beings and gods, stars, animals, objects, and other humans. Reciting the dream narrative to another person was thought to increase its potency, so a dream was rarely revealed except in an attempt to diminish its threatening quality.

The Mesopotamians had a ritual in which they told their dreams to a lump of clay for just that reason. The dreamer would take the lump of clay and rub it over his entire body, saying, "Lump! In your substance my substance has been fused, and in my substance your substance has been fused!" The dreamer

then told the clay all the dreams and said to it, "As
I shall throw you into the water, you will crumble
and disintegrate, and may the evil consequences of
all the dreams seen be gone, be melted away, and
be many miles removed from my body."[10]

As we have noted, the methods employed for incubating dreams included fasting, flagellation, and meditation.
In the case of the Greeks, these methods also included long
pilgrimages, intense concentration, and forbidden dormi-
tories filled with snakes. In Egypt, those unable to make a
pilgrimage sometimes sent surrogate dreamers to a temple
to incubate a dream for them. One incubation technique
reported in Egypt involved writing the names of five gods
on a linen bag. The bag was folded and dipped in oil to become the wick for a lamp; then the lamp was lit. The person
seeking the dream repeated a magical text seven times before putting out the lamp. Preparations complete, the
Egyptian rested, hoping to receive an answer while dreaming. In Tibet, yogic techniques were practiced to incubate
dreams; and the Chinese were known to employ dream temples. Incubation was generally reserved for important problems and concerns. Our ancestors conceived of a vast
difference between "ordinary" dreams and dreams containing spiritual significance. Only the latter were deliberately
sought.

In the West, the practice of dream incubation faded as
the dream world came to be understood as "unreal" under
the influence of Hellenistic philosophy.

We could re-create incubation using any number of
known methods. Most of us today are not inclined toward
prolonged periods of fasting, flagellation, pilgrimages to
distant places, or cohabitation with snakes—even innocu-
ous ones. Meditation seems more practical, but we are gen-

erally unfamiliar with its practice and often find it too time-consuming. Patricia Garfield, in her excellent book *Creative Dreaming*, suggests an alternative:

> Assuming that you value your dreams, and you accept that you can consciously influence them, and you have accumulated much that is interesting to dream about, you can hasten creative dreaming by immersing yourself in the specific subject you wish to dream of. Every system employs this step. Ancient dreamers concentrated on thoughts of the god they expected to appear in a dream to heal them; past creative dreamers... exerted intense efforts to invent a story for the few days prior to [their] induced dream; American Indian youths on their vision quests endured hungry days and nights thinking about and waiting for their spirit guide's arrival; the Senoi are occupied almost constantly with the subject of their dreams; don Juan urged Carlos to concentrate on his desired dream imagery; lucid dreamers... focused intensely on the... dreams [they] wished to produce; and Yogi dreamers meditate on the events of their dreams to come. Skills in meditation may increase dream control. *Whatever subject you wish to dream about, immerse yourself fully in it. Concentrate on it. Many creative dreamers stay deep in their subjects up until a few minutes before sleep.*[11]

This technique of focusing your thoughts and making creative dreaming your intention may serve the purpose. Obviously, the more resources you bring to the effort, the better. Finding a personal "high place" can help. Creating a ritual for preparation can help. And so on.

☽

The astonishment with which Jacob awakened while still dreaming is widely reported by those who have experienced lucid dreams. One dream researcher, Jayne Gackenbach, has suggested that women exhibit a greater "propensity to dream lucidly" than men. Nevertheless, her findings indicate that the regular practice of meditation can help people not only to recall more of their dreams but also to experience a greater number of lucid dreams.[12] Stephen LaBerge, the leading contemporary researcher of lucid dreaming, developed a method called *MILD*, the "Mnemonic Induction of Lucid Dreams." He recommends waking up from a dream; then visualizing yourself back in the dream becoming lucid, and repeating a mnemonic phrase such as, "Next time I dream, I want to recognize that I am dreaming." The mnemonic, a reminder to yourself, should be the same each time. LaBerge reported that, using this method, he could "reliably induce lucid dreams."[13]

In their book *Exploring the World of Lucid Dreaming*, LaBerge and Howard Rheingold, include a four-step method for employing lucid dreams to solve problems.[14] The first step is to *phrase your question*. Whether you wish to be able to better relate to a teenage child or need to know whether or not to quit your job and start your own business, you must phrase the question as simply as you can. Having phrased the question, write it down and memorize it.

The second step is to incubate a dream using your question as a mnemonic, while telling yourself that you wish to awaken to the answer.

The third step is to ask the question or seek the answer in the dream. When you awaken in the dream, you may find that the dream situation has nothing to do with your question. Nevertheless, being lucid, you can seek out a person within the dream, one who could answer your question, or you could search for a place that will give you some indication of the answer. So, for example, you might wish to consult with your mother or father to ask how they related to you when you were a teenager, or you could even summon your own teenager and pose the question directly. You could imagine yourself in the business you are considering and decide whether being in that business would be more comfortable than being in your present job. You might even find indicators of success or failure in the dream. LaBerge and Rheingold add, "Remember that you unconsciously know many more things than you imagine; the solution to your problem may be among them."

The fourth step is remembering to awaken and recall the dream and the answer you have received. You can call on yourself to awaken, or have your dream image remind you to wake up. You should immediately write down the dream segment that contained the answer. If you can't remember the answer or if you think that the dream did not provide the answer, you should still write what you can recall of the dream. On further analysis, you may find the answer by interpreting the dream narrative.

Creative problem-solving may be a benefit of lucid dreaming in modern terms. Our quest, however, runs more toward spiritual aims. In trying to re-create the transformative moments found in Bible dreams, we can profitably consider the lucid dreaming reported by Tibetan monks.

As early as the eighth century A.D., Tibetan Buddhists pursued the cultivation of dream lucidity. Achieving mastery of lucid dreams was considered a prerequisite to seeking enlightenment. As a monk increased the frequency of lucid dreaming and developed the ability to modify his dream imagery by willing it to change, he gradually recognized the illusory nature of the dream. This awareness similarly enabled the adept to recognize the waking world as an illusion. The monk would then recognize consciousness, which continues in both waking and dreaming states, rather than coarse material existence, as reality.[15]

LaBerge holds that "this capacity of lucid dreams, to prepare us for a fuller awakening, may prove to be lucid dreaming's most significant potential for helping us become more alive in our lives."[16] LaBerge estimates that, on the average, we enter our dream worlds half a million times in the course of our lives. Should we neglect the world of our dreams and allow it to become a wasteland, or cultivate it so that it becomes a forest of wonder? Many of us awaken, thinking with relief, "It was just a dream." But should we be relieved? As the Chinese sage Chuang-tzu said upon awakening, "I do not know whether I was then a man dreaming I was a butterfly, or whether I am now a butterfly dreaming I am a man."[17] There is infinite potential for wonder in the third of our lives that we spend sleeping. Should you close your eyes and sleep even while you are awake? Or should you open your eyes while you sleep and perhaps sense the astonishment that Jacob found?

)

In a brief span, we have penetrated far into the forest. Our dreams are not unlike those of ancient and preliterate peoples. In nearly every time and place, people of nearly every religion have accepted the idea that dreams connect us to an awareness greater than our own. Nearly every culture has some kind of *axis mundi* or sacred "high place" at which a special connection between earth and heaven can be achieved. Some distinction has nearly always been made between ordinary and extraordinary dreams. A great many cultures have believed that significant dreams should or could be incubated. A great many more dreams become available to us in those moments in our lives when we are faced by crisis or trauma or transformation. And almost all cultures believe that there is an art to finding the meaning in dreams: dreams must be interpreted.

Dream interpretation is not static. It is a process of developing an ever-increasing awareness of an array of meanings in every dream. Using our intellectual faculties, and "playing" with the text, we may arrive at more than one "true" interpretation—in fact, we *always* arrive at many "true" interpretations since any one that suits us is "true" *for us*, and each person reads a dream text a little differently. Two sculptors may take the same subject and produce entirely different statues. Each of them is a "true" representation. Two composers may take the same folk song and produce entirely different symphonies. Each of them is a "true" representation. And what is true of two is true of many; and what is true of many is true of one. For one person can interpret a dream today and find in it a resounding truth. And tomorrow the same person can interpret the same dream and find an entirely different and equally significant truth.

This is the shape-shifting nature of spiritual awareness. Its first principle is that *all truths are multifaceted*—things are more than they seem, many times more than they seem. There is no end to what may become sensible either to an individual or to a community of individuals. "It is crucial, then, for dream interpreters to have a sensitivity for radically new meanings, for meanings that are shockingly, dramatically different from our common understanding of ourselves and our world."[18]

Coming Home

JACOB'S DREAM
OF REINTEGRATION

)

As a large fish moves along the two banks of a river, the right
and left, so does that person move along these two states, the
state of sleeping and the state of waking.
— The Upanishads

Genesis 32 contains one of the Bible's most enigmatic passages: "Jacob was left alone, and a man wrestled with him
till daybreak." The tale of the wrestling match is often
lifted out of context and studied in isolation. In Genesis,
however, it is the final link in a tight group of three sequences. The text clearly indicates that each of the first two
sequences has a dream at its core. The wrestling sequence
is left unexplained. Was it, too, a dream?

Traditionally, Jewish commentary explained this incident in Jacob's life as a prophecy, despite its difference
from later prophetic utterances. This view considers the
conferring of the new name, "Israel," on Jacob to be the

most important element in the narrative. Genesis 32:28 reads: "Your name will no longer be Jacob, but Israel, for you have struggled with God and with men and have prevailed." Three chapters later, Genesis 35:10 reads: "God said to him: 'Your name is Jacob, but you will no longer be called Jacob; your name will be Israel.' So God named him Israel." Was Jacob named Israel by God or by his wrestling opponent? The traditional view is that God does nothing in a redundant way, therefore the first utterance of Jacob's new name must be a prophecy.

Modern Bible scholars often argue that the two versions of how Jacob received the name Israel stem from two distinct oral traditions preserved side by side in the Bible (just as two unique versions of Creation were preserved in the first two chapters of Genesis).[1]

Some traditional commentators, however, argued that Jacob's wrestling match can be nothing else than a vision or a dream.[2] One of the most interesting discussions is found in the work of the esteemed Jewish philosopher Moses Maimonides (1135–1204). For Maimonides, the power of the wrestling story derives from a secret concealed within the narrative. The key is in understanding the appearance of mysterious men in the Torah. Maimonides quotes Rabbi Hiyya the Great (2nd century B.C.E.) who commented on Abraham's three mysterious visitors.[3]

Genesis 18:1 reads: "And the Eternal appeared to him [Abraham] by the terebinths of Mamre." The verse says "the Eternal" appeared, but Rabbi Hiyya notes that the story goes on to describe the appearance of three "men." When he looked up to see the three men, Abraham ran to greet them. Since he bowed low to welcome them, Rabbi Hiyya said, Abraham had apparently realized that they were not ordinary men, but angels. He addressed "the greatest among them," calling himself "Your servant." It is strange, Rabbi Hiyya said, that Abraham then reverts to behaving toward the three as if they are ordinary men. He offered them the hospitality he would extend to any travelers—preparing and serving them food, and standing nearby in the attitude of an eager servant. Rabbi Hiyya concludes: Abraham's vacillation proves that even the great patriarch could not always distinguish an angel from a human being. Of course, being close to God, Abraham recognized the men as angels almost at once (though he behaved as if he had not), whereas some would realize that they had seen an angel only afterward, and some would never reach this realization at all. Maimonides commends Rabbi Hiyya's particular insight, adding:

> Understand this story [of Abraham and the visitors] for it is one of the secrets. I say likewise also of the story about *Jacob* in regard to its saying, *And there wrestled a man with him,* that it is in conformity with the form of prophetic revelation, inasmuch as it is finally made clear that he who was there was an *angel.*[4]

Whenever an angel is mentioned in the Bible, Maimonides continues, it is in relation to a vision of prophecy or a dream "whether this is explicitly stated or not." Sometimes a prophet immediately recognizes the angel. Sometimes the prophet thinks the angel is a person, though it later becomes clear that the person was an angel. In either case, "the event was from the first *a vision of prophecy* or *a dream of prophecy.*" And Maimonides hastens to add, "It should by no means occur to your thought that an *angel* can be heard except *in a vision of prophecy* or *in a dream of prophecy....*"[5]

Following the reasoning of Rabbi Hiyya and Maimonides—and for another reason that will unfold as we proceed—we will treat the wrestling story as a *dream* of Jacob.

☽

To interpret the wrestling dream, we need to step back and view the whole tapestry of three dream sequences. In his youth, Jacob was a competent cheat. His elder kinsman Laban, however, was a master cheat. At first, Jacob found himself overmatched. The general outline is well known: Jacob fell in love with Laban's youngest daughter, Rachel. He agreed to serve Laban for seven years in exchange for Rachel's hand in marriage. Laban arranged an elaborate ruse, substituting his first-born daughter, Leah, on the night of the wedding. To gain Rachel, Jacob agreed to a second round of seven years of servitude. Jacob served out his fourteen years, only then negotiating for wages.

Suddenly, God commands (Genesis 31:3), "Return to the land of your fathers where you were born, and I will be with you. "[6] From this moment forward, the biblical narrative fairly explodes with dream narratives.

In response to God's call, Jacob summons his wives, Rachel and Leah, to the field where they can confer on a touchy subject without fear of being overheard. The subject is their father, Laban.

"I served Laban with all my might," Jacob told his wives, "but your father has cheated me, changing my wages time and again." Jacob described how God foiled Laban's plans. When Laban offered to pay Jacob by giving him all the speckled animals, God caused the flocks to drop speckled young. When Laban changed his offer to give Jacob only streaked animals, God caused the flocks to drop streaked young. Despite Laban's wily maneuvering, Jacob told his wives: "God has taken away your father's livestock and given it to me." Jacob then relates a dream.

> Once at the mating time of the flocks, I raised my eyes and saw in a dream, behold, the he-goats mating with the flocks were streaked, speckled, and mottled. And in the dream an angel of God said to me, "Jacob!" "Here," I answered. And he said, "Note well that all the he-goats which are mating with the flock are streaked, speckled, and mottled; for I have noted all that Laban has been doing to you. I am the God of Beth-El, where you anointed a pillar and where you made a vow to Me. Now, arise and leave this land and return to your native land" [Genesis 31:10–13].

This dream begins in an odd way: "I raised my eyes and saw in a dream, behold...." There is no mention of Jacob sleeping. Nor do we think of receiving a dream by raising our eyes. So, the word "dream" here may have meant something else to Jacob and his wives. It seems to indicate "a moment of clarity" or "a realization." If we adopt this interpretation, Jacob's words make better sense. The "dream" would begin something like this:

> Once, at the mating time of the flocks, I raised my eyes and it struck me that the he-goats mating with the flock were streaked, speckled, and mottled. In that moment of realization, God's message came to me. ...

The new reading certainly "plays" with the text, but it has much to recommend it. "[I] saw in a dream, behold" is translated as "it struck me"; and "in the dream an angel of

God said to me" is translated as "in that moment of realization, God's message came to me." These changes are permissible since the words "dream, behold" seem to be a moment of inspiration and the biblical understanding of angels is that, at one and the same time, an angel is (1) an angel, (2) a messenger, and (3) a message.

It is in this dreamlike moment of clarity that Jacob recalls "the God of Beth-El" and the covenant he made there two decades ago. God promised to protect him and make him prosperous; he vowed to be loyal *while waiting for God's promises to be fulfilled*. This notion is also consistent with biblical belief: The truth of a prophecy is tested by whether or not it comes true. Looking back, Jacob knows that God has been with him all along. He left home empty-handed, but now he hopes to return with wives and children, servants, and flocks.

Of course, all of Jacob's wealth has come to him at Laban's expense. In his dream, Jacob hears the message that God has brought this to pass. But the real-world Jacob seems to question whether his title to all these possessions is free and clear.

We need a little more information here regarding Jacob's precise legal status. From archaeological records, we know of a form of marriage practiced in Assyria called *eribu* marriage.[7] In an *eribu* marriage, the husband agrees to leave his family and become part of his wife's family. This may be the kind of marriage referred to in Genesis 2:24, by the statement at the end of the second creation story: "Hence a man leaves his father and mother and clings to his wife, so that they become one flesh." If Jacob entered into an *eribu* contract with Laban in order to obtain his two wives, then he could only legally retain title to his "earnings" as long as he remained in Laban's household. In other

words, he would have no legal right to remove these possessions from Laban.

Rachel and Leah, however, come to his defense by
claiming all of Jacob's wealth on different grounds. They
claim that this is the dowry *owed* to them by their father,
Laban. They tell Jacob, "Truly, all the wealth that God has
taken away from our father belongs to us and to our children. Now, then, do just as God has told you" [Genesis
31:16].

Reading between the lines, it appears that Jacob, Rachel, and Leah have entered into a conspiracy to cheat
Laban.[8] Once more, Jacob stands to gain worldly wealth
through his old friend, trickery. He has worthy companions
in Rachel and Leah, for the two of them had learned deceit
at their father's knee and once even practiced it against Jacob. Of course, any trick succeeds only if you get away with
it. So Jacob waits until the most opportune moment, when
Laban is away from home. Then he packs up his whole camp
and flees.

It seems to the reader that Jacob, since leaving his parents, has hardly matured one iota. He is the same trickster
he was then, practicing the same kind of deceit against
Laban as he did against Esau and Isaac, using his obviously
considerable charms to lure his wives into conspiring with
him, and being once again forced to make a quick getaway.
A person of greater integrity might have negotiated with
Laban, despite the fact that Laban himself was deceitful.
We are left to contrast Jacob's leaving Laban with Abraham's leaving Haran. Abraham walks in God's way from the
very outset. Jacob is still a man of two minds—with an incli-
nation to trust in God but an obsession to win his worldly
way through trickery.

☽

The next sequence commences, "Jacob outwitted Laban the Aramean, not telling him that he was fleeing." Three days later, Jacob's flight was reported to Laban who gathered a posse of male relatives and pursued Jacob for seven days, catching up with him at last in the hills of Gilead. Jacob and his retinue were camped "on the Height" when Laban and his force appeared. Laban pitched his camp in the surrounding hills.

This time, it is Laban who has a dream. The Bible supplies no visual details of this dream (perhaps it is also a kind of realization). What is important is the message:

> But God appeared to Laban the Aramean in a dream by night and said to him, "Beware of attempting anything with Jacob, good or bad" [Genesis 31:24].

When Laban confronts Jacob, he repeats the dream message to him:

> I have it in my power to do you harm; but the God of your father said to me last night, "Beware of attempting anything with Jacob, good or bad" [Genesis 31:29].

As the sequence closes, Jacob and Laban conclude a nonaggression pact, in witness of which they set up a mound of stones to mark the boundary between them. They make a covenant, each taking an oath. Laban swears by the God of Abraham and the God of Nahor—calling on these two deities to judge between them if either should henceforth cross the boundary with evil intent. Jacob swears by the "Fear of his father Isaac."[9] Jacob then offers a sacrifice "on the Height," and invites Laban and all his relatives to partake of the sacrificial meal. Afterward, they all spend the night together "on the Height."

Why should the text specify that they all slept "on the Height?" Knowing what we do of the importance of "high places" in the Bible, we have to wonder whether some kind of ritual was being enacted. Were these two dreamers—Jacob and Laban—each incubating dreams, looking perhaps to reassure themselves that they had concluded a fair bargain? All we can really say is that some reason obviously existed for the two camps to spend the night together "on the Height." The incident might have had some obvious meaning for our biblical ancestors; for us, its intention is difficult to fathom.

This is the state of the tapestry as the sequence that includes the wrestling commences. As Nahum M. Sarna sympathetically characterizes it in his book *Understanding Genesis*:

> The biographical details of Jacob's life read like a catalogue of misfortunes. When he was finally able to make his escape and set out for home after two decades in the service of his scoundrelly uncle, he found his erstwhile employer in hot and hostile pursuit of him. No sooner had this trouble passed than he felt his life to be in mortal danger from his brother Esau.[10]

Since the narrative of the wrestling dream is long, it is best read once in its entirety, before we take it apart to interpret it.[11]

> Jacob went on his way, and the angels of God encountered him. When he saw them, Jacob said, "This is God's camp." So he named that place Mahanaim.

Jacob sent messengers ahead to his brother Esau in the land of Seir, the country of Edom, and instructed them as follows, "Thus shall you say, 'To my lord Esau, thus says your servant Jacob: I stayed with Laban and remained until now; I have acquired cattle, asses, sheep, and male and female slaves; and I send this message to my lord in the hope of gaining your favor.'" The messengers returned to Jacob, saying, "We came to your brother Esau; he himself is coming to meet you, and there are four hundred men with him." Jacob was greatly frightened; in his anxiety, he divided the people with him, and the flocks and herds and camels, into two camps, thinking, "If Esau comes to the one camp and attacks it, the other camp may yet escape."

Then Jacob said, "O God of my father Abraham and God of my father Isaac, O Lord, who said to me, 'Return to your native land and I will deal bountifully with you'! I am unworthy of all the kindness that You have so steadfastly shown your servant: with my staff alone I crossed this Jordan, and now I have become two camps. Deliver me, I pray, from the hand of my brother, from the hand of Esau; else, I fear, he may come and strike me down, mothers and children alike. Yet You have said, 'I will deal bountifully with you and make your offspring as the sands of the sea, which are too numerous to count.'"

After spending the night there, he selected from what was at hand this gift for his brother Esau: 200 she-goats and 20 he-goats; 200 ewes and 20 rams; 30 milch camels with their colts; 40 cows

and 10 bulls; 20 she-asses and 10 he-asses. These
he put in the charge of his servants, drove by drove,
and he told his servants, "Go on ahead, and keep a
distance between droves." He instructed the one in
front as follows, "When my brother Esau meets you
and asks you, 'Whose man are you? Where are you
going? And whose [animals] are these ahead of
you?' you shall answer, 'Your servant Jacob's; they
are a gift sent to my lord Esau; and [Jacob] himself
is right behind us.'" He gave similar instructions to
the second one, and the third, and all the others
who followed the droves, namely, "Thus and so
shall you say to Esau when you reach him. And you
shall add, 'And your servant Jacob himself is right
behind us.'" For he reasoned, "If I propitiate him
with this present in advance, and then face him,
perhaps he will show me favor." And so the gift
went on ahead, while he remained in camp that
night.

That same night he arose, and taking his two
wives, his two maidservants, and his eleven children, he crossed the ford of the Jabbok. After taking them across the stream, he sent across all his
possessions.

Jacob was left alone. And a man wrestled with
him until the break of dawn. When he saw that he
had not prevailed against him, he wrenched Jacob's hip at its socket, so that the socket of his hip
was strained as he wrestled with him. Then he said,
"Let me go, for dawn is breaking." But he answered, "I will not let you go, unless you bless me."
Said the other, "What is your name?" He replied,
"Jacob." Said he, "Your name shall no longer be Ja-

cob, but Israel, for you have striven with beings divine and human, and have prevailed." Jacob asked, "Pray tell me your name." But he said, "You must not ask my name!" And he took leave of him there. So Jacob named the place Peniel, meaning, "I have seen a divine being face to face, yet my life has been preserved."

The sun rose upon him as he passed Penuel, limping on his hip. That is why the children of Israel to this day do not eat the thigh muscle that is on the socket of the hip, since Jacob's hip socket was wrenched at the thigh muscle [Genesis 32: 2–33].

If Jacob's staircase dream dealt with estrangement, divorce, and the path to salvation, the story of Jacob's wrestling match deals with maturity, self-image, and reintegration. Taking a reverse page from Thomas Wolfe, this chapter might be called *You Can Go Home Again*, provided that we add: *but you will not be the same person who left, and home will not be the same as it was when you left it.* Jacob's struggle in the wrestling narrative portrays tests that all of us eventually face. What is more, as Jacob undergoes his transformation, the struggle itself undergoes a transformation—it models an opportunity to create a milestone in a spiritual life. Let's take the text apart piece by piece.

$$)$$

✹ *Genesis 32 [2]* **Jacob went on his way, and the angels of God [malachei-Elohim] encountered [vay-yifg'u] him. [3] When he saw them, Jacob said, "This is God's camp [mahaneh]." So he named that place Mahanaim.**

This third dream sequence opens with echoes of Jacob's dream at Beth-El. The word for "angels of God" is *malachei-Elohim*—literally, "divine beings." It is the same word that was used for the angels ascending and descending the staircase. The word *vay-yifga*—this time with a plural ending, *vay-yifg'u*—is repeated with its implication of "came up against" or "was touched by." At Beth-El, Jacob "encountered" the certain place; now he is "encountered" by the angels.

Professor Sarna believes the similarity between the opening verses of the Beth-El story and the first verse here serves to "bracket" the beginning and end of the Jacob and Laban "cycle of stories, which constitute a distinct unit within the larger biography of the patriarch."[12] While this is possible, the verses seem equally integral to the wrestling dream story that follows.

In 32:3—"This is God's camp [*mahaneh*]"—the word *mahaneh* has several possible meanings. Which of them we choose is critical since we encounter this same word seven times. It can mean a "camp," a place where tents or huts are set up by nomads, travelers, or armies. It can mean the people themselves, as in "the camp awakened." It is also used to mean "a military host," and we use it in this sense in English, as well, sometimes couching the word as "encampment." It can also mean a "troop," again in a military sense. For this reason, some interpreters translate the phrase as "This is God's host" or "This is God's army."

The normal plural for the word *mahaneh* is *mahanot,* but in naming the place, Jacob employs a special Hebrew usage, the dual, a form of the plural that signifies a pair. Thus, *mahanaim* literally means "a pair of camps"—it forms a collective noun with the sense of two parts. We have similar usages in English, for example, "trousers," a plural noun for a single garment with two legs. But these are rare, and never as explicit as the dual suffix is in Hebrew. *Mahanaim* could be just a place-name as our initial translation indicates: "that place Mahanaim." But it is possible that something more is intended.

The venerated commentator Rashi (1040–1105) suggested that Jacob actually encountered two camps of angels: those who had accompanied him while he was outside the Promised Land and those who waited to accompany him when he would again enter the Promised Land. Other classic commentators considered the name Mahanaim appropriate since this marked the meeting of Jacob's camp and a camp of angels. Several modern commentators believe that the encounter and the name are vestiges of a fuller story that has been lost.

There is another possibility. As Jacob approaches the Jabbok River, the historic boundary beyond which lies the Promised Land, he encounters a moment in which his spiritual self is revived. He feels himself being joined by a host of angels. His camp is now "two camps." His lower camp is earthly—it consists of his family and his flocks. His upper camp is heavenly—it consists of the angels that come to protect them. Perhaps this is the sense behind the word *mahanaim*, which implies "two camps-in-one."

✻ *[4]* **Jacob sent messengers *[malachim]* ahead to his brother Esau in the land of Seir, the country of Edom, *[5]* and instructed them as follows, "Thus shall you say, 'To my lord Esau, thus says your servant Jacob: I stayed with Laban and remained until now; *[6]* I have acquired cattle, asses, sheep, and male and female slaves; and I send this message to my lord in the hope of gaining your favor.'" *[7]* The messengers returned to Jacob, saying, "We came** to your brother Esau; he himself is coming to meet you, and there are four hundred men with him." *[8]* Jacob was greatly frightened; in his anxiety, he divided the people with him, and the flocks and herds and camels, into two camps *[mahanot]*, *[9]* thinking, "If Esau comes to the one camp *[mahaneh]* and attacks it, the other camp *[mahaneh]* may yet escape."

Jacob sends *malachim,* "messengers" or "angels" to his brother Esau. The word is equivocal. Were the messengers actually angels? Or is this just very effective wordplay?

> *Please forgive me for inserting a digression here: One of the problems of reading the Bible in English is that we lose the way it "sounds." In English transla- tions, the Bible appears to be a very noble, serious, and intense document. This is true, of course. But the translations also make it seem that the Bible has almost no sense of humor whatever. And this is en- tirely false. What made the Bible, and especially its stories, entertaining was the use of inventive puns, humorous little changes within words, puns, and wordplay. The reason I spend so much time defin- ing this Hebrew word or that, showing where one relates to another, or how one word plays off an- other, is that I want to share some of that humor with you. Interpretation, at its creative best, can be a very sophisticated art that "plays" with words and tweaks their meanings to bring us insight and pleasure simultaneously.*

The messengers return and report that Esau is ap- proaching with four hundred men. Jacob grows frightened. Some medieval commentators speculate that Jacob named the place Mahanaim because of the action he takes next.

Jacob divides his own camp in two camps, hoping that if Esau manages to attack one, the other might escape. This is suggestive—it is a military strategy, here applied to civilians and flocks. His spiritual encounter with the angels apparently gives way to a more pragmatic inspiration. Jacob behaves in his old ways and prepares a trick. Perhaps he can convince Esau that he has only half as much wealth as he really has.

We also get the impression that Jacob might be willing to sacrifice the first camp provided that he can save the second camp—the one that, presumably, includes his wives and children. Then, in a remarkable twist, as quickly as his old "trickster" self formulates a practical strategy and carries it out, Jacob's spiritual awareness suddenly comes to the fore again.

❋ **[10] Then Jacob said, "O God of my father Abraham and God of my father Isaac, O Eternal, who said to me, 'Return to your native land and I will deal bountifully with you'! [11] I am unworthy of all the kindness that You have so steadfastly shown your servant: with my staff alone I crossed this Jordan, and now I have become two camps [mahanot]. [12] Deliver me, I pray, from the hand of my brother, from the hand of Esau; else, I fear, he may come and strike me down, mothers and children alike. [13] Yet You have said, 'I will deal bountifully with you and make your offspring as the sands of the sea, which are too numerous to count.'"**

Jacob seems to have a realization: He can seek protection in the conditional covenant he made with God. His practical self subsides for a moment, and Jacob becomes a spiritual tactician. He prays for God to remember their covenant. He repeats phrases from his earlier dreams. *Return to your native land* reminds us of the message he received from the angel in 31:3, "Return to the land of your fathers where you were born" and in his dream of the flocks in 31:13, "Arise and leave this land and return to your native land." *The sands of the sea, which are too numerous to count* reminds us of the staircase dream in 28:14, "Your descendants shall be as the dust of the earth...." For a moment, Jacob becomes uncharacteristically humble, calling himself "unworthy," recalling that he left his home with nothing but his staff. But, since he is unworthy, he cleverly offers his prayer in the names of Abraham and Isaac as a reminder to God that he has been confirmed to be their successor.

Is there an epiphany in this prayer? Has the old Jacob who always viewed God in a conditional way ("if I return safe to my father's house—the Eternal shall be my God" [Genesis 28:21]) now decided to place his life and the lives of all who are with him entirely in God's hands? Will he now trust in God's protection, hoping that God will save him from Esau as God saved him from Laban?

Or perhaps the prayer just gives us another way to understand why Jacob calls the place Mahanaim? The name may refer to Jacob's existential condition. He is a man of two compartmented minds. One tells him to trust in God, to turn away from any thought of being murdered by Esau since God has promised to protect him. The other argues, it is all well and good to trust God, but when it comes to personal safety, it is best to trust yourself. One mind, two compartments—Jacob is at *Mahanaim*.

✢ *[14]* **After spending the night there, he selected from what was at hand this gift *[minhah]* for his brother Esau: *[15]* 200 she-goats and 20 he-goats; 200 ewes and 20 rams; *[16]* 30 milch camels with their colts; 40 cows and**

10 bulls; 20 she-asses and 10 he-asses. *[17]* These he put in the charge of his servants, drove by drove, and he told his servants, "Go on ahead, and keep a distance between droves." *[18]* He instructed the one in front as follows, "When my brother Esau meets you and asks you, 'Whose man are you? Where are you going? And whose [animals] are these ahead of you?' *[19]* you shall answer, 'Your servant Jacob's; they are a gift *[minhah]* sent to my lord Esau; and [Jacob] himself is right behind us.'" *[20]* He gave similar instructions to the second one, and the third, and all the others who followed the droves, namely, "Thus and so shall you say to Esau when you reach him. *[21]* And you shall add, 'And your servant Jacob himself is right behind us.'" For he reasoned, "If I propitiate him with this present *[minhah]* in advance, and then face him, perhaps he will show me favor." *[22]* And so the gift *[minhah]* went on ahead, while he remained in camp that night.

In this set of verses, it appears that Jacob has decided to trust himself. Shifting his allegiance away from the host of angels and from God's covenant, Jacob devises a new stratagem. Esau is a man, he reasons, and men can be flattered. Esau is a man, he reasons, and men can be impressed. Esau is a man, he reasons, and men can be bribed. He will bribe, flatter, and impress his brother.

The Hebrew word used for "gift," *minhah,* has been carefully chosen. A *minhah*-gift is propitiatory, as in a "tribute" or "offering." It is a gift given with the specific purpose of pacifying or influencing the receiver. Its most frequent use is to denote an "offering to God," a "sacrifice."[13] Jacob is not sending these gifts out of the goodness of his heart; he is making sacrifices intended to appease Esau. There may also be a hidden meaning here, an additional wordplay. By transposing the middle consonants, *minhah* ("gift") becomes *mahaneh* ("camp"). In fact, when spoken aloud, *minhah* and *mahaneh* are alliterative. If we interpret the verses with this in mind, the inference is that "Jacob is *sacrificing* one *camp* as a propitiatory *gift*."

Jacob sends forth a stream of servants (not "messengers" this time) to flatter Esau in his name. He sends forth a stream of wealth to bribe his brother. He sends forth a stream of men and flocks to show that he has abundant wealth; and to insinuate that his strength must be overwhelming, too. He divides the gift into a series of successive gifts to drive home his point. By the time the last gift arrives, he hopes that Esau will imagine that he has more to fear from Jacob than Jacob has to fear from him.

Has Jacob simply suffered a failure of nerve? He is still afraid, still unable to fully place his trust in God. What a picture the story paints! As Esau approaches, it is almost as if Jacob is frantically running up and down the staircase that joins earth and heaven. He meets angels (up the stairs), he divides his camp in two to deceive Esau (down the stairs), he prays for deliverance (up the stairs again), and he sends off tribute to bribe or intimidate Esau (down the stairs again). He waffles—now trusting God, now trusting himself. In this moment of crisis—as in any moment of transition—he must soon come to one conclusion or the other. "A house divided against itself," as both Mark and Abraham Lincoln observed, "cannot stand."

✳ *[23]* **That same night he arose, and taking his two wives, his two maidservants, and his eleven children, he crossed the ford of the Jabbok.** *[24]* **After taking them across the stream, he sent across all his possessions.** *[25a]* **Jacob was left alone.**

Jacob is still restive. Has he done everything in his power to protect the things he loves? He looks deep into his bag of tricks. No one, not even Esau, would cross the Jabbok River in the middle of the night. The military strategist in him takes hold again. At great risk, he takes his family across. He then returns and sends the rest of the camp across the Jabbok. He is alone again with his staff. He is physically separated from everything he achieved in the past twenty years.

Unexpectedly, the story begins to speak to us in all too familiar terms. We can easily empathize with Jacob at this moment. Whenever we approach our siblings after a separation, or whenever we return to our parents' home after being on our own, we often find ourselves unable to act with the maturity we believe we have won so dearly. We still carry a child in us, barely below the surface, impishly anxious to emerge. Going home almost inevitably means reverting to childhood behaviors.

Moreover, some folks do not wait for a physical journey home for this to be true. They never *stop* regarding themselves as children, whether they are thirty or forty or even fifty. They face the child within them whenever they stand before a mirror, whenever they are evaluated at work, whenever they telephone their aging parents, whenever they argue with a spouse, whenever they deal with a sibling. In a hundred ways, they feel immature; while in a hundred other ways, they know that they must act grown-up.

All of us experience a reversion to childhood at some time or another. Is there a way that we can approach "home"—the people and places of our childhood—without losing our sense of being adult? It is surely at times of crisis or moments of transition, standing alone as Jacob does now, that we eventually come to grips with this issue.

The precise moment, the specific crisis, differs for each of us. It could be the awful time when a parent must be deprived of independence and placed in a home for the aged or infirm. It could be at the loss of a parent, a spouse, or a sibling. It could be at the loss of a child, a niece, a nephew, an aunt, or an uncle. It could be in a painful negotiation over the will and last testament of a departed father or mother. Or our crisis could have nothing to do with aging and death. It could be in therapy, in the face of realizing that one is a habitual gambler or an alcoholic, is a drug addict or a dealer, suffers paranoia or depression, or has repressed a childhood of abuse or incest. It could be in response to the threat of a terminal illness. It could be when confronted by a crisis for one's child. It could even be in the loss of a job, in the search for a new job, or even in a moment of particularly low self-esteem. Any event that saps us of our trust in our spiritual and worldly maturity may be our turning point. At times like these, dreams tend to become archetypal and prophetic—they tend to bring us messages. As emotionally drained as we feel, the crisis or transition also represents an opportunity for the spiritual potential within us to radically transform our lives.

✳ *[25]* **Jacob was left alone. And a man wrestled *[vay-ye'avek]* with him until the break of dawn. *[26]* When he saw that he had not prevailed against him, he wrenched Jacob's hip at its socket, so that the socket of his hip was strained as he wrestled with him. *[27]* Then he said, "Let me go, for dawn is breaking." But he answered, "I will not let you go, unless you bless me." *[28]* Said the other, "What is your name?" He replied, "Jacob." *[29]* Said he, "Your name shall no longer be Jacob, but Israel, for you**

have striven with beings divine *[elohim]* and human, and have prevailed.”

We sense an immediate and qualitative difference between these verses and what came before. Verses 15 and 16 contain an enumerated listing of Jacob's gift. They read as if an accountant drew them up. Taken along with the very specific instructions Jacob gives his servants, those verses are grounded in common reality. By contrast, the dream verses are episodic, impressionistic, and (pun fully intended) disjointed. If we had no other reason to assume that this part of the narrative is a dream, the surreal imagery employed here might force us to that conclusion.

We also reach the same conclusion along another path: In 32:25 we hear, “And a man wrestled with him until *the break of dawn*.” In 32:27 the man says, “Let me go, for *dawn is breaking*.” Why repeat this idea? Is the dawn here just a poetic symbol for a time of new beginnings?

We know why Jacob is afraid of the dawn. At dawn, he expects to face Esau. But why should the dawn be so threatening to the man wrestling with Jacob? Or, perhaps, we should phrase the question another way: What is it that the man represents? What is it that must always disappear when we awake at the break of dawn? One answer, of course, is a dream.

The rabbinic sages adopted an entirely different point of view. They inherited a tradition that the “man” was actually an angel. When they noticed the angel's insistence on leaving at dawn, they explained that the angel was being called back to heaven to join the chorus of angels that sing God's praises each morning. Some cited yet another tradition that the angel who wrestled with Jacob was Samael (often identified with Satan), the angel who poisoned the world with death and who had become Esau's guardian angel. Their interpretation was that Jacob wrestled with his mortality that night, seeing Esau as the agent of his potential destruction. Bearing these ideas in mind, let's play with the text further to see what other possibilities may lay just below its surface.

The verb for "he wrestled," *vay-ye'avek*, is a wordplay on the name of the river that Jacob crossed, the Jabbok (*yabbok*). Folklorist Sir James Frazer noted that the literature of myth throughout the world speaks of river-spirits that contest with humans who attempt to ford their streams. Even the simplest water crossing can be treacherous, and mishaps were often attributed to malevolent demons identified with the water. Could Jacob have wrestled (*ye'avek*) the spirit of the Jabbok (*yabbok*)? The Jungian analyst M.-L. von Franz observes:

> The Self usually appears in dreams at crucial times in the dreamer's life—turning points when his basic attitudes and whole way of life are changing. The change itself is often symbolized by the action of crossing water.... Crossing a river is a frequent symbolic image for a fundamental change of attitude.[14]

Turning back to comparative mythology, Frazer also suggests that Jacob may have encountered a demon of the night, one who must depart by morning and who injures Jacob in his attempt to flee before the dawn. When a mythic hero can catch hold of such demons and detain them until the dawn when they must escape, the demons are often forced to give some kind of gift to the hero in return for their freedom.[15] Perhaps this is what is happening when Jacob demands a blessing.

The verb for "he wrestled," *vay-ye'avek,* comes from the root word *avek,* which means "dust." The derivation seems to be that wrestling is equivalent to rolling in or being covered by dust. This may also allude to Jacob's descendants, who are called the sand (the "dust" near the sea, see 32:13) and the dust of the earth (see 28:14, where the word for "dust" is *afar*). In the Creation story, too, Adam was created of the dust (*afar*) of the earth (see 2:7). Could we then interpret the verse to mean, "And Jacob wrestled with himself until the break of dawn to *re-create* himself and his descendants"? Might this capture the sense of the verse, if not its literal meaning?

Carl Jung spoke of an emanation from within ourselves that sometimes confronts us in our dreams. He termed it the "shadow." M.-L. von Franz explains Jung's concept, noting, "In dreams and myths ... the shadow appears as a person of the same sex as that of the dreamer." In seeing our shadow in a dream, we become "aware of (and often ashamed of) those qualities and impulses" we deny in ourselves "but can plainly see in other people." Among these are "unreal fantasies, schemes, and plots."[16] This would certainly include Jacob among those that might dream of their shadow wrestling with them.

In sum, Jacob may be wrestling an angel of God, a river-demon, a demon of the night, the angel of death, the guardian spirit of Esau, his "shadow," the child within him, or himself. Do we have an absolute need to know which of these is "true"? Not in our spiritual forest. As the contemporary Jungian James Hillman notes:

> "Literalism is sickness." Whenever we are caught in a literal view, a literal belief, a literal statement, we have lost the imaginative metaphorical perspective to ourselves and our world.[17]

To need to know for certain whom Jacob is wrestling is to be caught up in literalism, to succumb to our critical faculties alone. Each time we approach the dream, we need to hear it again, as if for the first time. Each time we hear it, the character of Jacob's adversary may differ *for us*. Which of the possibilities is the "true" adversary depends less on the story than on our own needs—the adversary that is true *for us now* is always the "true" adversary.

Jacob is alone, but someone is with him. He wrestles with a man. The pain is excruciating, the scar of it may last forever. For certain, Jacob will be deprived of something on account of this struggle. Neither of the wrestlers can prevail, yet Jacob refuses to let go of the man, refuses to allow the struggle to end without resolution. When the man cries out, "Let me go, for dawn is breaking," we know the moment of transition is at hand. The shadow will disappear inside Jacob, or the angel will vanish along with this opportunity, unless Jacob does something to break the deadlock.

Always resourceful, Jacob has a brainstorm. Through his father's blessing, he gained the strength to go out on his own. Through God's blessing, he gained the moral courage to leave his Promised Land. Why not demand another blessing, another source of strength? *I will not let you go, unless you bless me.* How will the man bless him? What will replace the loss of the child (the trickster) in him? Yet, no blessing follows; instead, the man offers a gift.

"What is your name?" the man asks. And suddenly so much becomes clear. The struggle we are witnessing has all along been a struggle for identity. Jacob's innermost being has all along been crying out, "Who am I? What am I?" Am I the part of me that has concluded a covenant with God? Or am I the part of me that continually attempts to deceive others? Am I a spiritual person, worthy of calling on the names of Abraham and Isaac? Or am I a fraud, pretending to be spiritual, while really attempting to make heaven do my will? "What is your name?" the man asks. But Jacob hears the question as, "How shall I really know myself?"

He replies, "Jacob," but we can imagine him holding on for dear life to hear the answer that he will really give himself. The man replies, "Your name shall no longer be Jacob, but Israel...." *Yisrael*, "the one who wrestles with God." *Yisrael* for "you have striven with beings divine and human." *Yisrael* for "you have prevailed." The *Odyssey* (4:397) states, "Hard is a god for a mortal man to master," yet the *Iliad* and the *Odyssey* both include accounts of famed warriors overmatching gods. The difference between these accounts and the biblical narrative, however, is stunning. The Greek warriors gain fame and, by defeating their gods, earn a place beside them. Jacob prevails, but it is clear from the context that he does not win. He has only become "the one who wrestles with God." From now on, to be Israel, he will have to continue to struggle against "beings divine and human."

A transformation has taken place, nonetheless. Beforehand, Jacob wrestled in the dust, an earthly being wriggling this way and that like a trapped worm. Now Jacob's wrestling becomes spiritual. He is Israel, "the one who wrestles with *God*." Beforehand, Jacob's name signified his struggle with his brother Esau—the Hebrew *Ya'akov* referred to his coming out of the womb grasping at Esau's heel (*ekev*). His new name ties him to God, instead. This is the inner message of the dream as it first appears. Even if we were unable to explore other possibilities, it would still be a significant moment of transformation. But what does it mean *for us*?

Like Jacob, in such moments, you are alone and yet not alone. You are of two minds. You face the choice of acting through the child in you or of exercising your most mature judgment. A person "who is not your self and yet is your self" struggles with you until dawn. You wake up sweating with the struggle, held in its eviscerating grip, having tossed and turned the whole night. Spiritual awareness can help you here. Wrestling with your own conscience is equivalent to wrestling with the prophetic message. To win through to an integrated personality, you must either release or integrate the child within. Though you have every reason to be insecure without the child, having never been without it before, at this moment there is a new possibility—the possibility of reintegration.

✽ *[30] Jacob asked, "Pray tell me your name." But he said, "You must not ask my name!" And he took leave of him there. [31] So Jacob named the place Peniel, meaning, "I have seen a divine being [elohim] face to face, yet my life has been preserved."*

The dream is not yet over. Why does the wrestler withhold his name, offering no clue to his identity? The sages speculated that the angel spoke for God, and human beings cannot know God's name. In Judges 13, an angel foretells the birth of Samson. Samson's father, Manoah, thinks the angel is a man and asks, "What is your name?" The angel responds, "You must not ask for my name; it is unknowable." Only later does Manoah realize that the man he spoke with was an angel. Then Manoah is frightened and tells his wife, "We shall surely die, for we have seen a divine being [elohim]." His wife assures him that if God had meant for them to die, they would already be dead.[18] The two stories bear close resemblance. Throughout history, it has been claimed that to know the true name of a person or a thing is to gain power over it:

> The essential character of things and of men resides in their names. Therefore to know a name is

to be privy to the secret of its owner's being and master of his fate. The members of many primitive tribes have two names, one for public use, the other jealously concealed, known only to the man who bears it....

To know the name of a man is to exercise power over him alone; to know the name of a higher, supernatural being is to dominate the entire province over which that being presides. The more such names a magician has garnered, the greater the number of spirits that are subject to his call and command. ... "Tell me, I pray thee, thy name," Jacob demanded of the angel with whom he wrestled, but the angel parried the question and his name remained his secret, lest Jacob invoke him in magical incantation and he be obliged to obey. ... Higher than all, however, stands God— and the names of God which Jewish ingenuity invented (or discovered?) placed in the hands of the Jewish magician unlimited powers to manipulate God's world.[19]

This may explain why the man withheld his name from Jacob. If he was an angel speaking for God, then the name would have been either too powerful for Jacob to understand or too dangerous to place at Jacob's behest. As with Manoah, the man's refusal to give his name, seems to have immediately tipped off Jacob that the disappearing man was an angel. He, like Manoah, remarks on the close call he had in seeing a divine being and being allowed to continue living.

All this makes sense, but we can say more. It is possible to surmise that the man cannot give his name because he has just given it to Jacob. His name was Israel, but now it is no longer his. The shadow is literally nameless, without an identity. *And he took leave of him there*—he has no identity any longer, his message has been delivered, and he vanishes with the dawn like the shadow that he is. Jacob would continue to struggle for the rest of his life, but his struggle from now on would *not* be against the child (or the shadow) within him; it would also be the struggle with the Image of God (or the Self) within him—a struggle for ever-increasing maturity.

❈ *[31]* **So Jacob named the place Peniel, meaning, "I have seen a divine being face to face, yet my life has been preserved."** *[32]* **The sun rose upon him as he passed Penuel, limping on his hip.** *[33]* **That is why the children of Israel to this day do not eat the thigh muscle that is on the socket of the hip, since Jacob's hip socket was wrenched at the thigh muscle.**

Jacob has named many places, and usually the names help us to understand the meaning of the events that took place in those places. Here, despite the parallel with the story of Manoah in Judges, the name, "Peniel" or "Penuel," remains confusing. We know that Jacob has seen God on other occasions. In what way does this revelation differ? For one thing, the name "Peniel" means only one part of what Jacob says it does. Literally, *peni-el* means "face of a divine being."

Without changing the Hebrew word, we can alter its interpretation just slightly to achieve a better reading. *Peni-el* can be translated as, "I have faced a divine being." This is slightly better. But a moment later the name of the place changes. Evidently, things are not the same in the light of dawn. *The sun rose upon him as he passed* Penuel, *limping on his hip.* Now the place is *Penu-el*, which must be translated as, "*They* have faced a divine being."

Why has the name of the place changed? Is it merely an error in the text, the errant pen stroke of a scribe, which was later retained by tradition? Is it to indicate that the dream is over? Is it a foreshadowing of the fact that Jacob's new name, *Israel*, will not be his alone, but the name of a whole nation? Or is it to symbolize the fact that Jacob is no longer alone?

It may be that, in the light of dawn, Jacob has realized that whatever his fate is, it will also determine the fate of his wives and his children. In the light of dawn, has he decided that he must face up to his responsibilities not only for his own sake but also for the sake of his family and his descendants? That would, in itself, represent a second major transformation.

The transformation from Jacob to Israel is more than a name change. It has a permanent effect on Jacob's family. Therefore, the moment is ritualized: His children memorialize it through a symbolic reminder. They create (or reinterpret) a taboo.

Most scholars agree that the word for "thigh," *yerech*, is a euphemism for the loins, the seat of procreative power. Jacob's limping fits this interpretation well. If in the wrestling, the man struck (the actual word means, "touched") Jacob in the genitals, Jacob's limping would be temporary and not permanent. Significantly, the Bible makes no issue of his limping after this incident. Not eating the genitalia of ritually slaughtered animals also serves as an appropriate taboo to memorialize the incident for the Children of Israel, who are, after all, the product of Jacob's loins.[20] It may be, as Sarna suggests, that the taboo was already in effect long before this line was added to the story.[21] That hardly diminishes the significant connection the Israelites drew between themselves as Jacob's children and the straining of Jacob's "loin muscle."

From our perspective, whatever the cost to us as we find our true potential in moments of crisis or transition, there is always a concomitant cost for the people around us. No one can undergo an integration of self without the transformation impacting on others. Transitioning to a new stage of maturity changes the way we treat parents, children, spouse, siblings, and friends. It changes the way we affect their lives, the way we make them feel when they are with us. It makes us more aware of their presence, more responsible to them, more responsive to them. It also finally reveals our human weaknesses—to us and to them. After the transition, like Jacob, we limp for a while. We are never again as certain of ourselves as when we were children. We are not as certain of our infallibility as when we were children. Nor are we ever quite as certain of our permanence as when we were children.

))

The staircase dream, occurring as Jacob leaves the Promised Land, is a dream of Jacob the child leaving home. The wrestling dream, occurring as Jacob reenters the Promised Land, is a dream of the adult Israel struggling to become fully mature as he returns home. In moments that try our souls, we have a tendency to behave as Jacob did, waffling between tricks that worked when we were children and the spiritual resources we need to approach the world as adults.

Jacob, the child, would have continued to rely upon his wits. Israel, the adult, must rely upon his integrity. This "integrity" has been available to him since he first left home. Jacob expressed it in the covenant he made with God at Beth-El. At that moment, he set a course that represented his ideals, his goals, and his aspirations. Yet in making that covenant, he withheld a part of himself. He did not fully commit, but set conditions for God to meet before he, Jacob, would take full responsibility.

We may recognize similar patterns in our own lives. As we enter on a new career or set long-term goals for ourselves, we always plan for success and seldom plan for failure. Our immature selves expect that "the world owes me a living." Or we believe that we have the right to demand "life, liberty, and the pursuit of happiness." As time passes, however, we begin to recognize the world for the harsh place it really is. There is no possibility of life without crisis, no chance of living a life entirely charmed. The poor suffer. The rich suffer. Disappointment and despair are nearly inevitable. Temptations lie like snares in our paths and almost all of us succumb to them at some time or other. We want to do right, but there is a child in us looking for shortcuts and loopholes. Eventually, like Jacob, we reach a breaking point.

Our dreams play an important role in this transition from childhood aspirations to adult inspirations. At moments of trial and travail our dreams confront us with what the Jungians call our inner "shadow," the unresolved child in us. We struggle against seeing this shadow because facing it implies facing ourselves. One commonly reported recurring dream involves "some unacceptable character knocking at a door, wanting to be let in." It takes moral courage to open that door.

Yet, so often, when let in, he or she turns out to be helpful, after all. It is a part of us, our own substance, and cannot be eliminated or removed. The task is to struggle towards seeing ourselves as we really are, "warts and all," instead of wishing or fantasizing about being something or someone else. This struggle ... is the first step in the journey toward wholeness, the first staging-post on the journey to meet the Self.[22]

After the wrestling dream, the text of the Bible wavers, sometimes calling Jacob by his original name, sometimes calling him Israel. The sages interpret this as an indication of Jacob's continuing struggle. At times when Jacob is totally immersed in the struggle he is called "Israel." At times when he acts on his own without reference to his spiritual covenant he is called "Jacob."

In our waking world, it is possible for us to reach maturity, integrate our personalities, and achieve a degree of mastery over ourselves. We can even do this without calling on dream resources (though our dreams may be helping us without our being fully conscious of their help). But when we learn to accept the help that our dreams can provide, we can accelerate our progress. We can struggle in our dreams, as Jacob did, taking that "first step in the journey toward wholeness" by involving our entire life—waking and dreaming—in the process.

What, then, is the powerful "secret" in this tapestry that Maimonides hinted at? At first, we apprehend a person in our dream. Some of us will ask no more. Those of us who are more spiritually adept may realize later that what we thought was a person was something more significant. But the truly spiritual adept will realize almost at once that the person we perceive is an angel, a messenger, a message *for us*. The secret may be that seeking spirituality is also the path to seeking maturity. It does not dawn on us all at once.

It comes as we struggle continuously up that staircase and across that river toward the light of higher awareness.

First Fruits

Visions, Prophecy, Gifts, and Landscapes

☽

Your old ones shall dream dreams, your young ones shall see visions. — Joel 3:1

We cannot ask of Jacob's wrestling narrative, "Is it a prophecy or is it a dream?" The Bible speaks of all visions and prophecies as "waking dreams." This is elegantly stated, though sometimes misunderstood, in the often-quoted verse from Joel: "Your old ones shall dream dreams, your young ones shall see visions." In this poetic language, it seems that Joel is saying that dreams replace visions with advancing years. Actually, the prophet has a different intention. When we read the verse in its original context, we more readily comprehend its meaning:

> After that, I will pour out My spirit on all flesh; your sons and daughters shall prophesy; your old ones shall dream dreams, your young ones shall see vi-

sions. Even on slaves—both men and women—I will pour out my spirit in those days [Joel 3:1–2].[1]

Joel understood dreams, visions, *and* prophecy as one phenomenon: the outpouring of God's spirit. This same meaning is conveyed in Numbers 4:6, where God explains to Miriam and Aaron: "When a prophet of the Eternal is among you, I reveal Myself in visions, I speak in dreams."

We find the same identification in Deuteronomy, a book associated with the priestly cult. We might not expect to find it here since the priests generally sought to diminish the role of prophets, soothsayers, necromancers, and witches. Inadvertently, however, in order to warn against false prophets, Deuteronomy 13:2 elucidates the term "prophet" when it states: "If a prophet, or a dreamer of dreams, arises in your midst...." The Hebrew word for "or" indicates the equivalency of the prophet with the dreamer of dreams.

Now, if we count all of these forms—dreams, visions, and prophecy—as types of dreaming, the number of biblical texts available for dream interpretation multiplies exponentially. A wiser, more narrow, assertion might be: *In the Bible, every dream or vision is a prophecy, but every prophecy is not necessarily a dream.* The Bible makes it clear that we cannot say less than this. And, since every prophecy is *potentially* a dream or vision, each instance of prophecy must be weighed independently. In other words, whether or not to view a prophecy as a dream or vision is left to the interpreter to determine. It depends on what the words mean *for us*.

☽

Maimonides considered Moses different from other prophets in four respects: (1) Moses received his illuminations while awake; the other prophets in dreams and visions. (2) Moses received direct instruction; the other prophets received allegory. (3) The other prophets were filled with fear when they received prophecy; Moses was not. (4) The other prophets received prophecy intermittently; Moses received it on request.[2] From the evidence in the Bible itself, then, Maimonides takes the broadest possible position on our question, namely, that prophecy *is* equivalent to the dream and the vision. His list also provides clues that can help us identify the hallmarks of a prophetic dream.

First, we can assume that a prophetic dream will be received as a message. Some prophetic messages are accompanied by elaborate imagery, as in Jacob's staircase dream. Some are brief flashes of insight or moments of clarity, as in Jacob's dream of the flocks. And some consist of a visceral feeling, an intuition, or a gut instinct that provides us guidance, as in Laban's dream.

Second, we can assume that prophetic dream messages will be indirect or allegorical. Brides-to-be, for example, often report what amounts to an archetypal dream. They dream that they are walking down the aisle or up the steps to the altar to be married, when they suddenly trip over their gowns. Reports of this dream are similar, but this does not mean that the dream has one message for all who dream it. It is allegorical, entirely open to interpretation for each dreamer. For one dreamer, it may indicate nothing more than an insecurity about wearing and being seen in a costume that is very different from her normal garb. For another, it may indicate a general insecurity about entering on a new role in life. For another, it may indicate a general resistance to ritual, pomp, and circumstance. For another, however, it may be prophetic in its message, a warning that the marriage is a false step. This is the kind of dream that may profitably be shared and discussed. Though we can never know our future for certain, the mere fact that fifty percent or more of all marriages end in divorce would seem reason enough for a bride-to-be to discover what the message of this dream is *for her*.

Third, we can expect that a dream that brings us a prophetic message will be accompanied with a strong physical sensation, often fear. I say, "often fear," because the word "fear" as Maimonides understood it does not mean outright terror. He uses fear in the sense of "awe," "amazement," "trembling," and "wonderment." Of course, we should number terror as a possibility as well. The physical sensation varies: We may awaken to wonder, as Jacob did after his dream of the staircase. Or we may awaken from a nightmare in a cold sweat. A dream may leave us with a vivid memory of light, a sensation of having been flushed with excitement, a sense of having been heartened, or a renewed sense of the joy of life. Such potent sensations accompanying a dream message are part of the dream's message. Reflecting on the feeling enables us to better interpret the dream.

Fourth, we cannot expect prophetic dreams to become a constant in our dream lives. They are intermittent. While it is possible to incubate them, they often come unbidden. Naturally, the frequency and intensity of these message dreams increases as we approach moments of transition, transformation, or crisis. It is no accident, for example, that almost all births of heroes in sacred texts are first predicted in their mother's dreams. This is not just true for the birth of heroes. Pregnant women typically report active dream lives in which memorable dreams become ever more prevalent as the time of birth nears. A large number of these dreams have to do with the anticipated child. Some are fearful anticipations, while others are visions of a bright future. It is a shame when such dreams are not shared and discussed with family members. When dreams with fearful anticipations are interpreted with others, they often turn out to be auguries of comfort. When visions of a bright future are shared, they often bring messages of great beauty not only to the dreamer but also to family and friends.

The dreams we are discussing generally fall into the dream categories that Hunt referred to as *prophetic* and *archetypal-spiritual.* They are similar to the prophetic dreams found in the Bible. In fact, even when a biblical dream seems on the surface to be *personal-mnemic,* the dream of an individual in response to a personal situation, the biblical narrative treats it as both *prophetic* and *archetypal-spiritual.*[3] In other words, both biblical dreams and our own prophetic dreams stand, so to speak, on sacred ground.

In the Bible, Abraham, Jacob, Solomon, Jeremiah, and Daniel all receive prophetic dreams; so do Abimelech, Pharaoh, Balaam, and Laban. Our ancestors clearly believed that prophetic dreams were available to people of all faiths—pagans and Jews alike. Simply put, prophetic or "message" dreams are indigenous to the human condition—we cannot help but experience them. This is an extremely liberal stance for a religious document. In our day and age, we could profit from a similar liberality in accepting one another's potential for spirituality.

"Message" dreams may be recognized by the four guidelines proposed by Maimonides. They may also be identified by comparing our dreams with those in the Bible. The dreams in the Bible are models in the same way that other parts of the life stories of biblical heroes and heroines are models. In the latter case, the Bible is saying, *This is how our ancestors lived in relationship with the sacred; at our best we should learn to walk in their ways.* In the case of dreams, the Bible is saying, *This is how our ancestors received divine inspiration; at our best we should learn to receive inspiration as they did.* Whether your spiritual search is for the word of God or personal satisfaction, for inner healing or peace of mind, biblical dreams provide invaluable touchstones.

☽

The dreams of Jacob ring true because they share a common symbolism and personality. They are dreams of home: leaving home or returning home. They involve angels or godlike beings. They involve gifts—the gift of God's protection or the gift of a new name. And they evoke blessings—God's blessing as Jacob leaves home and the angel's blessing that allows Jacob to return home with a new sense of maturity.

The Senoi tribes of Malaysia consider dreams the most important aspect of their daily lives.[4] Their interactions and decisions are actually guided by dreams. Because Senoi society places a high value on dreams, an individual's dreams are nearly always remembered. In fact, each day at breakfast, Senoi families relate and discuss their dreams. Children are encouraged to begin reporting their dreams from the time that they learn to speak, and their elders guide the Senoi young in dream practices.

Senoi dream practices can be summarized by three simple rules: (1) The dreamer should seek to confront and conquer danger in dreams. (2) The dreamer should attempt to move toward pleasurable experience in dreams. (3) The dreamer should attempt to make dreams lead to a positive outcome by extracting a creative product (a "gift") from the dream.[5] All of these involve forms of dream control, a close parallel to lucid dreaming.

Kilton Stewart, who studied the Senoi in the 1930s, reported that the Senoi people show remarkable emotional maturity. Psychosis and neurosis are rare among them. Among the Senoi, aggression is almost entirely worked out in dreams.[6] When Patricia Garfield studied their culture in 1972, she was told by a hospital worker at nearby Gombak that folks at the medical facility "could not remember ever having observed fighting among the Senoi themselves or with outsiders." Garfield comments:

> The effect of applying the Senoi system of dream control, according to Stewart (and the evidence of my own experience), is to reorganize the dreamer's internal experience in such a way that his personality becomes unified. The results of unpleasant experience in waking life are at first neutralized in his dreams, then reversed. Negative images, if they occur at all, are no longer frightening; tension is reduced. The energy that went into forming negative images is transformed into a positive creative product.[7]

The Senoi teach that dream enemies must be confronted and conquered. Once overcome, dream enemies should be forced to give a gift. This gift can take any form. It may be a poem or story, a song or dance, a design or painting, or even the solution to a problem. Garfield notes,

"The value of the gift should be such that the dreamer obtains *social consensus of its worth* in a waking state."[8]

The Senoi also share a concept espoused by Native Americans, namely, that any person or image encountered in a dream can become an ally. There is only one difference between these two traditions. To Native Americans, the dreamer "is the suffering *child* who is helped out of pity by the grandfather spirit." The Senoi believe that the dreamer "is the *father* who is helped out of friendship by the child spirit guide."[9]

The dream practices of the Senoi can be applied seamlessly to Jacob's wrestling dream. Jacob confronts the danger in his dream before confronting a similar danger in real life. He tests his mettle by wrestling with his dream image before facing Esau. He also asks for a "dream gift," a gift with positive value that will be recognized among the people in his waking life. The gift he receives is his new name.

Ironically, up to this point, Jacob was dependent on Esau. He was named Jacob, a derivative of the word for "heel" as we are told in the text, because he emerged from the womb "holding on to the heel of Esau" [Genesis 25: 26]. His dream adversary grants Jacob a new name—one that expresses no dependence on Esau. As the text has it: Henceforth, he will be called Israel so that all who meet him will know that this person has struggled with beings both divine and human and prevailed. Any Senoi would be pleased by this gift—it would be instantly recognized as important not only by one family but by the whole tribe.

If we continue to interpret Jacob's wrestling dream according to the Senoi system, Jacob would represent the father not the child. That is, the man he wrestles does not resemble the grandfather spirit of Native Americans but the child spirit likely to be encountered by the Senoi. The man-child emerges as an enemy but is soon transformed into an ally. Though neither can prevail, the man-child says that Jacob did prevail. Once the gift is given, the man-child simply departs, as if the gift was the message all along. Thus Jacob is transformed. He will confront his brother as an equal, not as one who clings to the heel of a superior.

For us, too, a new truth emerges from this interpretation. We can struggle to restructure our reality, to integrate our personality. As Garfield eloquently puts it:

> By deliberately changing elements in your dream life, you can learn to confront many of your problems at their origin—in your own mind, rather than years later in the therapist's office. Gestaltists regard each image in the dream as representing an aspect of the dreamer. Even if the dream image symbolizes another person, it is *your idea* of that person (not the person himself), thus, still you. When one dream image attacks another, you, the dreamer, are literally attacking part of yourself. These conflicting elements within your mind can be reorganized and unified in a positive way during the one and a half hours or more you spend dreaming each night, by applying the Senoi concept of dream control. The dreamer who uses his dreams properly can become integrated; in Stewart's terms, he can "work for peace on earth by first establishing peace inside the earth that is his body."[10]

☽

It is not unusual for dreamers to "favor" particular land-scapes—a playing field on which dreams commonly occur. You may have such a landscape, even if you are virtually un-conscious of it. Most of your dreams may be set in the desert or on some endless highway or in a house or in town. Perhaps it is a single room that frequently appears as your background; perhaps it is a richly realized set of surreal constructions, a garden, or a maze. Whatever it is, some landscape may reappear with regularity. As you look back through your own dreams or through a dream journal, try to identify any commonality in the setting of your dreams to see whether you can identify the landscape you encoun-ter most often.

When he was a child, Robert Louis Stevenson was haunted by frequent nightmarish dreams. In his memoirs, he recalls how he struggled to remain awake just to avoid these nightmares. During his medical studies at Edin-burgh, he was so terrified by a series of dreams that he sought the advice of a doctor. As he matured, he learned to control the content of his dreams—to induce them con-sciously, instead of "allowing them to happen."

His induced dreams were populated by little folk he called "Brownies." He would make up stories for them as he fell asleep each night. In turn, the Brownies would act out the stories he made up on a miniature theater stage com-plete with spotlights and changing scenery backdrops. He discovered that his most vivid dreams came at moments when he was especially hard-pressed for cash:

> The little people began to bestir themselves in the
> same quest and labour all night long, and all night
> long set before him truncheons of tales upon their

lighted theatre. No fear of his being frightened now; the flying heart and the frozen scalp are things bygone; applause, growing applause, growing interest, growing exultation in his own cleverness (for he takes all the credit), and at last a jubilant leap to wakefulness, with the cry, "I have it, that'll do!" upon his lips.[11]

Stevenson said that his Brownies often provided "better tales than he could fashion for himself." He dreamed the basic plot sequences of *The Strange Case of Dr. Jekyll and Mr. Hyde* while dozing at a window, allowing the little actors to play out the plot on his dream stage. The stage was the basic backdrop for Stevenson's dreams. Stevenson had only to hit upon the idea of incubating dreams to dream out his fantasies. The stage landscape was an unconscious but entirely suitable venue.

Seeing, as we think of it, doesn't happen in the eyes but in the brain. In one way, to see flamboyantly, in detail, we don't need the eyes at all. We often remember scenes from days or even years earlier, viewing them in our mind's eye, and can even picture completely imaginary events, if we wish. We see in surprising detail when we dream. Sometimes when I'm in a visually besotting landscape, somewhere out in nature and experiencing intense rapture, I close my eyes, and see the landscape parading across the inside of my closed lids. The first time this happened—on a 200,000 acre working cattle ranch, surrounded by pastel mesas, in the New Mexico desert—I was a little spooked. Wrung out from the rigors of the branding corral, I needed sleep, but all the day's images, gestures, and motions still blazed in my visual memory. It was not like dreaming: it was like trying to sleep with your eyes wide open during a fiesta in full swing.[12]

The stories of Jacob exhibit a preference for "high places" as the sites for dreaming high thoughts. Or else, as in the case of the stairway dream, the biblical character visualizes a height from which things can be seen differently. But would Jacob have been able to dream the wrestling match if he had remained only in the landscape of the heights? Or was it necessary for him to come to ground in order to deal with the man-child in him? In either case, the landscape of a dream often provides a significant context.

If, up to now, you have been dreaming against a recurring landscape—in a city or on a highway, in a garden or on a desert—one way to incubate new dream content may be to consciously alter the landscape in which your dreaming takes place. Our dream life is open to suggestion. Suggest a new landscape to yourself as you fall asleep. Visualize yourself on a mountain, on the heights. See yourself in a room attending a party filled with people you want to meet. See yourself in a laboratory filled with the chemicals you will need to alter the dream's "reality." Find a peaceful setting in a forest and surround yourself with comfortable forest sounds. "Rain" on your dream, have a "dark" dream in an inner daylight. By changing the scenery, you may encounter a whole new set of possibilities. You may even allow your dreams to speak to you in new ways.

Australian Aborigines speak of a "dreamtime" that preceded our present human existence. It ended only when the supernatural beings left the surface of the earth—or when they turned into rocks, trees, and sacred objects. Only through dreams and tribal rituals can the dreamtime be recovered. As tribe members study their own rituals, they become aware of their sacred history—they comprehend the meaning of rocks, plants, rituals, symbols, and tribal values. In *The Dreaming Universe,* Fred Alan Wolf points out:

> At a certain moment in their lives humans discover that before their birth they were spirits and that after their deaths they are to be reintegrated into the prenatal spiritual condition. They learn that the human cycle is part of a larger cosmic cycle, that creation was a "spiritual" act that took place in the dreamtime and that although the cosmos is now "real" or "material," it nonetheless must be periodically renewed by the reiteration of the creative acts that occurred in the beginning. This renovation of the world is a spiritual deed, the result of a reinforcing communication with the eternal ones of "dreamtime."[13]

The Aborigines have only recently returned to their sacred land, their "reality." Even their word for *reality* means something special to them; it is "a resourceful land formed, enriched, and consecrated by supernatural beings." As Wolf describes it, "Such a world has a 'center' or a structure—and for this reason it is 'oriented.'"[14] In other words, the Aborigines conceive themselves living continually—both in dreaming and in waking realities—oriented in the landscape of their dreams.

As moderns, we tend to move *through* our reality rather more than our ancestors did. We are familiar with various landscapes, various backdrops. All of these can be evoked in our "dreamtime." A fascinating example of what is possible emerges from the work of J. Allan Hobson. Through his research, Hobson has attempted to connect science to dreaming. Fearing that the public might view his results as dry science, he determined to create a "dreamstage," a living museum of what happens when a person dreams.

> The music and the sights of them [dreams] and the microscope and the neurons and all of that stuff, it just seemed to me that if I could just make a collage of all that, then it might have a direct appeal to people. The way that we decided to do it was to have a person sleep in public. Then we just let people watch.[15]

Hobson used the energy from the brain waves of the sleepers to run laser beams and a scanning mirror, exhibiting eye movements, muscle tone, and heart rate as a laser light show on the walls of the dreamstage. A synthesizer was added to produce the dream soundtrack. The landscape of the dream was represented through the electronic media. The result is arbitrary in the sense that it is controlled by people who are not dreaming. For example, in slow-wave sleep the sound assigned was a deep basso, while in REM sleep the frequency was increased. In another sense, however, the landscape was very much controlled by the sleeper, since it was based on the unique energy patterns emanating from the sleeper's brain.

Hobson's "dreamstage" is a landscape of our creation, an early peek at how our advanced technology may be able to enhance one of our most primitive and sophisticated resources. Dreams always occur in landscapes of our creation, so there is no reason why we should not intervene by suggesting new landscapes for our dreams. If this technique works especially well for you, and you find that you can encourage little people in your dreams to create wondrous stories that make you the next Robert Louis Stevenson, my publishers will gladly supply my address so that you

can share your royalties with me. It's the least we can do for
one another, isn't it?

The Interpreter

JOSEPH AND DREAMS

☽

A dream not interpreted is like a letter not read. — Talmud, Berachot, 55a

In 332 B.C.E., Alexander the Great laid siege to the Phoenician port of Tyre. During the siege, he had a dream in which a satyr stood at the edge of a wood mocking him. He chased the satyr. At first it eluded him, but in the end he grasped and held it. In the morning, he consulted his interpreters and asked to have the dream explained. The counselors divided the word "satyr" (in Greek, *satyros*) into two words: *sa* meaning "yours" and *tyros* meaning "Tyre." They declared that Alexander would soon possess the city of Tyre. Hearing this interpretation, Alexander redoubled his efforts and conquered the city.

Coincidentally, the Jewish sages recorded their impression of Alexander the Great in a dreamlike fable. Alexander, they said, wandered beyond the black mountains. He stopped beside a well to prepare some salted fish to eat, and as he washed them, he noticed a sweet odor. He thought, "This well must issue from the Garden of Eden." He followed the spring that fed the well until he came to the gates of Eden. He cried out, "Open the gates for me." From within, a voice answered, "This is the gate of the Eternal and only the righteous shall enter into it." Alexander replied, "I am a king; I am worthy. I have come far on my journey. At least, give me a token so that all may know that I have been here." The gates opened a crack and an object rolled to Alexander's feet. He picked it up and, dusting it off, was shocked to discover that he was holding a human eyeball. On his return, he consulted the Jewish sages. He told them the story of his journey, displayed the eyeball, and inquired, "How do you interpret this sign?" They told him to bring together all the silver and gold in his camp and place it on one side of a set of balances. On the other side, they placed the eyeball. Immediately, the scales tipped. The eyeball weighed more than all the silver and gold! The sages said to Alexander, "This is the eyeball of a human being. It is never satisfied." "How can you prove your interpretation?" Alexander demanded. The sages gathered a little dust and covered the eyeball. Immediately, the scale was tipped so that the silver and gold outweighed the eyeball. The sages quoted Proverbs (27:20): "The nether world and destruction are never satiated; so the human eye is never satisfied."[1]

These two stories about Alexander have much in common. Both involve interpretation and both interpretations rely on wordplay. As we interpret a dream, a story, a myth, a text, or even an event in our lives, we are inevitably limited by words. We have seen how important the *translation* of words from Hebrew to English may be. Slight variations in the meaning of any individual word, minor nuances that we take for granted in everyday speech, can result in vastly different interpretations. This is especially true when a dream account repetitively employs the same word, words that sound alike, or words with very similar meanings.

In the class of words with nuances, for example, think of the word *malach*, "angel," which we frequently encounter in Bible dreams. Having worked extensively with this word, we know that it can be translated in a number of ways. It can mean "angel," but also "messenger" or "message." In many cases, the Bible narrative allows the word to remain ambiguous—as a double entendre—as if to intimate that the word is intended to be understood in two or more of its senses.

In the class of sound-alike words, we recall the use of *adam*, "man" or "Adam," and *adamah*, "earth." When these words appear in close proximity, the Bible seems to be pointing to their linguistic relationship. Sound-alike words can also hint at differences, however, as in the case of *Peniel*, "I have faced God," and *Penuel*, "They have faced God." Or sound-alike words can be puns, as in the case of the dream about Cappadocia, where the interpreter broke the name of the city into two words—*kappa*, "a beam" and *dika*, "ten"—to formulate an answer to a dream riddle, or above where *satyr* is made to mean "possess Tyre."

In the class of words with similar meanings, a good example is found in the many ways that the stuff of human creation can be referenced. It is called *afar*, "dust"; *adamah*, "earth"; *avek*, "dirt"; and even *hol*, "sand." When one or more of these appear in close proximity in a dream, or when one appears in the same phrase in one dream as another appears in a second dream, it is often intended as parallelism, one of the hallmarks of biblical prose and poetry.

These are three ways in which the biblical language is manipulated to provide layers of meaning within a single text. Using language elegantly (and playfully) is a distinguishing feature of great literature.[2] We employ such language when we remind a friend not to "tilt with windmills" (referring to *Don Quixote*) or impudently dismiss someone with the remark, "Off with his head!" (referring to *Alice in Wonderland*). Depth of language is the *sine qua non* of great secular literature, and assuredly of almost all sacred literature.

In addition to depth of language in its dream sequences, the Bible includes instances of dreams that feature specific words or numbers. Word or number dreams are common even today, though they sometimes mystify the dreamer and seem unaccountable on a conscious level. In a dream, a word or number may become a symbol, as if it were a visual image. And words and numbers often prove the most difficult of all dream symbols for interpreters.

Exploring dream interpretation is tantamount to gazing at the underside of leaves; or looking at the patterns that fall to the earth as the sun casts shadows through the trees; or seeing why the water springs from one side of a rock and not the other. As much as the dreamer is a visionary, the interpreter is also a seer. Both sides of the same leaf exhibit an equal amount of the rational and the creative. We could ask for no better guide in this investigation than the son of Jacob the dreamer, Joseph the interpreter of dreams. The transformations in Joseph's life revolve around the interpretation of three sets of dreams that come in pairs. The place to begin is with the story of Joseph's birth.

))

Sarah, Rebecca, and Rachel—the favorite wives of the three patriarchs—all had difficulty in conception. Throughout the Bible, births are considered more than biological phenomena, they also involve God's blessing. In the story of Sarah's pregnancy, there may be remnants of pagan myth. As normally translated, Genesis 21 (1–2) begins:

> The Eternal took note [*pakad*] of Sarah as promised, and the Eternal did for Sarah as promised. Sarah conceived and bore a son to Abraham in his old age, at the set time of which God had spoken.

The verb "took note" in Hebrew, *pakad*, may also be translated as "visited." In Judges 15:1, this word is used (probably, euphemistically) when Samson "visits" his wife for the purpose of intercourse. The motif of three—the father, the mother, and God—being essential participants in childbearing may be more literal in the Abraham story than we would suspect. Coming from the earliest periods of the patriarchal narratives, the story may recall a time when heroes were ascribed two births, one by a heavenly father and one by an earthly father.[3]

Similarly, Isaac pleaded to God when Rebecca was barren, "and the Eternal responded to his plea" [Genesis 25:21]. And Rachel, too, is barren until God responds. Jacob makes direct reference to this in Genesis 30:1–2:

> When Rachel saw that she had borne Jacob no children, she became envious of her sister; and Rachel said to Jacob, "Give me children, or I shall die." Jacob was incensed at Rachel, and said, "Can I take the place of God, who has denied you fruit of the womb?"

Jacob baldly states that he has been doing his part. It is obvious from the text that Rachel was doing her part. Jacob is angry because Rachel refuses to see the obvious, namely, that it is God who is not yet ready. Joseph is finally born when God "remembered Rachel; heeded her and opened her womb." She calls him *Yoseph*, "[God] will add," in the hope that God would give her yet another son. Thus, in the birth of Joseph—as in the births of the other patriarchs—the presence of the divine will is early established.

Shortly after Jacob enters the Promised Land, Rachel dies in birthing her second child, Benjamin. Joseph is seventeen years old when his dreams commence. We are given the briefest sketch of his youth. Joseph evidently helps his brothers as they tend the flocks in the fields. In addition, Joseph seems to act as a spy on his father's behalf, as it is said, Joseph "brought bad reports of them to their father." Joseph is clearly his father's favorite son, in token of which Jacob makes "an ornamented tunic" for him.[4] Seeing that Joseph was wearing this symbol of their father's favor, the brothers "hated him so that they could not speak a friendly word to him."[5]

It is against this background that two dreams of Joseph appear in Genesis 37:5–11.

$$\textbf{\Moon}$$

❋ *Genesis 37* [5] **Once Joseph had a dream which he told to his brothers; and they hated him even more.** [6] **He said to them, "Hear this dream which I have dreamed:** [7] **There we were binding sheaves in the field, when suddenly my sheaf stood up and remained upright; then your sheaves gathered around and bowed low to my sheaf."** [8]

His brothers answered, "Do you mean to reign over us? Do you mean to rule over us?" And they hated him even more for his talk about his dreams.

In general, the Bible depicts the ancient Hebrews as having no need for interpreters. They seem to have understood their dreams. The brothers were angry with Joseph even before they heard this dream. As soon as they hear it, they draw the obvious conclusions and hate their brother even more than before. Nothing about the dream seems too difficult, and interpreting the dream poses no particular challenge. On the other hand, the agricultural setting is a bit unexpected. Since the brothers' lives revolve around being shepherds, we might have anticipated a dream in which animals played the parts of the brothers. The agricultural reference may be used to intentionally foreshadow the later dreams of Pharaoh.

God does not appear to Joseph in the dream, so the brothers attribute the dream to Joseph himself. They ask if he is so smug as to believe that he will rule over them. They may be implying that "ruling over them" is connected with the spying Joseph does for his father. They blame Joseph for his dream. But the last phrase uses the plural "dreams" which would mean that Joseph had shared other dreams besides the one told here.

We may intuit from this that dreams were often shared among the brothers. Of course, not every dream would be expected to be prophetic. Most were accepted as indications of the personality of the dreamer. If the brothers were not overly worried by this first dream, another soon followed it.

✺ *[9]* **He dreamed another dream and told it to his brothers, saying, "Look, I have had another dream: And this** time, the sun, the moon, and eleven stars were bowing down to me." *[10]* And when he told it to his father and brothers, his father berated him. "What," he said to him, "is this dream you have dreamed? Are we to come, I and your mother and your brothers, and bow low to you to the ground?" *[11]* So his brothers were wrought up at him, and his father kept the matter in mind.

Joseph dreams a second dream containing basically the same message as the first. Jacob's response is, "Are we to come, I *and your mother* and your brothers, and bow low to you to the ground?" How can his mother come to bow low to Joseph? His mother has already died. Is Joseph referring to his stepmother, Leah? Perhaps. But Jacob does not state his question with "and your stepmother" instead of "and your mother." Instead, Jacob "kept the matter in mind."

Joseph's dreams anger his brothers, but Jacob, an experienced dreamer, seems to sense that his son's dream may be a sign—all the more so, if he knew it was a "duplicate dream." The special nature of duplicate dreams was reported in Mesopotamian sources long before Joseph's time.[6] It was equally well known to the Jewish sages centuries later. They counted four kinds of dreams as prophetic and certain to be fulfilled: "an early morning dream, a dream which a friend has about one, and a dream which is interpreted in the midst of a dream ... also a dream which is repeated."[7]

In the Bible, dreaming the same thing twice seems both to indicate its importance and to underline its prophetic quality. Indeed, each of the three dream sequences in the Joseph narrative includes duplicate dreams. The dreams of Joseph's family bowing down comprise the first set of two, the next set is formed of the twin dreams of the baker and the cupbearer, and the two dreams of Pharaoh are the third set.

Some dream researchers believe that recurrent dreams signify issues with which we have not properly dealt.[8] Jung observed that repetitive dreams happen "particularly in youth, but the recurrence may continue over several decades." They are often "impressive dreams," which convince us that they "must surely have a meaning."[9] This fits well with Jacob's reaction to Joseph's dream.

Jacob seems to guess that the dream is prophetic, but he is unsure of its precise meaning. For the moment, the best he can do is to keep the matter in mind. For Jacob, as we know, dreams are complex and filled with meanings. They also resolve themselves over the course of time. If they are prophetic, they are best interpreted with hindsight.

If Jacob could see ahead, he would better understand the dream. In the end, the brothers bow low to Joseph not because Joseph reigns over *them* but because Joseph reigns over *Egypt*. They bow to him when they come to Egypt seeking grain to save their family from famine (Genesis 42:6). They bow low to him on their second journey to Egypt when they seek to return the silver coins they discover in their sacks (Genesis 43:26). And they throw themselves on the ground before him in terror when they are trapped with the silver goblet Joseph instructed his servants to plant in Benjamin's sack of grain (Genesis 44:14). On this occasion, we are told that this goblet was the very one Joseph used in divination. When the brothers are caught with the goblet, Joseph says, "What is this deed you have done? Do you not know that a man like me practices divination?"[10]

The only "divination" that we are aware of in the story of Joseph is the interpretation of dreams as portents of the future. Could Joseph be giving his brothers a hint here that he is Joseph, their brother? Could he be trying to remind them of the dreams he had in which they bowed low to him? It is possible.

Centuries later, the sages took up the question of how the dream of the sun, moon, and stars bowing to Joseph's star could be fulfilled since Rachel, Joseph's mother, had died. To answer, they cited Jeremiah 23:28, "Let the prophet who has a dream tell the dream, and let the one who has received My word report My word faithfully! How can straw be compared to grain?—says the Eternal."

> [Now,] what is the connection of straw and wheat with a dream? The truth is, said Rabbi Yohanan in the name of Rabbi Simeon bar Yohai, that just as wheat cannot be without straw, so there cannot be a dream without some nonsense. Rabbi Berekiah said: While a part of a dream may be fulfilled, the whole of it is never fulfilled. Whence do we know this? From Joseph, as it is written, "the sun, the moon, and eleven stars were bowing down to me." And at that time his mother was not living.[11]

Joseph's prophecy was eventually fulfilled, but the reference to Rachel made it impossible for it to be fulfilled exactly as it was dreamed. After all, "there cannot be a dream without some nonsense." At least, that was the view of the sages. From our perspective, we might say the whole prophecy was fulfilled since the reference to "the sun, the moon, and eleven stars" was symbolic, meant to represent the whole family of Joseph. Either way, the dream presages important events and, as usual, marks a moment of transition in the life of a patriarch.

Just after the dream, when the brothers see Joseph coming toward them, they call him *baal ha-halomot*, "Master of Dreams" [Genesis 37:19]. They are deriding him for his many dreams, but we are being told at the same time that Joseph has become a master of dreams, *an interpreter*. The brothers continue, saying, "Come now, let us kill him and throw him into one of the pits; and we can say, 'A savage beast devoured him.' We shall see what comes of his dreams!" [37:20].

☽

Things go from worse to bad to better to worse for Joseph. The brothers cast him into a pit and, deciding not to kill him, sell him to a passing caravan of slavers on their way to Egypt. There, Potiphar, a courtier of the Pharaoh, purchases him. Potiphar appoints Joseph his personal attendant since "the Eternal blessed his house for Joseph's sake." One day, when they are alone in the house, Potiphar's wife tries to seduce Joseph, managing to snatch his tunic as he flees from her. Scorned, she displays the tunic to her husband saying that Joseph attempted to seduce her. Furious, Potiphar throws Joseph in Pharaoh's prison.

Characteristically, Joseph manages to befriend the chief jailer, who places him in charge of the prisoners since "whatever [Joseph] did the Eternal made successful."[12]

Sometime later, Pharaoh is offended by both his cupbearer (*sommelier*) and his baker. Pharaoh sends them to prison where, in token of their high offices, the chief jailer assigns Joseph to wait on them. One night—on the selfsame night—each of them has a dream, "each his own dream and each dream with its own meaning" [Genesis 40:5]. This is the second set of duplicate dreams in the Joseph cycle.

✴ *Genesis 40 [6]* **When Joseph came in to them in the morning, he saw that they were distraught. *[7]* He asked Pharaoh's courtiers, who were with him in custody in his master's house, saying, "Why do you appear downcast today?" *[8]* And they said unto him, "We had dreams, and there is no one to interpret them." So Joseph said to them, "Surely God can interpret! Tell me [your dreams]."**

The cupbearer and the baker are "distraught" and "downcast." When Joseph inquires why, they reply that they had dreams and there is no one to interpret them. That is to say, what has really made them unhappy is the lack of a professional dream interpreter. This is in stark contrast to the first set of duplicate dreams. There, Joseph's family took it for granted that their interpretations would be accurate. Here, the Egyptians take it for granted that they need help in interpreting their dreams.

This is, however, altogether in keeping with archaeological data from the ancient Near East. We have extensive records of professional dream interpreters operating both in Mesopotamia and Egypt, but not in Canaan. In his book *Beggar to King,* Walter Duckat provides a brief description of the way in which a Mesopotamian or Egyptian dream interpreter operated:

> Clients came to him, usually troubled by their dreams, which they tried to reconstruct for his interpretation, as well as to give him other information about themselves. Basing his interpretation on their statements, along with his probably shrewd understanding of human nature, he may have employed some magical flourishes or incantations and come up with an acceptable interpretation.[13]

Where professional dream interpreters were available, most folk resorted to them to explain any but the most common dreams. This fact poses a difficulty. How did the people of Canaan manage to have their dreams explained? Joseph seems to suggest an answer when he points to God's part in dream interpretation. Many centuries later, the sages made a similar suggestion in regard to a recurrent motif in Genesis, God's statement to the patriarchs: "And all the families of the earth shall bless themselves by you" [Genesis 12:3].[14]

> Rabbi Nehemiah said: The Holy One, the Blessed, said to Abraham: *And all the families of the earth shall bless themselves by you.* Now if that is meant in respect of wealth, they [the other families of the earth] are surely wealthier than we! But it was meant in respect of counsel: when they get into trouble they ask our advice, and we give it to them.[15]

In other words, other nations were blessed by being able to use the Hebrews as a conduit to God's wisdom. Wisdom and dream interpretation are closely linked in the ancient Near East. And God, as Joseph pointed out, is the ultimate interpreter of dreams. Likewise, Joseph tells the cupbearer and the baker, "Surely God can interpret!" adding, "Tell me." With these words, Joseph implies that he *is* a dream interpreter. This may be the reason the Canaanites had no need of a professional class of dream interpreters—in patriarchal times, the Hebrews may have served as counselors and dream interpreters.

Could this be the reason that his brothers called Joseph, *baal ha-halomot*, "Master of Dreams?" Certainly, Joseph does not hesitate for a moment to speculate whether he can interpret the dreams of the cupbearer and the baker. He assumes that he can. This would also explain why Joseph prefaces his request to hear Pharaoh's dreams with "Surely God can interpret!" The cupbearer and the baker will need to accept his qualifications before they accept his interpretation. Since he will neither employ magical flourishes nor recite incantations, Joseph begins by citing his credentials for the job: Hebrews, he tells them, receive their dream interpretations directly from God. You can also understand from this why I remarked a few pages ago, "In general, the Bible depicts the ancient Hebrews as having no need for interpreters. They seem to have understood their dreams."[16] Whatever the cause, at this point in the narrative, Joseph reveals himself as a divinely-inspired interpreter of dreams.

✸ *[9]* **Then the chief cupbearer told his dream to Joseph, He said to him, "In my dream, there was a vine in front of me.** *[10]* **On the vine were three branches. It had barely budded, when out came its blossoms and its clusters ripened into grapes.** *[11]* **Pharaoh's cup was in my hand, and I took the grapes, pressed them into Pharaoh's cup, and placed the cup in Pharaoh's hand."** *[12]* **Joseph said to him, "This is its interpretation: The three branches are three days.** *[13]* **In three days Pharaoh will pardon you** *[yisa et-roshecha]* **and restore you to your post; you will place Pharaoh's cup in his hand, as was your custom formerly when you were his cupbearer.** *[14]* **But think of me when all is well with you again, and do me the kindness of mentioning me to Pharaoh, so as to free me from this place.** *[15]* **For in truth, I was kidnaped from the land of the Hebrews; nor have I done anything here that they should have put me in the dungeon** *[ba-bor]***."**

Joseph interprets most of the symbols in the cupbearer's dream. Some, however, go unremarked. Joseph does not seem to deal directly with the premature blossoming and ripening of the vines nor with the image of the cupbearer taking the freshly ripened grapes and squeezing them into wine for Pharaoh's cup. It is left for us to assume that Joseph's interpretation actually covered these symbols as well, but these particular details were not carried into the narrative by the editor.

The cupbearer and the baker were not minor officials in Pharaoh's retinue. We are given a hint of their importance when Joseph is assigned to serve them while they are in prison. Typically, cupbearers were constantly at the king's side, thereby wielding great influence at court. Their services went far beyond merely pouring wine.

> The cupbearer's duties probably included supervision of the supply and quality of the beverages served (usually wine), serving the king, and testing the beverages before serving them to forestall attempts at poisoning the monarch.[17]

As an overseer, the cupbearer had to be familiar with the growing and harvest cycle of the vines, the pressing of the grapes, and the fermenting of the wine. The dream bears this out, as the cupbearer correctly describes the foreshortened growth cycle of the three vines that appear to him.

Joseph commences his interpretation by focusing on the number of vines in the dream. In dream interpretation, as we have indicated, number symbols are important ciphers. When one patient reported a complex dream based on numbers, Carl Jung noted:

Even in his waking life the patient gave free rein to his number fantasies.... It is difficult to say where the borderline of [number] play begins—necessarily so, for an unconscious product is the creation of sportive fantasy, of that psychic impulse out of which play itself arises. It is repugnant to the scientific mind to indulge in this kind of playfulness, which tails off everywhere in inanity. But we should never forget that the human mind has for thousands of years amused itself with just this kind of game, so it would be no wonder if those tendencies from the distant past gained a hearing in dreams.[18]

Joseph assumes that the number of vines represent a time period. The shortness of the growing season of the vines must indicate that what normally would take months has been compressed. Hence, he interprets the three vines to mean three days. The rest of the dream seems fairly straightforward. The cupbearer will be restored to his former post, watching over the pressing of the grapes and serving the Pharaoh as before.

In his interpretation, Joseph refers to Pharaoh, saying, *yisa et-roshecha,* "[he] will lift up your head," meaning, "[he] will pardon you" or "[he] will restore you." Other phrases would have been less suggestive and more succinct, so we are alerted to a possible wordplay in Joseph's interpretation.

Prior to this, the prison has been called a *beit sohar.* From the context, we know this means "a prison," but the precise meaning of the phrase is unknown.[19] At the end of this interpretation, however, Joseph does not refer to the prison as a *beit sohar.* He asks the cupbearer to remember him to Pharaoh, saying, "nor have I done anything here that they should have put me in the dungeon [*bor*]." The word *bor* can mean "dungeon," but its basic meaning is "pit." Joseph thereby connects his present imprisonment with the time his brothers threw him into a *bor* ("pit").[20] This is a fine example of the kind of wordplay that connects so many of the Bible's narratives.

✸ *[16]* **When the chief baker saw how favorably he had interpreted, he said to Joseph, "In my dream, similarly [af], there were three openwork [hori] baskets on my head. [17] In the uppermost basket were all kinds of food for Pharaoh that a baker prepares; and the birds were eating it out of the basket above my head." [18] Joseph answered, "This is its interpretation: The three baskets are three days. [19] In three days Pharaoh will lift off your head [yisa et-roshecha me'alecha] and impale you upon a pole [etz]; and the birds will pick off your flesh."**

The position of chief baker was almost as significant at court as that of cupbearer. From what we know of Egyptian gastronomy, some fifty-seven varieties of bread and thirty-eight different types of cake were regularly prepared. No wonder the baker dreams of "all kinds of food for Pharaoh that a baker prepares."[21] The chief baker would be in contact with the Pharaoh's inner circle on a fairly regular basis and may have become an advisor on matters more important than just food.

Hearing the favorable interpretation Joseph has given to the cupbearer, and realizing that his dream is very similar, the baker expects a favorable interpretation. Joseph again begins with the number three, saying that the three baskets represent three days.

We do not know the precise meaning of the word *hori*, translated above as "openwork." If it comes from the Hebrew *hor*, "hole," it could indicate the baskets had "holes" in them. It could mean "openwork," but it could also mean "white" or "wicker." Joseph may have taken the word to signify that the baskets were hurriedly prepared (just as the three vines hurriedly ripened) and therefore not woven tightly. His interpretation of three days (as opposed to months, seasons, or years) would make sense in the same way it had for the cupbearer.

Unfortunately for the baker, Joseph believes this dream is inauspicious. He may be influenced by the baker's use of the word *af*. This word can mean "similarly" or "also." It may mean "but" or "by contrast." Additionally, it may mean "anger." And it is frequently used in imprecations and curses. The birds scavenging the baskets of bread may also influence Joseph's interpretation. He construes this as an evil omen. Also, the fact that the baskets were piled on the baker's head does not portend well. In Joseph's mind, the image of the baker with the baskets on his head seems to resemble a tree with the baker's head hung from its branches.

Duplicate dreams require closely intertwined interpretations, and Joseph delivers up an elegant example. He tells the baker: In three days (the same number as figured in the cupbearer's dream), your head will be lifted up (the same words, *yisa et-roshecha*, as in his interpretation of the cupbearer's dream)—but here the similarity becomes dissimilarity as Joseph adds the phrase *me'alecha*, "*from* you." We can imagine the baker's distress as Joseph proceeds. The baker's head will be impaled on a pole—but the word for "pole" is *etz*, which usually means "tree," so the phrase can be translated as "hung from a tree." Joseph concludes, the birds will pick off your flesh (we can imagine this as the "flesh" that the baker had gained through eating "all kinds of food").

Joseph's interpretations of the dreams of the cup-bearer and the baker receive scant attention from most commentators. They remain, nonetheless, a tour-de-force!

✸ *[20]* **On the third day—his birthday—Pharaoh made a banquet for all his officials, and he singled out [yisa et-rosh] his chief cupbearer and his chief baker from among his officials.** *[21]* **He restored the chief cupbearer to his cupbearing, and he placed the cup into Pharaoh's hand;** *[22]* **but the chief baker he impaled—just as Joseph had interpreted to them.** *[23]* **Yet the chief cupbearer did not think of Joseph; he forgot him.**

All that Jacob predicts comes to pass. Pharaoh's action of "singling out" both the cupbearer and the baker is expressed with the use of *yisa et-rosh*, "lifted the head[s] of." This is the same expression Joseph used in speaking of both dreams, and its appearance here clinches the fact that his interpretations were inspired. The dream sequence ends with the cupbearer showing an ungracious forgetfulness that will cost Joseph an additional two years in prison.

In the thirteenth century masterwork the Zohar, the Jewish mystics ask how Joseph knew to interpret the cupbearer's dream in a positive way and the baker's dream in a negative manner. "The explanation," they say, "is that these dreams concerned Joseph himself, and, because he penetrated to the root of the matter, he gave to each dream the fitting interpretation so that everything should fall in its place."[22]

The Zohar attempts to interpret the method of Joseph's interpretations. In Joseph's mind, the Zohar says, the three vines symbolized the three classes of the community of Israel—Priests, Levites, and Israelites. The premature budding showed that by virtue of these three classes the Children of Israel ascended on high to receive God's blessing—that is, they "blossomed." And the ripe grapes represented the grapes that were stored in heaven to be used for the banquet of the righteous in the world to come. Through these interpretations, the Zohar maintains, Joseph knew that the cupbearer's dream was positive; the rest of the dream had meaning only for the dreamer.

What of the baker's dream? The Zohar declares that Joseph understood the word *af* to indicate the "anger" that resulted in the destruction of the Temple. The birds scavenging the basket refer "to the other nations who would assemble against Israel, slay them, devastate their dwellings, and scatter them into the four corners of the world." In this way, Joseph knew the baker's dream was negative. The Zohar concludes: "Observe, then, that the two dreams belonged to two different grades: the one saw the upper grade ascending and the moon in its fullness of light; the other saw the moon in darkness and under the domination of the evil serpent."[23]

Of course, the discussion in the Zohar is based on factors like the Temple cult and events like the destruction of the Temple, which came long after Joseph's time. It would be of only passing interest to us except for its observation, "The explanation is that these dreams concerned Joseph himself." Though their application of this dictum is a projection backward in time, the dictum itself is an important insight into dream interpretation.

Like Joseph, when any interpreter explains a dream the base against which the interpretation must be tested is what the dream means *to the interpreter*. Only after this test is satisfied can the interpreter ask what the dream might mean *to the dreamer*. At first this may seem odd, but the more you ponder it, the more it reveals.

The dreams of the cupbearer and the baker are a duplicate dream, but the text warned us from the start not to be deceived by this. We were told that both the cupbearer and the baker dreamed in the same night, "each his own dream and each dream with its own meaning." And, having looked closely for ourselves, we can now comprehend this statement all too clearly.

)

Events in Joseph's life seem to happen in twos. Two dreams in his youth bring him to Egypt. Two tunics mark two downfalls. He goes from one pit to a second pit. He interprets two dreams for two prisoners. Two years pass. Pharaoh dreams two dreams. Then we hear these dreams two times— in the first few verses of Genesis 41 and again when Pharaoh repeats them for Joseph.

Pharaoh's dreams are well known even to modern readers. Seven fat cows emerge from the Nile to graze, and seven gaunt cows emerge to swallow them up. Seven healthy ears of grain grow on a single stalk, and seven parched ears of grain come and swallow them up. The Bible indicates that these two dreams are one by stating, "Then Pharaoh awoke: it was a dream!"

The next morning, Pharaoh is still agitated by his dreams. He sends for all the "magicians of Egypt and all its wise men." He tells them the dreams, but none can interpret them to Pharaoh's satisfaction. It is at this critical juncture that the cupbearer remembers Joseph, "a Hebrew youth," and the accuracy of Joseph's dream interpretations: "as he interpreted to us, so it came to pass." Pharaoh instructs that Joseph should be removed from the prison

forthwith. Joseph is dressed and groomed and brought before Pharaoh.

❋ *Genesis 41 [15]* **And Pharaoh said to Joseph, "I have had
a dream, but no one can interpret it. Now I have heard it
said of you that for you to hear a dream is to tell its meaning."** *[16]* **Joseph answered Pharaoh, saying, "Not I! God
will see to Pharaoh's welfare."**

As he did with the baker and the cupbearer, Joseph stresses
that his skills do not depend on magic or incantations. His
credentials are his faith in his God. Pharaoh has already
been told that this is a Hebrew youth; so hearing the word
"God," Pharaoh must know that Joseph means the God of
the Hebrews. This may have been impressive to the baker
and the cupbearer, but should it impress Pharaoh? After
all, in Egypt, Pharaoh was himself a god. Why is Pharaoh
not insulted by the suggestion that the God of the lowly Hebrews should see to the welfare of the god of mighty Egypt?

In other words, how cosmopolitan was the patriarchal
age? Was there a common language of theology to which
both Joseph and Pharaoh could refer? Cyrus Gordon notes:

> Wherever we find men of different religious back-
> grounds meeting each other in an international
> age, they have arrived at the conclusion that above
> national, local, and particularistic deities, there is
> the one God who rules the universe. Joseph and
> Pharaoh, therefore, speak of "God" without any
> need of explanation.[24]

This naturally leads to the question of which of the
many Pharaohs Joseph was addressing. To date, we have
discovered no Egyptian evidence pointing to a particular
prime minister named Joseph. Nevertheless, based on gen-

eral comparisons of the Bible and the archaeological record of Egypt—and cognizant of the approximate time of
the patriarchal age—we can guess that Joseph is speaking
to one of the Pharaohs of the New Kingdom (approximately
the second half of the second millennium B.C.E.), possibly
Seti I (1308–1291).[25] In the time of Seti I, the New Kingdom was marked as

> an age of royal ownership of the land, as depicted in
> Genesis 47:19–20, where the system is attributed
> to Joseph's planning. The people were nearly all
> serfs bound to the king who owned the land. The
> taxes included one fifth of the crops that the serfs
> had to pay into the royal treasury. ... The old nobil-
> ity [had] disappeared as such, but in its place came
> an officialdom. The king always needed an able
> prime minister, who in turn needed able civil ser-
> vants to administer the land. There was thus oppor-
> tunity for talented common people. As was typical
> throughout Egyptian history, a young man able to
> show his merit ... could aspire to the highest posi-
> tions. Accordingly, the rise of Joseph from a slave
> to the highest position next to the king fits in with
> the picture of Egypt as we know it from native
> sources.[26]

Generally speaking, the Egyptians of this period were a
pragmatic people, led by a pragmatic and worldly Pharaoh
who was less likely to be interested in the magic and incantations of the magicians than in the straight talk of a young
Hebrew who claimed no special skills save for being inspired by a universal God. Pharaoh takes no insult; he decides to hear the young man out.

❋ *[17]* Then Pharaoh said to Joseph, "In my dream, I was standing on the bank of the Nile, *[18]* when out of the Nile came up seven sturdy and well-formed cows and grazed in the reed grass. *[19]* Presently, there followed them seven other cows, scrawny, ill-formed, and emaciated—never had I seen their likes for ugliness in all the land of Egypt! *[20]* And the seven lean and ugly cows ate up the first seven cows, the sturdy ones; *[21]* but when they had consumed them, one could not tell that they had consumed them, for they looked just as bad as before. And I awoke. *[22]* In my other dream, I saw seven ears of grain, full and healthy, growing on a single stalk; *[23]* but right behind them sprouted seven ears, shriveled, thin, and scorched by the east wind. *[24]* And the thin ears swallowed the seven healthy ears. I have told my magicians, but none has an explanation for me."

Joseph's interpretation of Pharaoh's duplicate dream follows in the next set of verses. In the meanwhile, the sages of the Talmud posed a pertinent query. What interpretations put forward by the "magicians" of Egypt did Pharaoh reject? They conjecture:

> [The magicians consulted and advised Pharaoh], the seven good cows mean you will sire seven daughters; the seven ill-favored cows, that you will bury seven daughters. The seven full ears [mean] you will conquer seven provinces; the seven thin ears, that seven provinces will revolt against you. Thus it is written, *A scorner seeks wisdom, and finds it not* (Proverbs 14:6), which applies to Pharaoh's magicians.[27]

In the sages' imagination, the magicians made safe predictions: Pharaohs were always giving birth to daughters and sending armies to conquer provinces; likewise, provinces were always in rebellion, and children were always dying. The sages remark that it takes little wisdom to come to an interpretation that fits a dream, but this is not the way the wise interpreter proceeds. They obviously infer that Joseph's interpretation is an example of real wisdom.

Wisdom is the issue because, in biblical times, the word "magician" was used colloquially somewhat the way we use the word "scientist" today, to indicate a person trained to explain the way the world operates. Dream interpretation was within the provenance of the Egyptian magician since it was a matter for scientific examination. Of course, magicians who rise to prominence in the palace of Pharaoh are likely not only to be wise but also to be politic. The sages' guess—that the magicians of Egypt were "playing it safe" in their interpretations—is based on their often uncanny knack for intuiting the nature of human motivations in any given situation. In his demeanor and in his interpretation, standing before Pharaoh, Joseph would likewise combine polity with wisdom.

Pharaoh's dream, of course, reminds us of Joseph's childhood dream of the sheaves. Since Jacob's family engaged primarily in tending flocks, that dream presented a somewhat unexpected agricultural setting. As we noted, it may foreshadow these dreams of Pharaoh. Both of Pharaoh's dreams accurately reflect the nature of agriculture along the Nile—the cows grazing in the rich reeds growing at the river's edge and the rich gold of grain growing on the Nile's banks. In interpreting Pharaoh's dreams, Joseph seems to demonstrate a wide-ranging knowledge of Egyptian agriculture. But where would Joseph have gained such knowledge?

❋ *[25]* And Joseph said to Pharaoh: "Pharaoh's dreams are one and the same: God has told Pharaoh what God is about to do. *[26]* The seven healthy cows are seven years, and the seven healthy ears are seven years; it is the same dream. *[27]* The seven lean and ugly cows that followed are seven years, as are also the seven empty ears scorched by the east wind; they are seven years of famine. *[28]* It is just as I have told Pharaoh: God has revealed to Pharaoh what God is about to do. *[29]* Immediately ahead are seven years of great abundance in all the land of Egypt. *[30]* After them will come seven years of famine, and all the abundance in the land of Egypt will be forgotten. As the land is ravaged by famine, *[31]* no trace of the abundance will be left in the land because of the famine thereafter, for it will be very severe. *[32]* As for Pharaoh having had the same dream twice, it means that the matter has been determined by God, and that God will soon carry it out. *[33]* Accordingly, let Pharaoh find a man of discernment and wisdom, and set him over the land of Egypt. *[34]* And let Pharaoh take steps to appoint overseers over the land, and organize the land of Egypt in the seven years of plenty. *[35]* Let all the food of these good years that are coming be gathered, and let the grain be collected under Pharaoh's authority as food to be stored in the cities. *[36]* Let that food be a reserve for the land for the seven years of famine which will come upon the land of Egypt, so that the land may not perish in the famine."

The sages make an incisive observation regarding Pharaoh's dream. They ask, "Do not all people dream?" And they answer, "True, but a king's dream embraces the whole world."[28] It is from this premise that Joseph begins his interpretation of Pharaoh's dream. Seemingly without hesitation, Joseph assumes that the dream has nothing to do with Pharaoh's personal life or with Pharaoh's immediate family. Joseph makes other assumptions, too. He treats both dreams as one duplicate dream. He assumes that since the setting of both dreams is agricultural, they refer to agriculture.

With these four suppositions, Joseph's interpretation starts to take shape. Joseph next addresses the recurrent number seven, just as he did the number three in the prisoners' dreams. In the ancient world, even as in the modern world, the number seven generally was considered a fortunate or "lucky" number.[29] Yet Joseph was presented with dreams in which the number seven appeared both fortunate and unfortunate. Moreover, the dreams were agricultural, a fact that provided Joseph with an additional point of reference.

In the ancient world, professional dream interpreters relied on long-established traditions of dream symbols and their meanings. We have recovered books of dream symbols from Mesopotamia and Egypt dating from as early as the third century B.C.E. One Egyptian manuscript, now in the British Museum, includes some two hundred dream symbols and their meanings listed in two columns horizontally. Along the margin, written vertically, are the words, "If a man see himself in a dream...," which are meant to be read before each of the entries. A few samples should suffice to give the flavor of this work:

If a man see himself in a dream...

White bread being given to him—	Good—*it means things at which his face will light up*
Seeing a large cat—	Good—*it means a large harvest will come*

Seeing the moon as it shines—	Good—*forgiveness to him by his god*
Seeing his face in a mirror—	Bad—*it means another wife*
Seeing himself with a pain in his side—	Bad—*taking something away from him*
Seeing the catching of birds—	Bad—*it means taking away his property*
Looking into a deep well—	Bad—*putting him into prison*

Joseph's rapid rise to prominence in the home of Potiphar and later in prison, and his apparent ability to speak with Pharaoh without any interpreter, indicates that his Egyptian was fluent. His deep interest in dreams probably led him to at least read, if not consult, Egyptian books of dream symbols. These might have contained various interpretations for the number seven, but they were oriented to the fate of individuals, not of nations. Such dream books might have been consulted by Pharaoh's wise men and magicians before they proffered their interpretations.

Possibly because the number seven appears to be both good and bad, Joseph does not feel constrained by its normal symbolism in dreams. He turns, instead, to Egyptian traditions regarding a seven-year agricultural cycle. He may have been familiar with examples such as the one we know from an inscription dating from the Ptolemaic period, which purports to record events from the twenty-eighth century B.C.E. (Whether or not this claim is correct, the inscription represents a tradition of very long standing.) The inscription reads:

To let thee know, I was in distress on the Great Throne, and those who are in the palace were in heart's affliction from a very great evil, since the Nile had not come in my time [flooded its banks] for a space of seven years. Grain was scant, fruits were dried up, and everything which they eat was short. ...

The inscription then describes Pharaoh receiving a visitation from the god Khnum:

... As I slept in life and satisfaction, I discovered the god standing over against me. I propitiated him with praise; I prayed to him in his presence. He *revealed* himself to me, *his face* being fresh. His words were: "I am Khnum, thy fashioner ... I know the Nile. When he is introduced into the fields, his introduction gives life to every nostril.... The Nile will pour forth for thee, without a year of cessation or laxness for any land. Plants will grow, bowing down under the *fruit*. ... The starvation year[s] will have gone, and [people's] borrowing from their granaries will have departed. Egypt will come into the fields, the banks will sparkle, ... and contentment will be in their hearts more than that which was formerly.[30]

This tradition of a famine lasting seven years, to be followed by a time of great plenty is well-attested in Egyptian archaeological finds, and dates from periods long before Joseph. It is entirely possible that Joseph was acquainted with this tradition. And it could account for his interpreting the lean and ugly cows and the parched grain as years of famine that would swallow the cows and grain representing plenty without seeming to grow fatter or more prosperous.

Additional guidance might have been at hand in the form of Mesopotamian traditions that would have been known to Joseph since they stemmed from his ancestral home, but perhaps less known to the dream interpreters of Egypt. It is possible, for example, that Joseph was familiar with traditional stories like the legend of Utnapishtim (who alone survived the Flood) and the Gilgamesh epic in the same way we are familiar with the stories of Noah and the ark and the Tower of Babel. If so, Joseph might have re- called an incident in the Gilgamesh epic in which Ishtar, enraged at being rejected, asks her father Anu for permis- sion to use the Bull of Heaven to slay Gilgamesh.

> To extract permission from her unwilling father, she makes threats of violence. Anu, in granting permission, reminds her that the slaying of a hero will cause a seven-year famine. She had anticipated this dire consequence and assures Anu that she has laid up a seven-year supply of food.[31]

Armed with this text, or knowledge of similar sources, Joseph would have at hand not only the interpretation of Pharaoh's dream but also a plan to suggest to Pharaoh. He seized the opportunity to both interpret and suggest. He may not have been promoting his own candidacy for the job, which he said required "a man of discernment and wis- dom," but he clearly hoped to gain a favorable position with Pharaoh by laying out a course of action.

Lastly, Joseph calls upon the traditions of his own peo- ple as he tells Pharaoh that God has sent the dream twice to make two points: (1) that the matter is certain and (2) that the matter will soon occur. Here, he takes a calculated risk. If he is wrong, it will soon be known. On the other hand, if he is right, his reward is likely to be the greater. We can only wonder whether he had gauged his risk by observing that it had been seven or more years since the last time the Nile failed to flood.

❋ *[37]* **The plan pleased Pharaoh and all his courtiers.** *[38]* **And Pharaoh said to his courtiers, "Could we find another like him, a man in whom is the Spirit of God?"** *[39]* **So Pharaoh said to Joseph, "Since God has made all this known to you, there is none so discerning and wise as you.** *[40]* **You shall be in charge of my court, and by your command shall all my people be directed; only with respect to the throne shall I be superior to you."** *[41]* **Pharaoh further said to Joseph, "See, I put you in charge of all the land of Egypt."** *[42]* **And, removing his signet ring from his hand, Pharaoh put it on Joseph's hand; and he had him dressed in robes of fine linen, and put a gold chain about his neck.** *[43]* **He had him ride in the chariot of the second-in-command, and they cried before him, "Abrek!"[32] Thus he placed him over all the land of Egypt.**

Pharaoh responds to Joseph's dream interpretation in the most positive way possible. He answers by speaking of "the Spirit of God," simultaneously showing his respect for a universal conception of the deity and for Joseph's credentials as a dream interpreter. The honors that Pharaoh bestows are granted in quick succession—the underlying assertion is they can be removed with equal rapidity. We have already witnessed such action on the part of this particular Pharaoh when he demoted his cupbearer and his chief baker in a single day, sending both to prison. All will now depend on whether Joseph's interpretation proves to be correct. This is no small thing. But, it leads us to investigate one of the great secrets of dream interpretation. As one of the Talmudic sages later tells us:

> There were twenty-four interpreters of dreams in Jerusalem. Once I dreamt a dream and I went round to all of them and they all gave different in-

terpretations, and all were fulfilled, thus confirming the proverb, *All dreams follow the mouth.*[33]

The proverb is the key. It implies that, if the interpreter has worked well, then the interpretation will come to pass as the interpreter has spoken. That is, a good interpretation leaves room for many truths. The sage visited twenty-four interpreters and received twenty-four different interpretations, and every one of the interpretations became plausible. The question is not how can this be the case, rather when is this not the case? Only if the interpreter has not left enough slack in the rope.

In the case of Joseph's interpretation, for example, the number seven is symbolic. It will not matter if the seven years of plenty turn out to be seven or six or eight, or if the seven years of famine turn out to be five or nine. They will still be spoken of as "the seven years of plenty or famine which Joseph predicted." *All dreams follow the mouth.*

The sages tell of a case in which a woman came to Rabbi Eliezer and told him, "I dreamed that the loft of my house was split open." He interpreted: "You will conceive a child." A while later, she conceived a child. She came a second time with the same dream, and Rabbi Eliezer interpreted it in the same way. She conceived a second child. When she dreamed the same dream a third time, she came to seek Rabbi Eliezer, but the sage was not at home. His students listened to the dream and interpreted it: "Your husband will die." Rabbi Eliezer approached his house just then, and hearing a wailing, he asked his students what was amiss. They told him what they had done. He upbraided them, saying, "You have killed a man." *All dreams follow the mouth.*[34]

The sages felt that from the moment Joseph interpreted the dreams of Pharaoh there was only one possible outcome: since it was divinely-inspired, God would bring

Joseph's interpretation to pass. This seems to fly in the face of much of what we have said in this book so far, but we should not dismiss the idea out of hand. We are, after all, wanderers in a strange forest looking at shadows. Let's not take the sages' position literally. It may well be figurative. One more story may help to clarify my meaning:

> The Roman emperor said to Rabbi Joshua the son of Rabbi Hananiah, "You Jews profess to be very clever. Tell me: What shall I see in my dreams?" Rabbi Joshua said, "You will see the Persians making you do forced labor, despoiling you and making you feed pigs with a golden crook." The emperor thought about it all day and in the night he saw it in his dream. King Shapor I once said to Samuel, "You Jews profess to be very clever. Tell me: What shall I see in my dreams?" Samuel said to him, "You will see the Romans coming to take you captive and force you to grind date-stones in a golden mill." King Shapor thought about it the whole day and in the night he saw it in his dream.[35]

The point of this story is that we are all suggestible. An elegantly plausible interpretation plants a suggestion in us that tends to make us believe it will come to pass. When the outside world reflects the inner world of the interpretation, we attribute the truth not to the outside world but to the interpretation. Knowing this, a clever interpreter can also reverse the process, making the interpretation fit the reality of the outside world and thereby "bringing it to pass."

The Zohar acknowledged this phenomenon of suggestibility and applied it in commenting on Joseph's dream of the sheaves:

We see here how [Joseph] begged his brothers to listen to him, and insisted on telling them his dream, which, had they given it another meaning, would have been fulfilled accordingly. But they said to him, "Do you mean to reign over us? Do you mean to rule over us?" and with these words they sealed their own doom.[36]

In short, the dream and the interpretation are both real and unreal events. Both can be interpreted. Both come to pass in reality. And the reality in which they both exist is the existential conundrum in which we find ourselves, the existence in which we can never quite answer the question, "Are we dreaming the dream or is the dream dreaming us?"

✻ [44] **Pharaoh said to Joseph, "I am Pharaoh; yet without you no one shall lift up hand or foot in all the land of Egypt." [45] Pharaoh then gave Joseph the name Zaphenath-paneah; and he gave him for a wife Asenath daughter of Poti-phera, priest of On. Thus Joseph emerged in charge of the land of Egypt.—[46] Joseph was thirty years old when he entered the service of Pharaoh king of Egypt.—Leaving Pharaoh's presence, Joseph traveled through all the land of Egypt.**

Among all the gifts Pharaoh bestows upon Joseph, the Egyptian name Zaphenath-paneah stands out. Translations of this name vary. Some translate the Egyptian to mean "God speaks; he lives" or "creator of life." Since the Pharaoh was considered the god of Egypt, the name no doubt refers to the Pharaoh and should be rendered as "the god Pharaoh speaks; he [Joseph] lives." Attempting to derive the meaning of the name from three Hebrew words,[37] the Targum, one of the earliest translations of the Bible, interpreted the name as "the one to whom hidden matters are revealed." The sages, however, preferred to sidestep the matter of translation, using instead the consonants of Zaphenath-paneah to pay tribute to Joseph. They said the Egyptian name was an acronym for *zofeh* ("scout"), *podeh* ("redeemer"), *navi* ("prophet"), *tomek* ("supporter"), *poter* ("interpreter"), *'arom* ("skilled"), *navon* ("understanding"), and *hozeh* ("seer").[38]

This is a fitting conclusion to our close inspection of interpretation in biblical times. All interpretation is prophecy, even as all dreams and visions are prophecy. Joseph has provided us insights into the interpreter's art. We can begin to see what this means *for us* as we apply the acronym of "Zaphenath-paneah." We must begin our own interpretations as *scouts* and end with the talents of *seers*. In the course of interpreting, we need to be nothing less than *redeemers*, *prophets*, *supporters*, and *interpreters*—bringing to all of these both *skill* and *understanding*. As the proverb acknowledges, *All dreams follow the mouth.*

From Scout to Seer

IN THE FOOTSTEPS
OF JOSEPH

☽

As Thou didst turn the curse of the wicked Balaam into a
blessing, so turn all my dreams into something good for me.
— Talmud, *Berachot*, 55b

Is every dream important enough to be interpreted? This is
one issue that Franz Kafka addressed in his parable "An Imperial Message."

> The Emperor, so it runs, has sent a message to you,
> the humble subject, the insignificant shadow cow-
> ering in the remotest distance before the imperial
> sun; the Emperor from his deathbed has sent a
> message to you alone. He has commanded the mes-
> senger to kneel down by the bed, and has whis-
> pered the message to him; so much store did he lay
> on it that he ordered the messenger to whisper it
> back into his ear again. Then by a nod of his head

he has confirmed that it is right. Yes, before the assembled spectators of his death—all the obstructing walls have been broken down, and on the spacious and loftily-mounting open staircases stand in a ring the great princes of the Empire—before all these he has delivered his message.

The messenger immediately sets out on his journey; a powerful, an indefatigable man; now pushing with his right arm, now with his left, he cleaves a way for himself through the throng; if he encounters resistance he points to his breast, where the symbol of the sun glitters; the way, too, is made easier for him than it would be for any other man. But the multitudes are so vast; their numbers have no end. If he could reach the open fields how fast he would fly, and soon doubtless you would hear the welcome hammering of his fists on your door. But instead how vainly does he wear out his strength; still he is only making his way through the chambers of the innermost palace; never will he get to the end of them; and if he succeeded in that nothing would be gained; he must fight his way next down the stairs; and if he succeeded in that nothing would be gained; the courts would still have to be crossed; and after the courts the second outer palace; and once more stairs and courts; and once more another palace; and so on for thousands of years; and if at last he should burst through the outermost gate—but never, never can that happen—the imperial capital would lie before him, the center of the world, crammed to bursting with its own refuse.

Nobody could fight his way through here, least of all one with a message from a dead man.—But you sit at your window when evening falls and dream it to yourself.[1]

Kafka's point is that every dream is an imperial message. Every dream is so important that it is the dying wish of the Emperor that you should hear it perfectly. The messenger struggles to reach you, but the path is crowded with obstacles. So you dream the dream, and dream the message of the dream, and hope somehow to interpret both the dream and its message *for you.*

If every dream you have is an imperial message meant only for you, can you afford to ignore even a single dream? "A dream not interpreted is like a letter not read."[2]

☽

In the mystic atmosphere of the Upper Galilee in the sixteenth century, a student of the Kabbalah proposed that the holiest among us create angels through the sounds we utter. An angel such as this, created out of human holiness, was called a *maggid* or "interpreter" angel. Unlike God's angels, who are perfect in every way, angels created through human utterance are sometimes capable of deception, even as humans are.

Since the Torah's words were those of God, the shock that angels are born of its words might be somewhat lessened, except that the Kabbalists read not only the words but the letters, *and* the spaces in between the letters and words, and interpretations of these gaps also brought forth angels. Acts

of interpretation and good deeds hardly were distinguished by the Safed mystics, certainly an alarm-
ing tendency when professional interpreters stop
to consider the consequences of their labors. Angels upon angels, angels everywhere, thronged the
atmosphere of Safed in the sixteenth century, and
the most remarkable among them, like the *maggid*
of Joseph Karo [the leading Talmudist of the age],
made "mighty promises" as dream interpreters
prophesying the personal future....[3]

Angels emerged from the dream world to become quite
real to some of the mystics. So real, in fact, that the mystics
devised a carefully worded questionnaire to enable a mystic
to certify that a particular "interpreter angel" was truthful.
The mystic was admonished to actually administer the
questionnaire to any *maggid* who proposed to guide him!
Once he felt he could trust his angel, he would allow the angel to speak through him, to interpret through his mouth
and his pen. In this way, some mystics engaged in what is
called "automatic" writing or, as we might prefer, "inspired" writing. The interpreter angels served as muses for
the mystics. Even now, I can feel my interpreter angel dic-
tating these words for you as I am writing them; and you
should be aware that your interpreter angel is helping you
to make sense of the words—lifting them from the dream
of ink on paper to the dreamlike reality of your reading self.

This is not so strange as it might first appear. Consider
the word *enthusiasm,* which comes from the Greek meaning "ecstasy arising from possession by a god or spirit." The
notion of ecstatic possession brings to mind the essential
role of the *shaman* in many so-called primitive traditions.
In these societies, the shaman is both the healer and the

prophet. He derives his inspiration and his enthusiasm from the spirit that guides him.

> For instance, [an] Eskimo shaman reported that when his spirit came to him it was as though the roof of his house was suddenly lifted. Then he saw through the house itself, across the world, and into the far reaches of the sky. This supernatural power of vision was produced by a light shining from within him, flooding his being, and proceeding outward wherever he might direct it. The same experience comes to the Nuba of Africa when they shamanize. Their heads become opened, they say, and there is the light.[4]

Often, shamans possess not only spirit helpers, but also spirit wives whom they meet on their ascent. This places a shaman on the same mythological rung as a king. In ancient Mesopotamia the king had to sleep with his wife in the temple at the summit of the ziggurat. In ancient Egypt similar rites were performed. Thus, both king and shaman wed the powers of earth and heaven in their selves, rejoining what was separated at the moment of creation. They gain their powers through this union, making upward progress on the spiritual pathway of the rainbow that joins heaven and earth. In this dreamlike state, the rainbow's path is seen as so narrow that mystics call it, "the sword's edge."[5]

Ordinary folk also experience the presence of spirit guides in their dreams. The black South African minister and musician Joseph Shabalala, who founded the choral group Ladysmith Black Mambazo and served as its lead singer, said:

> Every time when I am sleeping, I have music in my mind. All the time, like when you sleep, like a

dream. There is a stage, but there are children not on stage. They are between the stage and the sky, floating and always singing. They are like my teachers who teach me exactly this sound.[6]

This, of course, reminds us of the "Brownies" of Robert Louis Stevenson who played upon the imaginary stage in his dreams. Stevenson once confessed that he was no storyteller at all, "the whole of my published fiction should be the single-handed product of some Brownie, some Familiar, some unseen collaborator, whom I keep locked in a back garret." Stevenson posed the obvious questions concerning his Brownies, "Who are they, then? And who is the dreamer?"[7]

Nor is it only in the arts that dream spirits inspire. Among religious and historical figures, inspiration was brought in a dream to Muhammad by the angel Gabriel who told him to leave Medina and lead an army to conquer Mecca. In the eighth century, Aubert, bishop of the French town of Avranches, was visited in his dreams by the archangel Michael, who ordered him to build a chapel. Inspired by this dream, he founded Mont-Saint-Michel. René Descartes decided to pursue a career as a mathematician and philosopher based on a dream in which a stranger appeared and recommended to him a piece of Latin verse. A Hindu goddess named Namakkal appeared in the dreams of the Indian mathematician Srinivasa Ramanujan to present him with mathematical formulae.

Among the Kalapalo Indians of central Brazil dreaming is thought to be a means of communicating with powerful beings who possess great properties that can be transferred to the dreamer's interactive self. These beings are also considered potentially dangerous to the dreamer since, in the transfer of their power, the dreamer's interactive self may not prove strong enough and the dreamer may fail to awaken forever. Special parts of the Kalapalo language are set aside for speaking only about the dream life, and interpretation is considered one of the powers bequeathed by their spirit guides.[8] Among Native American Indians, the spirit interpreter may be a part of nature or an animal spirit; and in nearly all shamanic traditions, the shaman's magic is considered most potent when a lordly spirit beast such as a lion or tiger guides the shaman.

Can we create our own interpreter angels? For us, the issue is one of belief and psychology commingled. As Joseph Campbell describes it:

> Protective and dangerous, motherly and fatherly at the same time, this supernatural principle of guardianship and direction unites in itself all the ambiguities of the unconscious—thus signifying the support of our conscious personality by that other, larger system, but also the inscrutability of the guide that we are following, to the peril of all our rational ends.
>
> The hero to whom such a helper appears is typically one who has responded to the call. The call, in fact, was the first announcement of the approach of this initiatory priest [the spirit guide]. But even to those who apparently have hardened their hearts, the supernatural guardian may appear.[9]

To be a spiritual seeker implies learning to communicate with the dream spirits that are created through your search. What kind of questionnaire will you have in mind for your *maggid* when your *maggid* appears to you? At what point will you allow your interpreter angel to begin to speak through you? These questions are more than mere bluff. They may very well determine the moment when your dreams begin to transform you, the moment when your dream reality will merge with your waking reality. Psychologists tell us that every figure we encounter in a dream is some aspect of ourselves. The breakthrough here, then, is not your creation of some interpreter angel but the recognition of the interpreter angel already in you.

☽

Comparing your dreams to Bible dreams can provide another kind of guidance, too. Like the dreams in the Bible, your dreams are narratives—texts open to interpretation. Interpretation, however, is not static. Take, for example, the following dream that I recorded in my journal some years ago:

> I saw a diamond in my hand. Looking into it, I thought I saw thousands of sparkling lights. Then a voice spoke from beside me, telling me a story. As I listened, my eyes remained fixed on the diamond, as if the story were in it. "In the beginning," the voice said, "there was God and a spark of light. God saw the spark and knew it was beautiful. Then God chiseled at the unhewn spark until a surface appeared. In the surface God saw the reflection of the Eternal shining out mysteriously and God saw that it was good—though God knew that if it would be good, it might also be bad. Nonetheless, God affirmed it.
>
> "Then God carved a second surface beside the first. Now the first reflected the second and the second the first; and both reflected the remainder

of the spark and it all reflected the Eternal God. So God carved again, affirming it by re-creating it.

"When all the surfaces of the spark were carved, God reached the inside of the spark and began to carve outward. And the splinters and shavings that gathered about the place God was carving each reflected the light of the other and of the large spark (which was all gone but the insides now) and of God. And God reaffirmed each reflection by carving a surface for it and then another until only the insides of the clippings remained.

"Then God carved the inner surfaces until the inner was all carved away and only the outer remained. It was a sparkling reflection of the inner and the former outer and of the Eternal and of the spark that had disappeared but was present in every shadow of every reflection."

When the voice finished speaking the diamond disappeared, and I saw my hand filled with sparkling lights. The lights poured through every pore of my skin as if my hand were transparent. I held up my hand and thought, "It seems solid, but it might just be a reflection." I woke with an incredible feeling of deep satisfaction.

I have interpreted this dream many times, its interpretation depending heavily on what was happening in my life at a given moment. As I have been writing this book, I have come to think that the voice came to teach me about interpretation itself. I held a diamond, a thing that seems at first perfectly clear, even transparent. But as I look into a diamond, I begin to see the colors of light sparkling at every edge of every surface—and the surfaces that seemed transparent also seemed as reflective as mirrors.

In the same way, dream messages sometimes appear at first to be clear and transparent. As we listen to them again, though, they begin to sound as complex as a carillon—a myriad of bells ringing at different times in different tones yet all in tune and overlapping in their resonance. Every sensitive interpretation is as "true" as every bell, and every interpretation is another graceful note enhancing all the others.

We all know that truth is ephemeral: what is true today may or may not be true tomorrow. Being imperfect is a part of the condition of being human. But that is not the point here. The point is that the narrative, the dream, the dream message, and the interpretation of a dream all take on a life of their own, as if they each are exquisite tones or reflective surfaces of light. Like an imperial message, they come from inside us carrying many facets of truths all meant *for us*.

))

In his study *The Wilderness of Dreams*, Kelly Bulkeley proposes six questions to guide us as we interpret dreams: (1) What are the pertinent images in the dream? (2) Do the images metaphorically express religious or existential concerns? (3) What is the emotional power of the dream? (4) Does the dream relate to a current life crisis or transition? (5) Does the dream relate to both the dreamer's past and the dreamer's future? (6) What potential does the dream have to transform the dreamer's waking life?[10]

(1) What are the pertinent images in the dream? As we saw in the case of Joseph's interpretation of the duplicate dreams of the cupbearer and the baker, and in the case of his interpretation of the duplicate dreams of Pharaoh, the first step in interpretation is identifying the central symbols or images in the dreams. These may be visual images or words or numbers. Paying attention to other details such as the setting, the colors, the time, and so on may also provide clues to the possible messages in the dream. Consider the way in which Joseph envisioned the baker's head hanging in the tree from hearing the description of the baker crowned with three large openwork baskets above his head and the birds feeding from the uppermost basket.

(2) Do the images metaphorically express religious or existential concerns? Joseph was able to identify the existential concerns of the dreamers whose dreams he was interpreting. Though the dreams did not seem to be religious, he credited his interpretation to God, expressing the belief that the messages were heaven-sent. Even dreams that on the surface do not seem religious may metaphorically express existential concerns. Joseph provides us with good examples of this kind of dream in his duplicate dream of the sheaves of wheat and the sun, moon, and stars.

(3) What is the emotional power of the dream? Prophetic dreams often leave strong emotions in their wake. The specific emotion can provide a hint of how the dream can best be interpreted for the dreamer. Pharaoh was extremely agitated by his dream, and the cupbearer and the baker were downcast because they felt the dream needed interpretation and could find no one to interpret it. In waking from my diamond dream, I experienced a feeling of intense satisfaction. These feelings provide clues to the ways in which the interpretation should proceed.

(4) Does the dream relate to a current life crisis or transition? As we have observed, dreams seem to increase in intensity and frequency at moments of transition in our lives. Consider the moments at which the three sets of duplicate dreams appeared to Joseph. The first came as the boy Joseph began to envision his adult life. According to the text, Joseph was seventeen years old, a perfect moment for him to wonder about his future. Of course, we may well question his wisdom in sharing these dreams with his already jealous brothers. But who would mistake youth with wisdom?

"In crisis" is a phrase that well describes the existential condition of the cupbearer and the baker. By contrast, the dreams of Pharaoh seem to come at an unexpected moment, one unrelated to any apparent transition or crisis. It is only through Joseph's interpretation that Pharaoh's crisis is exposed.

(5) Does the dream relate to both the dreamer's past and the dreamer's future? One sign that a dream carries a prophetic message is the way the message for the future "fits" with the past of the dreamer. When Joseph goes to interpret the message of Pharaoh's dreams, it soon becomes apparent that the dreams relate to the past history of Egypt and the future of the nation. In their wisdom, the sages noted that "a king's dream embraces the whole world." The other two sets of duplicate dreams—Joseph's own and those of the baker and cupbearer—fit with both the past and future of the dreamers without a doubt. They are personal messages in the cases of the cupbearer and the baker, and both personal and prophetic for the nation in the case of the duplicate dreams of Joseph's youth.

(6) What potential does the dream have to transform the dreamer's waking life? A prophetic message is a forceful one whether it comes in a dream or in a vision. It demands attention and interpretation. Often, it demands that we make real changes in our lives. The plan Joseph puts forward to Pharaoh means that a whole nation must force itself to be austere in the midst of years of plenty in order to be prepared for a time of famine to come. To enact such a plan of action requires stores of faith.

In my case, the diamond dream adjures me to endlessly "hear again" the messages in my dreams for ever-emerging meanings. This separates me from my youth when what I most sought was certainty in my life and work. Today, I consciously seek uncertainties, delighting in the beauty of available alternatives, willing to live with ambiguity. In the sense that I have actualized the many messages of the diamond dream, the dream has proved to be prophetic *for me*.

Apply these six questions to your dreams. You will soon discover the dreams that are particularly likely to be prophetic for you. As you proceed, question-by-question, you will be "hearing again" the dreams. If you approach this as Paul Ricoeur suggested—with a second naïveté—you will begin to connect the dreams with your past and with your future. When a dream connects in both directions, eureka!, you are examining a "message dream." It is time to begin carving surfaces in the unhewn spark.

In these six questions, you may hear echoes of the questions proposed by Artemidorus, the Greek scholar of dreams. This should not be surprising. We have learned that societies modern and primitive, literate and preliterate, all have traditions of dream interpretation, and none of these traditions are ever cast off lightly. In our search to become the interpreters, we must be scouts studying the terrain to find the best way to proceed and seers opening our eyes and our ears to messages that may be true *for us*. The imperial message has been whispered to the messenger, and the messenger is struggling through obstacle after obstacle, but the only way you can ever hope to receive the message is to dream it to yourself.

Dream Symbols

SAMUEL AND SOLOMON
HEAR THE CALL

☽

A dream is a wish your heart makes ... if you keep on believing, the dream that you wish will come true. — Cinderella

The Bible contains no list of dream symbols and their meanings. Instead, it employs language to create images that fairly leap into the imagination, a vocabulary of fully-realized dream symbols: the flaming torch and the smoking oven, Jacob's staircase, Jacob's wrestling match, the sheaves of wheat bowing to Joseph's sheaf, the heavenly luminaries bowing to Joseph's light, the three vines and the three baskets, the seven lean and ugly cows swallowing the seven fat cows, the seven wind-scorched ears of grain swallowing the seven healthy ears. These are the handful we have examined. Along with dozens more, they are engraved in our cultural memory—many of them from childhood on.

If the redactors of the Bible had chosen to include lists of dream symbols, such lists were readily available. Judging by their format, the earliest lists seem to have been memorized and passed from generation to generation orally long before being committed to clay or papyrus. We have already examined an Egyptian example.

Unlike the Bible, the Talmud does include a list of symbols for Jewish dream interpretation. The sages felt free to borrow from earlier Mesopotamian lists, but their list gains its main distinction through its use of Hebrew wordplay. A brief sampling will suffice:

If a nose [af] falls off in a dream, fierce anger [af] has been removed from you. If both hands are cut off, you will not require the labor of your hands. If you see the month of Adar and not the month of Nisan, you will die in all honor [adruta] and not be brought into temptation [nisayon]. If you see a well, you will find peace or life. If you see a river or bird (or a pot in which there is no meat), you will find peace. If you see grapes, they represent the Children of Israel—if they are white it always a sign of good; if they are black and in season it is a sign of good; if they are black and out of season, it is an evil omen. If you see mountains, good tidings will come to you. If you see dogs, the greed of others will harm you. If you see lions, you should be afraid. If you see a reed [kaneh], a pumpkin [kara], a palm-heart [kora], or wax [kira] [all of which sound alike], you should hope for wisdom. If you see several reeds, hope for understanding. If you see an ox eating its flesh, hope for riches. If you dream of riding on an ox, you will rise to greatness. If an ox rides on the dreamer, it signifies death. Riding on an ass means salvation. If you dream of a cat from the region where the cat is called shunara, you will hear a beautiful song [shirah na'ah]; but if it is from the region where the cat is called *shinra*, it portends a change for the worse [*shinnui ra'*]. A white horse is a good sign, and so is a red horse that is walking; but a red horse galloping is an evil omen. A dream of one elephant (*pil*) portends wonders [*pela'ot*]; other beasts are good omens, except for the ape.[1]

The list continues. It indicates the meaning of seeing a particular sage in a dream—each sage mentioned by name is assigned a different meaning. It lists specific words that may be seen in a dream—each word is assigned a special meaning. The Talmud's list of dream symbols is presented in authoritative tones, and, in typical fashion, many of the interpretations are accompanied by proofs adduced from biblical verses.

Modern lists of dream symbols and their corresponding interpretation derive from ancient and medieval sources. Generally, they are edited and altered to appear modern. It is popular now, for example, to include symbols mentioned by Freud, Jung, and other modern interpreters of dreams. In many of these lists, the compiler's goal seems to be ambiguity, that is, making the interpretations broad enough to suit almost any combination of events that might overtake a dreamer subsequent to the dream.

> Milk is knowledge; a key means change; hair is worry; an arrow is pleasure; cats are bad luck; pins mean quarreling; iron is power; cheese is disappointment; a sneeze denotes a change in plans; a clock is danger; bread is happiness; a steeple predicts sickness; a thread signifies a road and the course of life.... As in so many other forms of fortune-telling, the dream prophecies are familiar ones. You will go on a trip, meet a stranger, receive something of value. Any or all these fore-

casts could hardly fail to come true during the course of a lifetime.[2]

Comparing lists of dream symbols can be a fatuous task. They often directly contradict one another. To the sages, dreaming of an owl meant misfortune. A recent list in *The Dream Encyclopedia* defines an owl as

> a symbol of wisdom and virtue, as a nightbird the owl is also a natural symbol of the unconscious. Solemn and wide-eyed, the owl may bear a message the dreamer needs to hear.[3]

The Dream Encyclopedia contains no mention of vines or baskets, torches or ovens, parched grain or ugly cows. Presumably, we are on our own when it comes to many of the symbols encountered in the Bible. Modern science may have come a long way, but it is fair to say that whatever wisdom can be gained from modern lists of dream symbols is almost entirely derivative. *The Dream Encyclopedia*, for example, contains no interpretation for chancing on radar, computers, cellular phones, or the Internet in a dream. Given a few more years, however, the lists will probably include these, deriving their meanings from more ancient symbols in the same way that *The Dream Encyclopedia* includes a definition for a spaceship:

> Spaceships in a dream may indicate a spiritual journey into the realms of the mysterious and the unknown. Spaceships (or flying saucers) have become, according to Carl Jung, the technological equivalent of angels in the modern world.[4]

Even from this cursory inspection, it is safe to say that when we rely on lists of dream symbols we often lessen our ability to hear what a dream is saying *for us*. Ironically, however, the lists do serve a useful purpose: They remind us that the visual images we see in our dreams are likely to be conditioned by the society in which we live; which, in turn, reminds us that human dreams have always been conditioned by social norms.

The dreams we have examined and interpreted thus far come from Genesis, by far the richest mine of dream data in the Bible. In this chapter, however, we turn to two dreams from other books in the Bible. These dreams amplify some of the concepts we have already encountered. They also form a natural bridge from what the dreams in the Bible can mean *for us* to what *our* dreams can mean *for us*. The first of these is the famous dream of King Solomon.

))

❋ *1 Kings 3 [2]* **The people, however, continued to offer sacrifices at the open shrines *[bamot]*, because up to that time no house had been built for the name of the Eternal. *[3]* And Solomon, though he loved the Eternal and followed the practices of his father David, also sacrificed and offered at the shrines *[bamot]*. *[4]* The king went to Gibeon to sacrifice there, for that was the largest shrine; on that altar Solomon presented a thousand burnt-offerings. *[5]* At Gibeon the Eternal appeared to Solomon in a dream by night; and God said, "Ask, what shall I grant you?" *[6]* Solomon said, "You dealt most graciously with Your servant my father David, because he walked before You in faithfulness and righteousness and in integrity of heart. You have continued this great kindness to him by giving him a son to occupy his throne, as is now the case. *[7]* And now, O Eternal my God, You have made Your servant king in place of my father David; but I am a young** lad, and do not know how to go out or come in. *[8]* **Your servant finds himself in the midst of the people You have chosen, a people too numerous to be numbered or counted.** *[9]* **Grant, then, Your servant an understanding mind to judge Your people, to distinguish between good and bad; for who can judge this vast people of Yours?"** *[10]* **The Eternal was pleased that Solomon had asked for this.** *[11]* **And God said to him, "Because you asked for this— you did not ask for long life, you did not ask for riches, you did not ask for the life of your enemies, but you asked for discernment in dispensing justice—** *[12]* **I now do as you have spoken. I grant you a wise and discerning mind; there has never been anyone like you before, nor will anyone like you arise again.** *[13]* **And I also grant you what you did not ask for—both riches and glory all your life—the like of which no king has ever had.** *[14]* **And I will further grant you long life, if you will walk in My ways and observe My laws and commandments, as did your father David."** *[15]* **Then Solomon awoke: it was a dream! He went to Jerusalem, stood before the Ark of the Covenant of the Eternal, and sacrificed burnt-offerings and presented offerings of well-being; and he made a banquet for all his courtiers.**

At the moment this dream occurs, the tensions that would eventually split the southern tribes from the northern tribes of Israel were already rife. King David showed his political acumen by selecting the ancient Canaanite city of Salem as his new capital, renaming it "the City of David." The city had never belonged to either the northern or the southern tribes, yet it was located in the Judean Hills almost midway between them. While David reigned, the northern and southern factions held together, albeit in a strained alliance.

To fully comprehend what David had in mind when he chose Solomon as his successor, we must go beyond the nearly identical accounts in Kings and Samuel and examine the narrative in Chronicles. According to Chronicles, David purchased the land for the Temple ("the House of the Eternal") from a Jebusite who was using the site as a threshing floor. The text continues:

> For David thought, "My son Solomon is an untried youth, and the House to be built for the Eternal is to be made exceedingly great to win fame and glory throughout all the lands; let me then lay aside materials for him." So David laid aside much material before he died. Then he summoned his son Solomon and charged him with building the House for the Eternal God of Israel [1 Chronicles 22:5–6].[5]

Kings and Samuel do not include David's instructions to Solomon, though both clearly state that David had hoped to build a Temple. Chronicles, reputedly the court annals of the House of David, is much more specific: David intended the Temple to be "exceedingly great to win fame and glory throughout all the lands." David may also have had a spiritual motivation, but the record here reflects a carefully calculated political agenda. It also notes David's characterization of his son Solomon as "an untried youth." If this was David's perception, it was no doubt also the political wisdom of the day. There is no reason to believe that Solomon's accession to the throne would go unopposed. Solomon would have to prove himself worthy of trust.

Solomon wisely cements his international position by marrying a daughter of the Pharaohs. Backed by his alliance with the powerful Egyptian nation, he next turns to the problem of reassuring his own people that he is the right king for all the tribes, north and south. He does this by touring the country's "shrines" to offer sacrifices. This tour of sacrifice is the ancient equivalent of kissing babies on the American political circuit.

The Hebrew word for shrines is *bamot,* which literally means "high places"—and many such high places were scattered throughout the land. Ostensibly, all these high places were now dedicated to the worship of the God of Moses. In actuality, a great number of them had formerly been used by the Canaanite nations to worship local deities and, to one extent or another, the worship of local gods was commingled with the newer Israelite religion.[6]

Our narrative begins as Solomon arrives at Gibeon, purportedly the largest of all the local high places. The holy site of Gibeon boasted possession of the tabernacle that Moses had constructed in the wilderness and also the traditional altar of burnt-offerings.[7] As a token of his kingship and wealth—and to pay the proper homage to the site and its priests—Solomon offers nothing less than "a thousand" burnt sacrifices.

The dream comes to Solomon at a moment of transformation, when he must make the transition from insecure youth to able leader. In the dream, he expresses his uncertainty. Is he ready to lead the people of Israel? Will he be recognized as the supreme judge over all the land? He asks, "Who can judge this vast people of Yours?" We can imagine what he has in mind when he uses the word "vast." He would obviously want to avoid saying the word "divided" out loud.

Solomon seems, nonetheless, willing to share his personal insecurity. He intimates his concern in unspoken questions we can read between the lines: Will he appear regal in the eyes of the court? "I am a young lad, and do not know how to go out or come in." Is he kingly enough to be

king? "Your servant finds himself in the midst of the people
You have chosen, a people too numerous to be numbered or
counted."

From the outset, we sense a certain amount of disin-
genuousness in his insecurity. It may be that he wants the
leaders of the tribes to believe that he is insecure in order
to entice them into reassuring, and thus confirming, him.
If so, it is a politic maneuver.

In the dream, God replies, "Ask, what shall I grant
you?" And Solomon is ready with an answer. He knows that
to govern his people he requires wisdom and understanding, discernment and judgment. God is pleased by Solomon's answer—an answer that shows that the young king
already has much wisdom—and the dream gift is granted.
The Senoi people would have been pleased by Solomon's
dream, for Solomon can now return to his people with a gift
easily recognized as valuable.

Solomon's response is so pleasing that God bestows additional dream gifts on Solomon, "riches and glory all your
life—the like of which no king has ever had." God then
makes a covenant with Solomon, which reminds us of the
patriarchal covenants we encountered in the dreams of
Abraham and Jacob. It reminds us of them, but is not identical with them. In the earlier covenants, God promised
that, in return for the obedience of the patriarchs, the nation would prosper and endure forever, growing too numerous to ever be counted—as numberless as the stars in the
heavens or the sand on the ocean's shores. Here, God promises Solomon long life. The implication is that the fate of
the nation is secure—it is *Solomon's* fate that hangs in the
balance.

Solomon awakens with the realization that he has been
dreaming. He celebrates by returning to Jerusalem and

making a banquet for his courtiers. It doesn't require too much imagination to see that the purpose of the feast was to provide him a proper setting in which to repeat the dream to the entire court (and, through them, to the entire nation). His prophetic dream could not help but ingratiate him with the tribes, north and south.

In fact, Solomon's dream reads like the work of an advertising genius. An almost identical account of the dream is repeated in Chronicles, without the banquet, but with the conclusion: "From the shrine at Gibeon, from the Tent of Meeting, Solomon went to Jerusalem and reigned over Israel."

Others who dream are sometimes granted spiritual guidance by angels or strangers, but a king can properly receive the word of God directly. So we are told, "the Eternal appeared to Solomon in a dream by night." And the striking thing about this dream, what makes it essential that it be included in our forest of dreams, is that for all of its elaborate detail there is no visual image whatever—no symbol that could appear in a list of symbols, no vision that gives us focus for our eyes. The message *is* the dream; the dream *is* the message.

Different in kind from the other dreams we have inspected, this one may also deliver a powerful message *for us:* In a prophetic dream it is not what we *see* that is of supreme importance, it is what we *hear.* Even when visual symbols are present, they are there to be interpreted in language, in sound that makes sense. Our other senses are all wonderful—taste, smell, touch, and sight—but it is through *hearing* the message that prophetic dreams transform us. The importance of hearing the message is further elucidated in a dream of Samuel the Prophet.

)

✳ *1 Samuel 3 [1]* Young Samuel was in the service of the Eternal under Eli. In those days the word of the Eternal was rare; prophecy was not widespread. *[2]* One day, Eli was asleep in his usual place; his eyes had begun to fail and he could barely see. *[3]* The lamp of God had not yet gone out, and Samuel was sleeping in the temple of the Eternal where the ark of God was. *[4]* The Eternal called out to Samuel, and he answered, "I am here *[hineni]*." *[5]* He ran to Eli and said, "Here I am *[hineni]*; you called me." But Eli replied, "I didn't call you; go back to sleep." So he went back and lay down. *[6]* Again the Eternal called, "Samuel!" Samuel rose and went to Eli and said, "Here I am *[hineni]*; you called me." But he replied, "I didn't call, my son; go back to sleep."—*[7]* Now Samuel had not yet experienced the Eternal, the word of the Eternal had not yet been revealed to him.—*[8]* The Eternal called Samuel again, a third time, and he rose and went to Eli and said, "Here I am *[hineni]*; you called me." Then Eli understood that the Eternal was calling the boy. *[9]* And Eli said to Samuel, "Go, lie down. If you are called again, say, 'Speak, Eternal, for Your servant is listening.'" And Samuel went to his place and lay down. *[10]* The Eternal came, and stood there, and God called as before: "Samuel! Samuel!" And Samuel answered, "Speak, for Your servant is listening." *[11]* The Eternal said to Samuel: "I am going to do in Israel such a thing that both ears of anyone who hears about it will tingle. *[12]* In that day I will fulfill against Eli all that I spoke concerning his house, from beginning to end. *[13]* And I declare to him that I sentence his house to endless punishment for the iniquity he knew about—how his sons committed sacrilege at will—and he did not rebuke them. *[14]* Assuredly, I swear concerning the house of Eli that the iniquity of the house of Eli will never be expiated by sacrifice or offering. *[15]* Samuel lay there until morning; and then he opened the doors of the House of the Eternal. Samuel was afraid to report the vision to Eli, *[16]* but Eli summoned Samuel and said, "Samuel, my son"; and he answered, "Here I am *[hineni]*." *[17]* And [Eli] asked, "What did the Eternal say to you? Keep nothing from me. Thus and more may God do to you if you keep from me a single word all that God said to you." *[18]* Samuel then told him everything, withholding nothing from him. And [Eli] said, "It is the Eternal; God will do what God deems right."

How did Samuel come to be in the service of God? Like the matriarchs, Samuel's mother Hannah was barren for many years. She was married to an observant man named Elkanah who loved her deeply. Elkanah had another wife, Peninah, who gave him daughters and sons. Peninah taunted Hannah for her barrenness. Year after year, Elkanah took his wives to the local shrine at Shiloh. There, he offered sacrifices to God. One night at Shiloh, after dinner, Hannah slipped out to weep and pray to God to grant her a child. Eli the priest was sitting by the door of the House of God. Seeing her swaying, Eli concluded that Hannah was drunk and he scolded her. But when she explained that she was praying in anguish for God to send her a child, Eli relented and blessed her.

In the course of time, Hannah conceived and gave birth to a boy. She named her child Samuel, meaning, "I asked the Eternal for him." After Samuel was weaned, Hannah brought him to Shiloh and presented him to Eli, dedicating Samuel to God's service. The Jewish historian Josephus informs us (based on traditions that we no longer possess) that several years passed so that Samuel was twelve years old at the time that his dream occurred.

If there is a central symbol in this dream narrative, it is the Hebrew word, *hineni*, which can be translated as "here I am" or "behold, it is I" or "I am present." An entire book could be written on the interpretation of this word in the Bible. Its every appearance is fraught with meaning. It occurs in Genesis 22 when God decides to put Abraham to the test by asking the patriarch to sacrifice his son Isaac. God calls, "Abraham." And Abraham answers, *hineni*. A few verses later, as Abraham and Isaac climb the mountain together, Isaac says, "Father," and Abraham answers, *hineni*. A few verses later, as Abraham lifts the knife to slay his son, an angel of the Eternal calls to him, "Abraham! Abraham!"—again Abraham answers, *hineni*.[8]

In Genesis 27, Isaac has grown old and his eyes have dimmed. He calls his son Esau and Esau answers, *hineni,* "I am present." Isaac sends Esau to hunt for game, promising to give him the patriarch's blessing when he returns from the hunt. In the meanwhile, Rebecca and Jacob cook up a meal and a scheme. Jacob dresses like Esau and disguises the soft flesh of his arm with goatskin. When Jacob brings the food to his father, he says, "Father?" And Isaac replies, "*Hineni,* which of my two sons are you?" [Genesis 27:1, 18]. In Genesis 31, when Jacob has worked for Laban for many years, he has a dream at the time of the mating of the flocks. An angel says, "Jacob!" Here, too, Jacob answers, *hineni* [31:11].

In Genesis 37, when Jacob decides to send Joseph out to see his brothers where they are pasturing the flocks, he says to Joseph, "Come, I will send you to them." Joseph answers, *hineni* [37:13]. This is, of course, the trip that will end in Joseph being sold into slavery. In Genesis 46, Jacob arrives at Beersheba on his way to Egypt to join his son Joseph. He is nervous about leaving the Promised Land. God calls to him in a dream, "Jacob! Jacob!" and here, again, Jacob answers, *hineni* [46:2].

Every instance of the use of *hineni* in the Bible occurs at a moment of crisis or transition. It is always a moment that requires the person answering the call to be fully present—alert and aware. And the word is used nowhere more frequently than in this dream of Samuel.

The half-blind priest Eli is asleep. Samuel has been assigned to sleep near the Ark where he can tend the lamp of God. The priestly code provided that the lamp should not be allowed to go out until morning and Samuel's task was to add oil from time to time to ensure that it would burn through the night. But on this night God calls out to Samuel, and Samuel is confused. He imagines that it is Eli who has called him.

The dream comes at a moment when Samuel is poised for transition. After the dream, he will become a judge, a priest, a prophet, and even (reluctantly) a kingmaker. Moreover, it comes at a moment of transition for Eli. Just before Samuel's dream, Eli received a visit from "a man of God" who told him that the sins of Eli's sons had not gone unnoticed. "A time is coming when I will break your power and that of your father's house, and there shall be no elder in your house." Eli realized that he and his sons were doomed, and it must have weighed heavily on his mind. The same stranger also told Eli that God would raise up a faithful priest, one "who will act in accordance with My wishes and My purposes."[9] So the moment of Samuel's ascension to power will also be the moment of the utter destruction of his master, Eli, and Eli's house.

It is this tragic coincidence that confirms the meaning of Samuel's dream for Eli. As he hears Samuel describe the words that God has spoken, Eli intuits that these words have been sent *for him*. Even more, he realizes that the words were sent in order that he might know that Samuel's dream was truly prophetic.

In describing the many biblical passages in which the word *hineni* figures, I saved one very important occurrence for this moment. In Exodus 3, when Moses turns aside to take a closer look at the burning bush, God calls out of the bush, "Moses! Moses!" and Moses answers, *"Hineni"* [Exodus 3:4]. In the present dream, too, we are told, in verse 10, God calls "as before," and the call is, "Samuel! Samuel!" and then Samuel answers, *"Hineni."*

This is how momentous transformations begin. The hero is beckoned. Joseph Campbell terms this "the call to adventure" but perhaps he should have termed it "the call to journey." As he demonstrates, the call typically begins with a heralding voice:

> The herald's summons may be to live ... or, at a later moment of the biography, to die. It may sound the call to some high historical undertaking. Or it may mark the dawn of religious illumination. As apprehended by the mystic, it marks what has been termed "the awakening of the self."[10]

Campbell continues by saying that this first stage of the mythological journey

> signifies that destiny has summoned the hero and transferred his spiritual center of gravity from within the pale of his society to a zone unknown. This fateful region of both treasure and danger may be variously represented: as a distant land, a forest, a

kingdom underground, beneath the waves, or above the sky, a secret island, lofty mountaintop, or profound dream state: but it is always a place of strangely fluid and polymorphous beings, unimaginable torments, superhuman deeds, and impossible delight. The hero can go forth of his own volition to accomplish the adventure ... or he may be sent or carried abroad by some benign or malignant agent.... The adventure may begin as a mere blunder ... or still again, one may be only casually strolling, when some passing phenomenon catches the wandering eye and lures one away from the frequented paths of man.[11]

In Samuel's dream, the journey begins with a blunder. He mistakes the voice of the Eternal with the voice of Eli. In Moses' case, the journey begins when he is tending the flocks and turns aside to notice a little bush that seems to be burning without being consumed. In both cases, the vision is not one of seeing, but one of hearing. The voice that calls is the real image that remains imprinted in the mind of the spiritual seeker. The hearing of the seeker's own name is the beginning of the journey of the self to the self's destiny.

At that moment, at that magical juncture of the divine and the human within us, whether we are awake or dreaming is of no real importance. Lists of symbols and their meanings cannot help us. Visual images must be translated into messages to make real sense to us.

Perhaps you have witnessed a radiant sunset. You have seen a rainbow in its full glory. You have heard bars of music that seemed to emanate from some celestial sphere. You have reached the top of a mountain to look out over an endless horizon. You have tasted a wine that left you breathless with its depth and complexity. You have smelled a perfume that instantly elicited emotions you thought long dead. You have touched a miraculously luxuriant cloth. To share these sensual perceptions, you must put them into *messages*, language that can be shared from mouth to ear. To behold something is to be challenged to interpret it. To interpret it is to transform it into a story, an adventure, a journey that can inspire and intrigue and enthuse. To interpret it is to embed it in your personal archaeology. To interpret it is to incorporate it into your self, into your own adventure, into your own journey. To interpret it is to make it possible to share it.

It is essential at the moment of hearing that you be fully present, fully aware, fully *here*. At that moment, the world stands still, waiting for you to take up the challenge. Your name is being called! It is up to you to answer, *"Hineni."*

Your Name Shall Be "Incredulous"

THE POTENTIAL FOR HEALING AND TRANSFORMATION

☽

The vision that he sees is for many days from now, and he prophesies of times far off. — Ezekiel 12:27

We have focused on dreams and visions in the Bible. In due course, we have brought to bear passages from the Talmud and Jewish texts through the ages; and materials from dream researchers, ethnographers, anthropologists, and archaeologists to amplify the discussion. Overall, we have demonstrated how the dreams in the Bible may become a framework for understanding our own dreams and for allowing our own spirituality to surface.

Although we provided no "recipes" or "instructions," as such, the materials suggest various methods for recording and interpreting dreams; and a number of ways in which you may compare your dreams with those found in the Bible. You and those with whom you choose to share your dreams already possess the wisdom of your life and experience, and that wisdom is the first and finest resource for analyzing your dreams. No set of recipes would work for everyone, and typical lists of dream symbols can only suggest, never decipher, what the symbols in your dreams mean. Your imagination—coupled with techniques culled from many cultures, times, and places—is really all you need to make the dreams of the Bible speak *for you.*

In addition to the dreams we encountered, the books of Jeremiah and Daniel, for example, contain many excellent dream narratives. In fact, Jewish tradition regards Daniel as Joseph's equal when it comes to interpreting dreams. Here and there, it is even said that Daniel was the Bible's greatest interpreter of dreams. On one occasion, Daniel proved his mettle by managing to accurately describe a king's dream before interpreting it. It seems that Daniel was deeply perceptive when it came to the kings he served. Of course, if your life depends on serving kings, you had best be perceptive. As we noted, the same was true in Joseph's presentation before Pharaoh.

You may wish to examine other Bible dream and vision narratives on your own or with a dream group. Moses' vision at the burning bush is one of the great transformational visions in the Bible. Greater still, for its lasting impact, is the vision that was granted to the Children of Israel as they stood at the foot of Mount Sinai. We think of Native American Indians dreaming of a trickster rabbit as a comic dream; in the Bible, the greatest comic dream is Balaam's vision of the talking donkey. When we think of visual images in dreams, we recall how the Chinese report seeing fire-breathing dragons, and the peoples of pre-Columbian

America dreamt of vividly colored feathered serpents; in the Bible, Ezekiel's dream of the chariot is similarly outstanding for its imagery. The list goes on.

The dreams we chose to analyze present a fairly unitary conception. They describe our biblical ancestors' understanding of the spiritual quest. In the case of the patriarchs, Solomon, and Samuel, individuals stand poised at a moment of transition. Based on dreams and the interpretations of dreams, they commence, reconfirm, or continue their spiritual quests, yielding individual and collective meaning. The quests are spiritual for two reasons: (1) in every case the Bible attributes dream answers to heaven; (2) in every case the Bible describes a matching quest on God's part, as divinity reaches out to infuse human beings with spirituality. It might be said that when a human being quests for spirituality, heaven joins the quest. Or, conversely, when heaven is ready for an individual to find spirituality, heaven elicits a human spiritual quest. Both of these statements are "true" in a metaphysical sense. When you are ready, heaven is ready; and when heaven is ready, you have no choice but to be ready.

This book, then, describes a mutual quest linking earth and heaven. The same mutual quest is found in varying degrees in the New Testament, in the Dionysian myths, in Jewish and Islamic mysticism, in the *Tao Te Ching*, in the writings of Chuang-tzu, in warrior messiah traditions such as those in the Dead Sea Scrolls and among the Samurai in Japan, in the dream world of the Aborigines, in the healing of primitive shamans, and so on. The same mutual quest is portrayed on the ceiling of the Sistine chapel; in the architecture of synagogues, churches and mosques; in icons and ritual objects; and in the many worlds of the arts throughout the ages.[1]

It is only in the last few centuries, and especially in the West, that the quest for spiritual enlightenment has been consigned to humans alone. But what is the effect when individuals and communities enter on the spiritual quest with no expectation of a mutual response from above? The goal of the quest is then limited to perfecting the individual or the group, to becoming superhuman, in other words, to becoming our own idols. Witness the ironically prophetic words of Friedrich Nietzsche: "Once spirit was God, then it became man, and now it is even becoming mob."[2] In our time, this kind of godless quest has been put to the test on numerous occasions. In every case, we have tasted only bitter fruit.

From the beginning, my hope has been to show that the mutual quest remains available to us, even in our modern situation. Bible dreams provide a rich resource for this— the eloquence and simplicity of biblical narrative works on us even as we strive to make meaning of it. Miraculously, after all our interpretation, the dreams in the Bible remain unchanged—pristine, solid, immutable—as if *they* are real and *we* are ephemeral. Each time we turn to these narratives they reveal still more to us; each time we approach them with a "second naïveté," we "hear their messages again."

)

Except for scientific work on the frequency of dreams, we have sidestepped the work of most scientific dream researchers. Surprisingly, much of it seems idolatrous, at least in the classic understanding of idolatry.

We normally think of idolatry as the worship of idols, but the term derives from the Greek word *eidolon* or "phantom." Idolatry is the worship of something visible which has no substance. By this definition, modern scientific dream research and ancient Near Eastern idolatry may sometimes occupy common ground. The idol-worshiper who brings a sacrifice to the statue of a god bears a marked resemblance to the dream researcher who sets up an "observable" experiment. Both conceive of their special space as sacred—the high place and the temple are analogous to the laboratory. The idol-worshiper and the scientist both approach their respective sacred spaces with devotion and awe. And for both, the issue at hand is practical. "Will the experiment succeed?" is very much the same question as "Will the god be pleased?" The idol-worshiper and the scientific dream researcher both rely only on observable results.

Likewise, both aim to gain human control of events: The idol-worshiper seeks to appease, propitiate, or celebrate the god for some functional advantage. The scientific dream researcher seeks some mastery of our dream lives through experimentation or through the discovery of new "laws." Both are aware that the system being used is only "representative" or "symbolic"—in other words, that the visible has but little substance. The idol-worshiper knows that an idol is not the god but only an image of the god. The dream researcher knows that the experiment is not reality but only a representation of what happens when reality is transferred into a laboratory or a controlled environment.

This is not to dismiss out of hand either idolatry or dream research. Both may bring benefits to those who believe in them. The spiritual quest, however, takes place in the fuzzy nexus between internal and external realities. Events in this nexus—visions and dreams—have the potential not only to *inform* us, but also to *transform* us. In this realm, scientific data such as data on REM dreaming cannot help us progress. Indeed, the data-driven "science of the observable" can only disorient the spiritual traveler.

Interpretation is a richer approach to spiritual awareness. Interpretation can involve us body and soul. For instance, when Jacob received a new name as a gift in his wrestling dream, the name itself did not confer power on Jacob. Instead, the name became a symbol. It offered Jacob and his children the power to transform themselves through the ways in which they interpreted it. Reading the narrative leads us to wonder how we may be transformed by interpreting the names we call ourselves, and the names that others give us. In the same way, it seems that Joseph adopted a pragmatic approach to warding off Egypt's approaching famine. Yet it was actually Joseph's skill in interpretation that led him to his destiny. Likewise, our personal destinies ultimately depend on the way we interpret the symbols in our lives.

It is still intriguing to believe that, sooner or later, some scientific dream research will lead to a significant breakthrough even in spiritual questing. It may be, for example, that science will eventually enable us to decipher our dreams and their symbols with a high degree of precision. (In the next chapter, we will glimpse a scientific path that holds real promise for the mutual quest.) In general, however, scientific dream research must learn to avoid manipulating dream data to find a single truth or a comprehensive scientific law (an idol)—instead, dreams should be allowed to open to a multiplicity of truths without end.

With this in mind, let us summarize what technology is available to aid us in our quest.

☽

Dream Recall. As we noted, "message" dreams tend to occur with the greatest frequency precisely when we need them the most. The mother or father before childbirth, the person faced with seeking a new career, the person coping with the loss of a loved one, the person in the crisis of separation, the person approaching midlife, the person passing from adolescence to maturity—these are individuals in transition, and the evidence indicates that they are the most likely to experience message dreams. There is a sense, however, in which nearly all dreams bring us messages. However, recognizing the messages depends on how well we can recall the dreams.

Dr. Patricia Garfield studied the dream journal of Julius Nelson, an American psychologist. In it, Nelson recorded over 1,000 dreams in the years from 1884 to 1887. He noted "a curious fluctuation in the *amount* of his dream recall," which seemed to rise and fall with the lunar cycle. Nelson speculated that this fluctuation might also occur in women, "since their menstrual cycle follows a lunar month." Garfield turned to her own dream diaries and discovered that she could indeed detect a definite pattern.

> The value of this discovery, at least for women, is an awareness that low dream recall is common during and prior to a menstrual period and that dream recall will return to normal and reach a peak in mid-cycle. A woman who feels "flooded" with dreams can rest assured that dream recall will not continue to build but will soon abate for a period of time. As for men, we simply do not yet know whether others, like Nelson, have a rhythmic shift in dream recall.[3]

Dr. Garfield was able to make these statements because she had kept a dream journal. Referring to it, she could hear the dreams again in a new way—in this case, in light of Nelson's suggestion.

In addition to providing a treasure-house for potential connections, the act of keeping a dream journal tends to increase dream recall for *all* dreamers, male and female. Those who compile dream journals over a course of time— several weeks, several months, several years—report that their recall grows greater in volume and in accuracy whether or not they are in the midst of major life passages. It stands to reason that we uncover more symbolic material worthy of interpretation as we recall more of our dreams.

Personal Archaeology. Keeping a dream journal also provides us with a *series* of dreams to interpret. Over the course of time, dreams seem to connect into larger sequences—sharing landscapes, symbols, messages, characters, colors, and feelings. This is an important aspect of the fuzzy nexus between the dream world and the waking world. In our waking world, we do not expect each day or even each week to form a separate story. Our ongoing personalities are made up of characteristics that regularly change, some that change sporadically, and some that change slowly, if at all. Our dream lives seem to mirror this. Therefore, dream journals can help us capture a significant part of what Paul Ricoeur calls our "personal archaeology."

We should say that symbols carry two vectors. On the one hand, symbols repeat our childhood in all the senses, chronological and non-chronological, of that childhood. On the other hand, they explore our adult life: "O my prophetic soul," says Hamlet. But these two functions are not external to one

another.... These authentic symbols are truly re-
gressive-progressive; remembrance gives rise to an-
ticipation; archaism gives rise to prophecy.[4]

Looking back through a journal, we can grasp an over-
view of our history unfolding in our dreams. This can be im-
mensely helpful in our work of interpretation.

The "Growing Edge." The patterns exposed in dream journals over a course of time may be significant in other ways,
too. Patricia Garfield observes: "Each idiosyncratic dream
image offers us a chance to learn more about ourselves.
When similar images recur over a series of dreams, they are
shouting ... for attention." Ernest Rossi proposed that
unique dream images are the "growing edge" of the
dreamer's personality. New learning gleaned from dreams
can be incorporated into our waking personalities, providing new behaviors in our waking lives and leading to "new
sensations and emotions, and eventually to new and different dream images."[5] The production of new images and
feelings may seem an admirable goal, but it is far less inspiring than the mutual spiritual quest found in Bible
dreams. It may even be somewhat self-deceptive. As Jung
incisively points out:

> [A dream] may either repudiate the dreamer in a
> most painful way, or bolster him up morally. The
> first is likely to happen to people who ... have too
> good an opinion of themselves; the second to those
> whose self-validation is too low.

On the other hand, in examining a journal of dreams we
may find what Rossi called the "growing edge." If so, we can
interpret our dreams in the context of our present state of
awareness—to examine what they mean *for us now*—even

as we reserve for ourselves the right and the responsibility to revisit the same dream material in the future to discover what it means *for us then*. It is clear that in order to discover any edge, growing or otherwise, we must have some record to analyze.

☽

A parable: The year is 1799. Your desk at the Institute of Egypt at Paris is piled high with papers, and your calendar is crowded with the many things you must yet accomplish today. You glance at the mail and notice a letter from the army engineers telling you of "the discovery at Rosetta of some inscriptions that may offer much interest." You set the letter aside. The key to linking the future with the past has been in your hands for a brief instant, but you are entirely unaware of it. "That will have to wait," you think as you get back to working on the budget.

It was only a letter, but it represented a 1,500-pound block of polished basalt chiseled with characters, which would one day be known as the Rosetta Stone. The writing on the stone was merely a decree announcing the official coronation of Ptolemy V in 197 B.C.E., but it prophesied years of dedication and destiny. It would be 1822 before the marks on the stone were deciphered and still many more years before the modern world would at last encounter ancient Egypt in its own voice.

Jotting down a dream or two first thing in the morning may seem far less important than the things that normally crowd our calendars. But there is no telling when you will glance back at a dream you recorded, and suddenly a link between your past and your future will be at hand. It was just that way with me. It was my dream of climbing Mount Sinai that put me on the path to examining the dreams in the Bible. Each of us needs a touchstone (though, we hope that few of these stones will be as heavy as that piece of polished black basalt from Lower Egypt). If ours is to be a mutual quest—one that seeks heaven, even as heaven seeks us—then something like a dream journal may be a prerequisite. Keeping a record of dreams may open you to an inner voice that speaks outside of hearing.

$$\mathcal{D}$$

I wish I could make some sweeping claim regarding the potential for healing and transformation possible in comparing the dreams in the Bible with your own dreams and visions. I would like to assure you that interpreting your dreams along the lines we have interpreted the Bible's dreams will change your life by lightening and enlightening your spirit. I would like to assure you that interpreting your dreams can bring you the only real riches that a person ever truly attains: wisdom. I would like to assure you that interpreting your dreams can bring you the only real strength that a person ever truly attains: tolerance. I would like to assure you that interpreting your dreams can bring you the only real fame that a person ever truly attains: respect. I would like to assure you of these things, but I would feel like a snake-oil salesman if I did. You would surely find any such assurances incredulous.

Many chapters back, we spoke of the incubation of healing dreams at the Temple of Asclepius at Epidaurus. You may recall that, "near the entry to the temple itself, the pilgrim encountered tablet after tablet describing mi-

raculous cures which had been effected for previous pilgrims."[6] These tablets seem to have served the purpose that
advertising billboards do along a modern highway. In that
less hurried time, though, they contained longer inscriptions. Here is the text of one of the tablets from Epidaurus,
dating from the late fourth century B.C.E.:

> A man whose fingers, with the exception of one,
> were paralyzed came as a suppliant to the god.
> While looking at the tablets at the Temple he ex-
> pressed incredulity regarding the cures and scoffed
> at the inscriptions. But in his sleep he saw a vision.
> It seemed to him that, as he was playing at dice be-
> low the Temple and was about to cast the dice, the
> god appeared, sprang upon his hand, and stretched
> out all his fingers one by one. When he had straight-
> ened them all, the god asked him if he would still
> be incredulous of the inscriptions on the tablets at
> the Temple. He answered that he would not. "Since,
> then, formerly you were incredulous of the cures,
> though they were not incredible; for the future,"
> he said, "your name shall be 'Incredulous.'" When
> day dawned he walked out sound.[7]

For about ten years now, I have conducted "Bible
dream weekends," seminars built around the ideas in this
book. I often begin these workshops on Friday night with
Jacob's dream of the staircase and continue on Saturday
morning with Jacob's wrestling dream. Typically, on Friday
night and Saturday morning the participants have hardly
warmed to the process. Many believe that I am using the al-
lure of "dreams" just to present Bible study. Generally po-
lite, they "go along" with my supposed ruse, still reserving
judgment. By Saturday afternoon, however, a few participants tend to become more vocal. "When are you planning

to tell us what *our* dreams mean?" "Why do you keep turning aside questions about the things *we* have dreamed?" I answer politely that their dreams are very important to the process, but I am not really prepared to interpret them. By the end of the day on Saturday, as we encounter Joseph the Interpreter, a few participants begin offering fragments from their remembered dreams to help interpret the Bible texts. At this point, a few more heads bob in unspoken agreement; and, if a particularly fine insight is offered by one of the participants, the group seems to smile in satisfaction. Sunday morning is always tumultuous. There is hardly time to look at Samuel's call. So many dreams visited the participants during the night, and they have so much to share, that the day passes before we know it. The change in the quality of the interpretations is so regular and so overwhelming that it always reminds me of the first thaw of spring in the Swiss Alps when every hillside throbs with the rushing sound of rivulets. It is all I can do to convince the participants that the weekend is only a beginning for them.

If you have not kept a dream journal while reading, it may seem to you that I have spent most of this book interpreting the Bible. You are among the Friday night and Saturday morning crowd.

If you have kept a dream journal, then it may seem to you that your dreams have begun to flow more freely and the symbols in them have begun to etch themselves more deeply in your mind than they did before you began reading this book. What can I say? If you think your dream symbols are becoming richer *because you are keeping the diary*, then at least you have taken that much from our time together. You are part of the Saturday afternoon crowd.

It may be, however, that you are now immersed in the intuitive process we have been developing. You may realize that your dream symbols are becoming richer because you are *hearing* more of the messages that you normally regarded as things *seen*. That is, you are already incorporating the ideas of the Senoi, the Navajo, and the Aborigines; the principles of lucid dreaming; the techniques of dream incubation; the search for dream gifts; the process of sharing your dreams; the exhilaration of letting many truths arise through many interpretations; and more. If so, you are of the Sunday morning crowd and, forever more, your name shall be "Incredulous."

Out of the
Dream Forest

THE MEANING OF
THE SPIRITUAL QUEST

𝄪

The opposite of a small truth may be a lie, but the opposite of
a great truth is also a great truth. — Niels Bohr

The Nuclear Age began with the detonation of the first
atomic bomb at Alamogordo, New Mexico, on July 16,
1945. After the explosion, the man who spearheaded the
bomb's development, J. Robert Oppenheimer, quoted the
Bhagavad Gita: "If the radiance of a thousand suns were to
burst forth at once in the sky, that would be like the splendor of the Mighty One."[1] Later, Oppenheimer recalled the
enormity of the scientists' emotions at that moment:

> We knew the world would not be the same. A few
> people laughed, a few people cried. Most people
> were silent. I remembered the line from the Hindu

scripture, the *Bhagavad Gita* [in which Vishnu says:] "I am become Death, the destroyer of worlds." I suppose we all thought that, one way or another.[2]

Lecturing at Massachusetts Institute of Technology on November 25, 1947, Oppenheimer opined:

> In some sort of crude sense which no vulgarity, no humor, no overstatement can quite extinguish, the physicists have known sin; and this is a knowledge which they cannot lose.[3]

Knowingly or unknowingly, Oppenheimer, the nuclear scientist, had co-opted the language of religion. His words signaled something new in Western culture. For most of the twentieth century, we have been urged to turn aside from that which is not observable. We have felt reasonably assured that individuals are the moral, if not the physical, axis of the world. Oppenheimer evoked a new spirit as he spoke of the "splendor of the Mighty One," quoted Vishnu's exclamation, and stated that scientists "have known sin." Even more striking is the fact that his was not the first voice of the Nuclear Age to do this.

Albert Einstein's theory of relativity foreshadowed the nuclear revolution. His formula "$E=MC^2$" entered the world as a scientific symbol only to become a cultural icon, adorning mugs, T-shirts, baseball caps, and screen savers. Yet it is questionable whether the masses of people who recognize Einstein's formula as a symbol actually comprehend its full implications. Behind the formula is the proposition that nothing in our world is as solid as it seems. Things we call solid are merely energy moving at rates lower than the speed of light. Also, the equation sign indicates that the transformation of matter into energy can be reversed—everything that seems evanescent to us can be made solid.

Einstein's formula is a symbol of the potential for transformation manifest in all things.

While the masses accepted the new symbol as an icon, physicists studying the laws of quantum mechanics were faced with a more difficult puzzle. They discovered that at the point where energy and matter transform, the universe seems to behave in dreamlike ways. They were forced to ask: Does the universe actually behave strangely as we observe it, or is the mind of the observer unable to grasp the meaning of what is being observed? Two giants of physics, Albert Einstein and Niels Bohr, wrestled with this issue. Einstein maintained that there is an objective (real) world "out there" even if we are unable to grasp it all the time. Bohr agreed that there may be an objective world "out there," but he maintained that as humans we cannot describe it since we cannot reliably observe it.

> Their argument had to do with the nature of observation. It seems that a quantum mechanical system such as an atom or a subatomic system (later this was quite generalized to include large objects as well) undergoes a rapid and unpredictable change whenever it is observed. This rapid change cannot be encompassed within the equations that describe quantum systems. It lies embarrassingly outside of the domain of mathematical representation. Somehow the very act of observing something causes an irreversible and uncontrollable change in the system, and this change effects and, for that matter, affects the relationship that exists between the observer and the observed.[4]

This is difficult ground to traverse. It is dreamlike enough that we almost wish a spirit guide would appear to point the way. If I understand it correctly, the scientists are beginning to say that their entire elaborate structure of physical laws arrived at through observation were actually arrived at through interpretation. The scientific schema— on which we rely every time we start our cars, boot up our computers, turn on our televisions, accept our doctor's advice, and call on our military to protect us—is no more than a composite conception of reality based on intuitive guesswork. Physicist Fred Alan Wolf describes this in his book *The Dreaming Universe*:

> When physical research is carried out, measurements must be made and are the result of psychic actions within the brains of the experimenters. So also are the concepts and theories that are invented by physicists to describe nature.[5]

This realization is like entering an entirely new and fertile grove in our dream forest. Here, the plants seem to have substance until we approach them. The closer we draw, the less substantial they appear to be. Extending a hand to touch one, the hand passes right through the plant turning green in the process. The trees in this grove are substantial, wearing proudly their mighty crowns of leaf and branch. Yet we can walk through a tree's trunk without hesitation and without producing any noticeable effect on the branches or the leaves, though our skin turns to bark as we move through the space we thought was occupied by the tree trunk. We can form theories about the behavior of the plants and the trees. For as long as we remain in the grove, the trees and plants will act according to the theories we form. The moment we leave the grove, the grove continues to act as it did before we entered it. Of course, that is assuming that the grove actually exists—for, if it was nothing more than a dream landscape of our own creation, then the process of leaving it does not necessarily mean that it is leaving us.

Linger for a while in this unusual grove. Sit and rest your back against a tree. As long as you believe that the tree is solid, your back is supported. If you wish to continue sitting upright, this is no time to think of Einstein's theory. The moment it enters your mind that the matter on which you are resting is actually energy in slow motion, your support vanishes and you find yourself fallen back and lying flat on the ground. The moment it enters your mind that the ground on which you are resting is energy in slow motion, you find yourself sinking slowly in an endless vastness that seems to envelope you. True, you can still see the grove with its plants and trees, but you can also see the roots and the water table and the earth itself. You now realize that the grove is like a city of skyscrapers and that, at first, you had been lying near the top of the city, admiring the spires.

The moment it enters your mind that you yourself are actually energy in slow motion, you understand why each time you placed your hand in a plant it turned green and why your skin turned to bark as you passed through the trunk of a tree. Having awakened to this knowledge of yourself as pure energy, you have become entirely yourself, which means that you are the grove and the ground and the plants and the trees and the forest and the mountains and the rivers beyond. You are the cloud passing overhead and the water running beneath. You are the lava that flows from the volcano and the mushroom that springs up after the rain. As you lie, encompassing all, the need for naming things passes away from you. Names separate matter from matter; but matter no longer matters; one energy flows through all.

The Tao has no name; it is a cloud that has no
　shape....
Things have been given names from the beginning.
We need to know when we have enough names: this
　is wisdom.[6]

Something prods you to remember that you are in the
dream forest and you may be dreaming. You look around;
you are suddenly not alone. There is a person with you,
wrestling with you. There is an angel beside you, speaking
in your ear. There is a voice calling you. There is a broad
staircase with a hundred copies of you ascending and descending on it.

Knowing you are dreaming seems like a blessing. You
are no longer falling into the forest world; you are floating
on the gentle breeze. Your spirit travels to where you
started this journey. There was a question in your mind.
There was a reason for your quest. Will you know the answer
if you awaken? You know now that you have a dream gift,
one that will return with you.

If it was your self that you were seeking, you know now
that you will never finish the quest for your self. Each time
you enter the grove of your dreams, you will find another
self that is also your self. It may be as peaceful as the one
you feel now, or it may be a self that is thundering with anger or flaming with the torches of resentment. You may become a whirlwind instead of a gentle breeze. Your wrestling
shadow may become your enemy trying to bruise you. An
emerald-skinned dragon may rise up in your dream with the
fire of terror gleaming in its eyes and the breath of madness
scorching its teeth. Look again. Your dragon is not matter,
and neither is your whirlwind. Reach out and touch them
and they vanish.

If you were to awaken now, you would find some way to interpret what has happened to you—you would be able to give it a name. But if you were to awaken now, who would be awakening? And if you were to awaken now, would you be awakening to your waking self or to another dreaming self? There is no way to know. You may already be awake.

))

When you entered this dream forest you had no need to suspend your belief in science or in your individuality. As you read the dreams of the Bible, you brought yourself to them so that every interpretation that you heard became your interpretation and not mine. True, the words were the words of the Bible and the interpretations of the words were mine, but your mind was necessarily engaged in rendering the words and their interpretations in ways that made sense *for you*. This was never my book and it was always yours—or, more accurately, we have shared this dream work in the same way in which the scientists have pooled their observations to interpret a world that makes sense for them. As long as we share their conception, their interpretation of the world will be ours, too.

You have experienced a transformation just by entering the dream forest, just by reading this book, whether or not you have examined your own dreams. That transformation is in the realization that if you seek yourself in your spiritual quest, you cannot help but find it. Your self is actively seeking you. As Kelly Bulkeley concluded:

> The growing interest in the religious dimension of dreams reflects a profound desire, in Ricoeur's words, "to be called again," a belief "that *being* can

still speak" to us. Many Westerners are dissatisfied with the existential meanings provided by their culture. The rationalism, commercialism, and individualism promoted so vigorously in the modern West do not always lead to a fulfilling, meaningful life. Many people have looked for religious rituals, mythological symbols, and spiritual teachings that can reconnect them with the sacred and provide them with existential meanings to guide their lives. Dreams, as we have abundantly seen, have always been an outstanding source of religious images and symbols.[7]

We have gone beyond Bulkeley's search for "an outstanding source of religious images and symbols." We have discovered that in biblical dreams when we encounter a symbol and interpret that symbol, the symbol not only has meaning for us but actually becomes us. In "hearing again" the interpretation, we are called to transform ourselves. Is this really possible? Can the listener actually become the speaker? Yes, this is exactly what the physicists say. In observing the experiment, the scientist becomes the data, influences the outcome, interprets the result, alters the world. This echoes what we learned from the Joseph narrative, as well. In interpreting the dream, the interpreter determines the outcome, speaks the truth from the interpreter's heart, makes the dream his own, and shapes his own destiny. When we share dreams, we enable others to join the same process; as others interpret our dreams they become a part of us, shaping us, and linking their destinies to our own. It is a truism that every person you meet in a dream is actually yourself, since every person you meet—in or out of a dream—is also yourself. All of us, though we appear to be separate matter and have separate names, are a part of the same energy.

)

In the closing pages of his book, Fred Alan Wolf recalls an episode from the television series "Star Trek: The Next Generation." In this fictitious series, the ship includes a "holodeck" where generated holographs become so "real" that they can interact with members of the crew. In the episode that Wolf describes, the captain encounters a holographic entity who admits to knowing that he is a computer-generated image, but claims that he has become self-conscious. This entity wishes to enter the "real world." The captain warns the holograph that he will cease to exist the moment he leaves the holodeck, but the holograph insists that this is not true, saying, "I think, therefore I am." With this, the holograph opens the door to the holodeck and walks through into the ship itself, where it takes control of the ship's computer. At first, it seems that the holograph actually has dreamed itself into existence. Soon, however, we are led to an even more convoluted truth.

The holograph has actually programmed the computer to create a copy of the ship's interior complete with crew, and it was the holographic copy of the interior of the ship that the holograph actually entered. The captain now steps in to make things even more complex. Sympathetic to the holograph's will to exist, the captain programs the computer to create a virtual universe where the holograph not only can continue not only to exist, but also move about freely and exercise free will. Wolf ends his description of the episode by remarking:

The whole [computer] program is kept running for the entity and eventually placed inside a small cube. The entity has no way of knowing this. But the captain and the crew of the "real" ship do. However, at the end of the program, they all wonder if they, too, are just images inside of some unimaginable technology themselves. And of course as I watch the show, I realize that they are inside my box, the television set I observe.[8]

Are we inside the dream when we think we are awake? Are we outside the dream when we are dreaming? Is our waking consciousness our real consciousness, or is it as illusory as the dream world of our nights?

I feel guilty as I ask these questions. If you and I were to behave as if the waking world were nothing but a dream, we might easily become callous and abusive. If the real world *is* a dream we control through our interpretation, then it is a sin that we have collectively allowed pain and hunger, disease and poverty, cruelty and suffering to exist. I am forced to take the side of Einstein in his debate with Bohr. The real world must be "out there" somehow, even if we fail to grasp how.

On the other hand, the world "out there" is a dream, too. When we collectively dream that we can do the impossible, we manage to do it. We learned to fly. We split the atom. We conquered polio. We imprinted our footsteps on the moon. Each time a dream like one of these was achieved, it became necessary for us to move a token from the column marked "symbolic" to the column marked "real." We had to reinterpret the world to make space for a new reality. If enough of us wanted to dream the dream, we might yet conquer prejudice, relieve suffering, clothe the needy, feed the hungry, and outlaw war. This is how I interpret one dream in my dream journal, the one that I entitled, "Inter-connectedness."

> In my dream, I see that it is not gravity that holds people bound to the earth. I realize that people have souls which begin somewhere above their heads and continue down through their feet to the center of the earth where they are all joined together as one soul. I realize that if I hurt another person, the pain travels down through their soul to the center of the earth where their soul is joined to my soul. Hurting someone else makes me feel worse in the end. And helping someone else makes me feel better. So I realize that I had better spend my time helping people because that is the best thing I can do—not only for them, but for me.

To heal the world is an awesome goal. In a sense, of course, it is the ultimate purpose of the Bible. The prophets exhort us to create collective dreams, to stand together at the feet of holy mountains, to cry out against impropriety and injustice even if our cries seem like lonely echoes in a wilderness of indifference, to bring the wicked to task, and to remove the yoke of poverty from our midst. But the words of the prophets would be only bombastic sentiment if the Bible had not first addressed personal goals and needs. Before we can transform our world, we need to transform ourselves. The dreams in the Bible hint at what is possible for each of us to achieve—the mutual quest that can take us even beyond ourselves. We stand at the top of that human pyramid, outside the forest, back in the world of reality. Still, a voice calls to each of us to pool our knowledge and share our dreams. If we cannot reach the end of our spiritual quest, we can at least make a fine beginning.

Notes

)

Shattering Idols:
Bible Dreams and Our Own

1. Joseph Campbell. *The Mythic Image*. Princeton, NJ: Princeton University Press, 1974, p. 497.

2. Roland Cahen. "The Psychology of the Dream: Its Instructive and Therapeutic Uses," in G. E. von Grunebaum and Roger Caillois, eds., *The Dream and Human Societies*. Berkeley and Los Angeles: University of California Press, 1966, pp. 119–120.

3. Cahen, p. 121.

4. Idries Shah. *The Pleasantries of the Incredible Mulla Nasrudin*. New York: E.P.Dutton & Co., Inc., 1971, p. 26.

5. Campbell, p. 497.

Dreamwork:
Using This Book

1. James R. Lewis. *The Dream Encyclopedia*. Detroit: Visible Ink, 1995, pp. 157–158.

Are We on the Right Path?
Abraham's Midlife Crisis

1. The Epic of Gilgamesh, Tablet I, in *Ancient Near Eastern Texts Relating to the Old Testament*, edited by James B. Pritchard. Princeton, NJ: Princeton University Press, 1969, p. 76.

2. The Epic of Gilgamesh, Tablet V, in Pritchard, p. 83.

3. Throughout the discussion of the vision in Genesis 15, and wherever else the context requires, I use the name "Abram." In practice, both names identify the same person, and sometimes, for the sake of clarity, I use the name "Abraham." In Genesis 17:5, God gives Abraham his new name, indicating that it means "a father of many nations." Literally, *Abram* means "exalted father" and *Abraham* means "father of many."

4. A. Cohen, ed. *The Soncino Chumash*. London: The Soncino Press, 1947, pp. 72–73.

5. Toufy Fahd. "The Dream in Medieval Islamic Society" in *The Dream and Human Societies*, edited by G. E. Von Grunebaum and Roger Callois. Berkeley: University of California Press, 1966.

6. Berthold Laufer. "Inspirational Dreams in Eastern Asia." *Journal of American Folk-Lore*, 44, 1931, pp. 208–216.

7. Theodore Papadakis. *Epidauros, The Sanctuary of Asclepios*. Athens: Art Editions, Meletzis-Papadakis, 1971, p. 5.

8. In the course of my studies of Jewish folklore in the Talmud and Midrash, I have found many stories and legends identical with Persian and Indian (Aryan) myths. Especially the talmudic stories of Rabbi Akiba are often close parallels to stories found in Indian texts. This would indicate that, by the early centuries of the Common Era, there was discourse not only along the Mediterranean basin but also along the caravan routes to the Far East. In reading the literature of the Sufis, I have often encountered stories later reworked and used by the Hasidic Jews of Eastern Europe. One of my teachers, Joseph Campbell, would no doubt have considered many of these parallels as basic myths

that reverberate through all cultures (a Jungian approach with which he closely identified). Another of my teachers, Cyrus Gordon, would probably have taken a far different tack. He would no doubt counsel us to look for a possible common background for the stories. In suggesting the Phoenician link between the Greeks and the Hebrews, I have adopted the system of Gordon. In thinking about dreams that are at the same time more and less than structured stories, we should not discount either possibility. In general, my only problem with the Jungian approach is that many of its practitioners tend to impose symbolic meaning on common objects and elements of all dreams. As we shall see later, Jung, at least in his theoretical writings, attempts to avoid such an imposition of one culture upon another.

9. Raymond De Becker. *The Understanding of Dreams*. London: Allen & Unwin, 1968, p. 166.

10. See Norman MacKenzie. *Dreams and Dreaming*. London: Aldus Books, 1965, p. 43.

11. Patricia Garfield. *Creative Dreaming*. New York: Ballantine Books, 1974, p. 21. Garfield herself points out that the earliest stelae do not necessarily relate to impotence at all, but to problems like lice and pleurisy.

12. Carl G. Jung, ed. *Man and His Symbols*. Garden City, NY: Doubleday & Company, Inc., 1964, p. 52.

13. Jung, p. 14.

Dream Types

1. Rosalind D. Cartwright. *Night Life*. Englewood Cliffs, NJ: Prentice-Hall, 1977.

2. Harry Hunt. *The Multiplicity of Dreams: Memory, Imagination, and Consciousness*. New Haven, CT: Yale University Press, 1989, p. 4.

3. Hunt, pp. 95–96.

4. Hunt, p.160.

5. Cicero. *On Divination.* 1.64.

6. Georg Luck. *Arcana Mundi: Magic and the Occult in the Greek and Roman Worlds.* Baltimore: The Johns Hopkins University Press, 1985, p. 275.

7. Cicero, 2.127–128.

8. Common Era.

9. Luck, p. 292.

10. Artemidorus, Book 4, Chapter 3.

11. Artemidorus, Book 1, Chapter 2.

12. Joseph Campbell. *The Hero with a Thousand Faces.* Cleveland and New York: The World Publishing Company, 1949, p. 3.

The Stairway to Heaven: The Sages Interpret Jacob's Dream

1. "Stairway to Heaven," words and music by Jimmy Page and Robert Plant, 1972.

2. Cited in Geoffrey A. Dudley. *How to Understand Your Dreams.* North Hollywood, CA: Wilshire Book Company, 1957, p. 58.

3. It became conventional for collections built on biblical books to add the popular word *rabbah,* meaning "great," to the name of the Bible book to derive a title for the collection. Thus, *Exodus Rabbah, Leviticus Rabbah,* and so on. As a group, the *Rabbah* commentaries form a small library known as the *Midrash Rabbah.*

4. Louis Ginzberg. *The Legends of the Jews.* Philadelphia: Jewish Publication Society of America, 1925, Vol. 5, "Jacob," note 134, pp. 290–291.

5. See Genesis 25:29–34.

6. See Genesis 27.

7. Genesis 27:41.

8. The translation is my own—a combination of several traditional sources with the interpolation of an occasional modern idiom that attempts to be faithful to the flow of the text while pointing at what the Hebrew language intends.

9. The Bible relates Abraham's death before telling of the birth of his grandsons, Esau and Jacob. This seems to indicate that Abraham had no contact with Jacob. Some commentators hold that there was an estrangement between Isaac and his father after Abraham bound him up as a sacrifice. Indeed, Scriptures omits any reference to Isaac receiving the special blessing, the *berachah*, from his father. Some arithmetic is necessary to see another possibility. Abraham was one hundred years old when Isaac was born (21:5), Isaac married at the age of forty (25:20), and Abraham lived to the age of one hundred and seventy-five (25:7). Thirty-five years remained, while both Isaac and Abraham lived in proximity to one another. Noting this, the sages postulated a close relationship between Abraham and his grandson Jacob. In the Book of Jubilees, Jacob is said to be the favorite grandson of Abraham. An account is given there of Abraham passing his blessing directly to Jacob in the presence of Rebecca. Abraham also instructed Rebecca to watch over Jacob. Jubilees, redacted around the time of the Second Temple and available to the sages, includes an account of Abraham's death in which the young Jacob is admonished not to marry a Canaanite woman, then comforts Abraham as he dies. According to Pesikta Rabbati 74, Esau and Jacob were fifteen years old when Abraham died. In Genesis Rabbah 63:9, Jacob is said to have attended the academy of Shem and Eber. Yashar Toledot 51a indicates that the latter should be read as the academy of Abraham. My speculation that Abraham may have described the wonders of Mesopotamia to Jacob is based on this tradition, but there is little doubt that Abraham would have shared these memories with Isaac—and that Rebecca would have brought some of the memory of these wonders with her when she left to marry Isaac—so they

could have easily been handed down to Jacob through his parents. If so, we can assume that Isaac would have been able to repeat the memories of Abraham nearly verbatim, since oral transmission was still considered a sacred trust at this early period.

10. Midrash, Genesis Rabbah 68. The setting is reproduced from archaeological data. The presence of Rabbi Judah and the advice of his physicians is cited in the Talmud (Ketubim 103b). This scene was repeated many times, but the conversation as I reconstruct it never actually took place. The Midrash is a compilation of discussions, texts, and sources that span centuries of time. The homilies of many generations of rabbis are included. Still, in viewing this as one conversation we are not breaching the basic tenet of the rabbis. Their rule was simple: *There is no earlier or later in the Bible* (see note below). The concepts are important. The preservation of the name of the person who spoke them is important. But when and where they were actually spoken is of little or no importance. One can learn from something said a century ago as much as from something said today. One can quote the prophets to understand better what is written in the Torah, or quote another sage to understand better what the prophets meant. Chronology makes no difference whatever. In this spirit, the conversation might as well have taken place all at once. It does for us as we study it. What follows is a very loose rendition of the discourse on Jacob's dream. It is by no means comprehensive. There is much more in the original. I have purposely removed the names of the rabbis who spoke and the names of the rabbis they cited in order to simplify the text for the modern reader. I have also edited the discourse, taking the liberty of removing repetitious parts that merely amplified a point. The translation is accurate in what is quoted or appears as a citation; otherwise it is a paraphrase of the original that tries to recapture the spirit of the interpretive process, including the spirit of the wordplay, which does not easily translate.

11. This identification of Jacob with the sun (and later with the chariot of the sun) was common in Jewish legend. It shows a Greek influence in which Jacob has gained the attributes of Apollo. Other Jewish legends identify Jacob with the moon, especially with the so-called man in the moon suggested by the shadows that fall on the full moon that cause it to look like a face with eyes, nose, and mouth. In both cases, the tendency to identify Jacob with a stellar luminary seems to have had a Hellenistic influence.

12. Talmud, *Eruvin* 13b; *Gittin* 6b.

13. The Egyptians worshiped the Nile as a god.

14. Talmud, *Pesahim* 6b. Literally, "There is no earlier or later in the Torah," but Torah is understood in its broadest sense to mean all of Jewish learning, encompassing the entire Bible and every teaching of the Pharisees, too.

15. Mishnah, *Avot* 2:4.

Paths of Interpretation

1. Cited in S. Carl Hirsch. *Theater of the Night: What We Do and Do Not Know about Dreams*. Middletown, CT: Xerox Educational Publications, 1976, p. 112.

2. Paul Ricoeur. *The Symbolism of Evil*. Boston: Beacon Press, 1967, p. 351.

3. Talmud, *Hagigah* 9b.

4. In Hebrew, these decorations are called *taggin*. They consist of three small strokes written on top of seven specific letters of the alphabet in the form of crowns. Six other letters of the alphabet are decorated with only a single stroke or *tag*. The significance of the *taggin* seems to be veiled in kabbalistic mysticism. In English the *taggin* are referred to as "tittles," as in the phrase, "jot or tittle." (For a fuller explanation of the phrase, see the beginning of the last chapter.)

5. Talmud, *Menahot* 29b. The story has a sad conclusion. Moses asks to see what will become of Akiba in the end, and God allows him to witness the martyrdom of Akiba by the Romans and the way Akiba's flesh is sold in the stalls of the marketplace. Moses asks God if such wondrous learning deserves such a terrible reward. God replies as before, "Be silent, for this is My decision."

6. Genesis Rabbah 48:12.

To Awaken Transformed:
Jacob's Dream of Separation and Divorce

1. Lewis Mumford. *Technics and Human Development*. New York: Harcourt Brace Jovanovich, 1966, pp. 48–51.

2. The prevailing rule in religion is that once a "high place" is established, it remains a "high place," no matter what religion uses it. Thus, a site like the Temple Mount is holy to more than one religion. This rule continues to the present day, as most buildings built as churches or synagogues retain their use even after being sold by one religious group to another.

3. The heavenly chariot first appeared when Elijah was swept up in a whirlwind, 2 Kings 2:11. Ezekiel later encountered it (chapters 1, 8, and 10). Jewish and Gnostic mystics especially prized the Ezekiel texts, making them the subject of deep contemplation. The Greeks had similar legends regarding Apollo and the heavenly chariot. See Louis Ginzberg, *The Legends of the Jews*. Philadelphia: Jewish Publication Society of America, 1925, Vol. 5, "Jacob," note 134, pp. 290–291.

4. The sages had commented that God stood beside or "on" Jacob. The Hebrew can mean either of these two, but "above" would best be expressed by a different Hebrew word. In the context of the sentence, this word almost certainly means, "beside him."

5. James B. Pritchard, ed. *The Ancient Near East in Pictures Relating to the Old Testament*. Princeton, NJ: Princeton University Press, Second Edition with Supplement, 1969, Figure 541, p. 182.

6. Compare this to Genesis 26:4: "I will make your descendants as numerous as the stars in the sky and will give them all these lands...."

7. These are all found in Genesis Rabbah 39:12.

8. Stephen LaBerge. *Lucid Dreaming*. Los Angeles: J. P. Tarcher, 1985.

9. Harry Hunt. *The Multiplicity of Dreams: Memory, Imagination, and Consciousness*. New Haven, CT: Yale University Press, 1989, p. 4.

10. Stephen LaBerge and Howard Rheingold. *Exploring the World of Lucid Dreaming*. New York: Ballantine Books, 1990, pp. 67–68.

11. LaBerge and Rheingold, pp. 1–2.

12. See Leviticus 6:5: "The fire on the altar shall be kept burning, not to go out..." and Leviticus 6:6: "A perpetual fire shall be kept burning on the altar, not to go out."

13. Leviticus 6:8, 14, 15.

14. In theory, the messiah would also be anointed.

15. Ginzberg, Vol. 5, "Jacob," note 134, pp. 290–291.

16. Patricia Cox Miller. "A Dubious Twilight: Reflections on Dreams in Patristic Literature." *Church History*, 55 (2), 1986, p. 156.

Preparing for Dreams and Visions

1. See Genesis 25:22–23.

2. A. L. Oppenheim. "The Interpretation of Dreams in the Ancient Near East with a Translation of an Assyrian Dream-Book,"

Transactions of the American Philosophical Society, 46, part 3, 1956, pp. 179–373.

3. Francis Huxley. *The Way of the Sacred.* Garden City, NY: Doubleday and Company, Inc., 1974, p. 118.

4. Cyrus Gordon. *The Common Background of Greek and Hebrew Civilizations.* New York: W.W. Norton & Company, Inc., 1965, pp. 232–233.

5. Karen Armstrong. *A History of God: The 4,000-Year Quest of Judaism, Christianity and Islam.* New York: Ballantine Books, 1993, p. 16.

6. Samuel A. B. Mercer. *The Pyramid Texts in Translation and Commentary,* 4 vols. New York: Longmans, Green and Co., 1952, vol. I, p. 169.

7. Zohar, *Beha'alotcha* 148b.

8. *Black Elk Speaks: Being the Life Story of a Holy Man of the Oglala Sioux, as Told to John G. Neihardt.* New York: William Morrow and Co., 1932, p. 38.

9. A. L. Oppenheim. "Mantic Dreams in the Ancient Near East," in *The Dream and Human Societies*, edited by G. Von Grunebaum and R. Callois. Los Angeles: University of California Press, 1966.

10. Robert L. Van de Castle. *Our Dreaming Mind.* New York: Ballantine Books, 1994, p. 51.

11. Patricia Garfield. *Creative Dreaming.* New York: Ballantine Books, 1974, p. 201.

12. Jayne Gackenbach. "Women and Meditators as Gifted Lucid Dreamers," in *Dreamtime and Dreamwork,* edited by S. Krippner. Los Angeles: Jeremy Tarcher, 1990, pp. 244–251.

13. Stephen LaBerge and Howard Rheingold. *Exploring the World of Lucid Dreaming.* New York: Ballantine Books, 1990, p. 73.

14. LaBerge and Rheingold, pp. 214–216.

15. Van de Castle, p. 441.

16. Stephen LaBerge. *Lucid Dreaming.* Los Angeles: Jeremy Tarcher, 1985, p. 279.

17. Chuang-tzu (369–286 B.C.E.), "On Leveling All Things."

18. Kelly Bulkeley. *The Wilderness of Dreams: Exploring the Religious Meanings of Dreams in Modern Western Culture.* Albany: State University of New York Press, 1994, p. 117.

Coming Home:
Jacob's Dream of Reintegration

1. See the discussion in Nahum M. Sarna, *Understanding Genesis: The Heritage of Biblical Israel.* New York: Schocken Books, 1966, pp. 202–206.

2. See Julian Morgenstern, *Book of Genesis.* Cincinnati: UAHC, 1919, pp. 270 ff.; also the commentary of RALBAG (Rabbi Levi ben Gershon, 1288–1344). These, in addition to Maimonides.

3. For the exact verses and their order, see Genesis 18:1 ff.

4. Moses Maimonides. *The Guide of the Perplexed*, trans. by Shlomo Pines, 2 vols. Chicago and London: University of Chicago Press, 1963; II, 42, p. 389. The italicized passages are present in the translation to denote terms discussed in other places in the *Guide*.

5. Maimonides, II, 42, pp. 388–390. The italicized passages are present in the translation to denote terms discussed in other places in the *Guide*.

6. This and the account that follows are from Genesis 31.

7. Cyrus H. Gordon. *The Common Background of Greek and Hebrew Civilizations.* New York: W. W. Norton & Company, Inc., 1965, pp. 249–250. This is also attested by Speiser, Sarna, Malamat, and others. The evidence comes from Middle Assyrian archaeological finds at Nuzi.

8. This impression of a conspiracy is further reinforced when Rachel steals her father's household gods: see Genesis 31:19. For

the importance of household gods, see Sarna, *Understanding Genesis*, pp. 200–202.

9. The meaning of the Hebrew word *pahad*, translated as "fear," is uncertain. Some interpreters translate it as "kinsman" to stress the close relationship between Isaac and God. This reading relies on cognate words and is unlikely. It probably refers to the way in which Isaac related to God, so it is possible to translate it as a name of God—hence, "Fear." Later, the Bible uses the term *yirah,* another word for "fear" (in the sense of "awe"), to mean "religion." It serves this purpose because there is no direct word in biblical Hebrew for religion. This may have been an earlier way of phrasing the same idea—namely, religion *is* the fear of God.

10. Sarna, p. 184.

11. Oddly enough, identifying the unit is made difficult because of the way the Bible is divided. In translating the Hebrew original, chapters and verses were artificially imposed on the text. They form the notation that we use today, but the verses as given in Christian translations do not always correspond to the Hebrew text. Thus, our translation begins with Genesis 32:2 in Jewish translations, while in most Christian translations it is given as Genesis 32:1. Jewish readers may find this even more confusing since the traditional division of the Torah for synagogue reading starts a new "portion" (*Vay-yishlach*) at Genesis 32:4. In effect, the opening two lines of the dream sequence are read in the synagogue on one week, while the rest of the sequence is not read until the following week. The division of the text into weekly portions, like its division into chapters and verses, was imposed somewhat arbitrarily.

12. Sarna, p. 203. This is evidently the view taken in Jewish tradition. In the division of weekly readings (*parshiot*) of the Torah for synagogue use, these two verses are the last of a weekly Torah reading (*parashah*) called *Vay-yetsei,* which begins with the staircase dream. (See note 11.)

13. The three daily prayer services of the Jews are each named after a different sacrifice that was offered in the Temple. The morning service is called *Shaharit*. The evening service is called *Ma'ariv*. And the afternoon service is called *Minhah*.

14. M.-L. Von Franz. "The Process of Individuation" in Carl G. Jung, ed., *Man and His Symbols*. Garden City, NY: Doubleday & Company, Inc., 1964, pp. 198–199.

15. Sir James G. Frazer. *Folklore in the Old Testament*, 3 vols. London: Macmillan & Co., 1919, pp. 410–425.

16. Von Franz, pp. 168–169.

17. James Hillman. *Loose Ends*. Dallas: Spring Publications, 1967, p. 57.

18. The story is found in Judges 13. The quotes come from verses 17 and 22.

19. Joshua Trachtenberg. *Jewish Magic and Superstition: A Study in Folk Religion*. New York: Atheneum, 1975, pp. 79–80.

20. In typical fashion, the taboo was misunderstood in later times and transferred to the site of the euphemistic muscle. Jews who maintain the dietary laws (*kashrut*) today do not eat the part of the thigh of large and small cattle that is served by the sciatic nerve. Birds are entirely excluded from this prohibition. See Talmud, *Hullin* 89b ff. and Yoreh Deah 65:5–7.

21. Sarna, p. 206.

22. Peter O'Connor. *Dreams and the Search for Meaning*. New York: Paulist Press, 1986, p. 136.

First Fruits:
Visions, Prophecy, Gifts, and Landscapes

1. Joel's vision in chapter 3 is concerned with the End of Days. Our interest is not in eschatology but in the close association of prophecy, dreams, and visions—and in the statement that Joel

makes, which demonstrates that in the time of the prophets they were all one and the same phenomenon.

2. Moses Maimonides. *Yad,* "Yesodei HaTorah" 7:6.

3. See the chapter entitled "Dream Types."

4. Patricia Garfield. *Creative Dreaming.* New York: Ballantine Books, 1974, p. 80. Some recent anthropological studies indicate that the role of dreams in the Senoi tribal life is not as all-encompassing as the early anthropologists believed. This falls into the category of "the researchers found what they were looking for." Yet, even if the Senoi take their dream practices for granted—and even if the Senoi dream practices do not account for the lack of depression, neurosis, and war among their tribes—the Senoi dream practices provide inspiring models for us. In many cases, their practices serve to remind us of what we have sacrificed in the course of becoming a technological society.

5. Garfield, p. 112.

6. Kilton Stewart. "Dream Theory in Malaya," in *Altered States of Consciousness*, edited by C. Tart. New York: Doubleday, 1972, pp. 161–170.

7. Garfield, p. 92.

8. Garfield, p. 89. Emphasis added.

9. Garfield, p. 91.

10. Garfield, p. 95.

11. Robert Louis Stevenson. "A Chapter on Dreams" in *Memories and Portraits, Random Memories, Memories of Himself.* New York: Scribner, 1925, p. 167.

12. Diane Ackerman. *A Natural History of the Senses.* Random House: New York, 1990, p. 234.

13. Fred Alan Wolf. *The Dreaming Universe: A Mind-Expanding Journey into the Realm where Psyche and Physics Meet.* New York: Simon & Schuster, 1994, p. 145.

14. Wolf, p. 146.

15. Wolf, p. 135.

The Interpreter:
Joseph and Dreams

1. Talmud, *Tamid* 32b.

2. I do not mean to imply that the use of literary devices is the only difference between great literature and entertaining but more commonplace writing. There are other distinguishing features, of course, among which are elegance of style, subtle characterization, and complexity of plot. It is interesting to note that when we recognize great literature, we speak of it as well "realized."

3. This was known throughout the ancient world. It is frequently attested in Greek myth where, for example, Odysseus is born after Zeus "visits" his mother. In the *Iliad* (10:144), Odysseus is called *diogenes laertiade*, "Zeus-born son of Laertes." Similarly, Jesus is considered divine because of his heavenly Father, but derives the kingship of the Jews from the mortal Joseph (Matthew 1). For further analogies, see Cyrus Gordon, *The Common Background of Greek and Hebrew Civilizations*. New York: W. W. Norton & Company, Inc., 1965, pp. 243 ff.

4. The precise definition of the adjective "ornamented" is unknown. The classic translation, of course, is "a coat of many colors." More likely it was a "striped tunic," such as princes of Egypt wore. If so, it might presage Joseph's sojourn in Egypt in the same way the ziggurat presaged Jacob's sojourn in Mesopotamia.

5. The citations and the account in this paragraph are from Genesis 37:1–4.

6. In the Gilgamesh epic, the hero's duplicate dream appears to form the backbone of the entire narrative. See Cyrus Gordon,

The Common Background of Greek and Hebrew Civilizations.
New York: W. W. Norton & Company, Inc., 1965, p. 64.

7. Talmud, *Berachot* 55b.

8. Peter O'Connor. *Dreams and the Search for Meaning.* New York: Paulist Press, 1986, p. 225.

9. Carl G. Jung. *Dreams.* New York: MJF Books, 1974, pp. 69–70.

10. See Genesis 44 for the sequence.

11. Talmud, *Berachot* 55a–b.

12. All this is encompassed in Genesis 39. In light of this, one might wonder what the Bible is trying to tell us about tunics. First, a tunic (the ornamented coat) makes Joseph's brothers jealous, then a tunic (grabbed by Potiphar's wife) lands Joseph in prison. Does this mean that flashy dressing leads to disaster? Or is it a symbol of Joseph's pride getting the better of him? This is not an issue for a book on dreams, but it is a fascinating instance of the application of biblical texts to our everyday lives.

13. Walter Duckat. *Beggar to King: All the Occupations of Biblical Times.* Nashville and New York: Abingdon Press, 1971, p. 70.

14. See also Genesis 22:18, 26:5, and 28:14.

15. Genesis Rabbah 39:12.

16. Despite my thesis and its proofs, several scholars argue against the idea that Hebrews may have served as professional dream interpreters. They note that dream interpretation played no part in the definition of biblical wisdom or in the skills required of a prophet or sage. Some also note that prophecy received in dreams was generally considered less accurate than that received in visions or through direct communications. In rebuttal, I note that the sages spend a great deal of time discussing which dreams will come true, what the various symbols mean in a dream, and how dreams should be properly interpreted—all this they considered a part of their work. That they were consulted by non-Jews for their interpretations is attested three times in this chapter and quite frequently throughout rabbinic literature. As for the prophets, we are unsure how much of their

vision came through dreams, but clearly those prophecies that were received by dreaming played an important role in their work, too. In any case, my argument is generally strongest for the patriarchal period in which dreams played a pivotal role.

17. Duckat, p. 64.

18. Jung, *Dreams*, p. 17.

19. The word *beit* is Hebrew for "house of." The word *sohar* occurs nowhere else in the Bible except in reference to this Egyptian place of imprisonment. If it is Egyptian, the word may derive from the root meaning "round," indicating that the prison is a fortress of some kind. Alternatively, it may have been the recognizable name of or epithet for a specific prison, in the way that we today speak of "Sing-Sing" or call the prison at Alcatraz "the Rock."

20. For uses of the word *bor,* see Genesis 37:20, 24, 28, and 29. The intention to link this dungeon with that pit is unmistakable.

21. Nahum M. Sarna. *Understanding Genesis: The Heritage of Biblical Israel.* New York: Schocken Books, 1966, p. 218.

22. Zohar, *Bereshit*, Section 1, p. 191b.

23. Zohar, *Bereshit*, Section 1, pp. 192a–b.

24. Gordon, p. 105.

25. Cyrus Gordon and Gary A. Rendsburg. *The Bible and the Ancient Near East.* New York: W.W. Norton & Company, Inc., 1997, p. 139.

26. Gordon and Rendsburg, pp. 63–64.

27. Genesis Rabbah 89:6.

28. Genesis Rabbah 89:4.

29. There was even a god named *Sheva*, "Seven." We have reminders of this in names like Bathsheba, meaning "daughter of the god Seven," and Elisheva, meaning "my god is Seven"; and in place-names like Beersheba, "fountain of the god Seven." (As an aside, the god Seven or Sheba seems still to be worshiped in places like Las Vegas and Atlantic City.) The sages in Talmud,

Berachot 55b, ordain a prayer to be said on receiving a bad dream: "May the All-Merciful turn it to good; seven times may it be decreed from heaven that it should be good and may it be good." The instances of the use of seven to bring luck in Jewish practice are numerous and include the bride circling the groom seven times during the marriage ceremony, carrying the scrolls of the Torah around the synagogue seven times during the festival of the Rejoicing in the Torah (*Simhat Torah*), and so on. No doubt, the Jews connected the good fortune of seven to the seven days of creation and the fact that the Sabbath—the ultimate Jewish institution—fell on the seventh day. The tradition of seven as a lucky number, however, was already well established by the time of the patriarchs. Indeed, everything that has been said of seven applied also to the number three. By the time of Joseph, both of these numbers were widely respected as good omens.

30. James B. Pritchard, ed. *Ancient Near Eastern Texts Relating to the Old Testament*. Princeton, NJ: Princeton University Press, 1969, pp. 31–32.

31. Gordon and Rendsburg, p. 46.

32. The meaning of this word is unknown. It is not found in Egyptian texts. If it is derived from the Hebrew, *berech*, which means "knee," then it could be translated as "Bow down!" or "Bow low!" It is often translated as "Make way!" just from the context. There have been some suggestions of late that it may be a northern Mesopotamian word meaning "Hail the prince!" but as yet there is no reason to believe that this word would have made its way to Egypt.

33. Talmud, *Berachot* 55b.

34. Genesis Rabbah 89:8.

35. Talmud, *Berachot* 56a.

36. Zohar, *Bereshit*, Section 1, p. 183b.

37. The three words are *zefunot* ("hidden things"), *mofi'a* ("he reveals"), and *nohot* ("easily").

38. Genesis Rabbah 90:4.

From Scout to Seer:
In the Footsteps of Joseph

1. Franz Kafka. *Parables.* New York: Schocken Books, Inc., 1947, p.268 ff.

2. Talmud, *Berachot* 55a.

3. Harold Bloom. *Omens of Millennium: The Gnosis, Dreams, and Resurrection.* New York: Riverhead Books, 1996, p. 89.

4. Francis Huxley. *The Way of the Sacred.* Garden City, NY: Doubleday and Company, Inc., 1974, p. 255.

5. Huxley, p. 257.

6. Robert L. Van de Castle. *Our Dreaming Mind.* New York: Ballantine Books, 1994, pp. 14–15.

7. Robert Louis Stevenson. "A Chapter on Dreams" in R. L. Woods, ed., *The World of Dreams.* New York: Random House, 1947, pp. 876–877.

8. See Ellen B. Basso, *The Kalapalo Indians of Central Brazil.* New York: Holt, Rinehart & Winston, 1973. Also on the Kalapalo, see Barbara Tedlock, ed., *Dreaming: Anthropological and Psychological Interpretations.* Santa Fe, NM: School of American Research Press, 1992.

9. Joseph Campbell. *The Hero with a Thousand Faces.* Cleveland and New York: The World Publishing Company, 1949, pp. 73–74.

10. Kelly Bulkeley. *The Wilderness of Dreams: Exploring the Religious Meanings of Dreams in Modern Western Culture.* Albany: State University of New York Press, 1994, pp. 185–186.

Dream Symbols:
Samuel and Solomon Hear the Call

1. Talmud, *Berachot* 56b.

2. S. Carl Hirsch. *Theater of the Night: What We Do and Do Not Know about Dreams*. Middletown, CT: Xerox Educational Publications, 1976, p. 27.

3. James R. Lewis. *The Dream Encyclopedia*. Detroit: Visible Ink, 1995, p. 335.

4. Lewis, p. 353.

5. The Chronicles were obviously a court history, and the same charge can be leveled at the Book of Kings. Their historical accuracy is open to challenge. We have not addressed the question of biblical historicity in this work on dreams. Was there an Abraham, an Isaac, a Jacob, or a Joseph? Are the accounts of their lives accurate? The suggestion has been made that the patriarchal history is a composite of earlier tribal histories in which the patriarchs represent whole tribes that later combined to become the Jewish people. We have no way of denying this as a possibility. Outside of relying on the biblical account, we have no way of "proving" the historicity of Moses or Joshua, either. The account of King David given in Kings and Chronicles has the "feeling" of history, but even here there is also the prejudice of the historians to consider. A lengthy examination of the text, the archaeological data, outside sources, and more, would leave us hardly closer to the "facts." Since the examination of dreams is not a historical exercise, the question of historicity only impinges on this study indirectly. I only add this note to remind the reader that history resembles dreaming in that it also requires interpretation.

6. It is convenient to call the "Tribes of Israel" or the "Children of Israel" *Israelites* at this point, even though they still very much thought of themselves as a loose confederation of tribes rather than as a single nation.

7. See 1 Chronicles 21:29.

8. See Genesis 22, verses 1, 7, and 11.

9. 1 Samuel 2:27 ff.

10. Joseph Campbell. *The Hero with a Thousand Faces*. Cleveland and New York: The World Publishing Company, 1949, p. 51.

11. Campbell, p. 58.

Your Name Shall Be "Incredulous": The Potential for Healing and Transformation

1. The "mutual quest" is given lavish and eloquent treatment by my late teacher Joseph Campbell in his wide-ranging four-volume work, *The Masks of God*. To complement these excellent interpretations of literature, Campbell examined world art and architecture for the motif of the "mutual quest" in his book *The Mythic Image*. Readers of Campbell will find that he was heavily influenced by Jung and by Eastern thought. He hardly touches on post-biblical Jewish literature. Nevertheless, his work is outstanding for its breadth of scholarship and fluency of style.

2. Friedrich Nietzsche. *Thus Spoke Zarathustra*, edited by Walter Kaufmann, part 1, "Of Reading and Writing." New York: Viking Press, 1972, p. 18.

3. Patricia Garfield. *Creative Dreaming*. New York: Ballantine Books, 1974, p. 194.

4. Paul Ricoeur. *Freud and Philosophy: An Essay on Interpretation*. New Haven: Yale University Press, 1970, pp. 496–497.

5. Garfield, p. 196.

6. See the chapter entitled "Are We on the Right Path? Abraham's Midlife Crisis."

7. Luther H. Martin. *Hellenistic Religions: An Introduction*. New York: Oxford University Press, 1987, pp. 51–52.

Out of the Dream Forest:
The Meaning of the Spiritual Quest

1. *Bhagavad Gita* (250 B.C.E.–250 C.E.), 11, 12.

2. Len Giovannitti and Fred Freed. *The Decision to Drop the Bomb*. New York: Coward-McCann, 1965, p. 212.

3. *Time*, February 23, 1948.

4. Fred Alan Wolf. *The Dreaming Universe: A Mind-Expanding Journey into the Realm where Psyche and Physics Meet*. New York: Simon & Schuster, 1994, p. 285.

5. Wolf, p. 285.

6. Lao Tzu. *Tao Te Ching* 32.

7. Kelly Bulkeley. *The Wilderness of Dreams: Exploring the Religious Meanings of Dreams in Modern Western Culture*. Albany: State University of New York Press, 1994, p. 213.

8. Wolf, p. 344.

Index

𝄐

A

Aaron, 103, 218
abaton, 57
Abbahu, Rabbi, 131
Abimelech, 134, 221
abode of the gods, 172
Aborigines, 228-229, 303, 314
Abrabanel, 147
Abraham, 8, 42-53, 55, 60-63,
    65, 67, 72-73, 78-80, 86-88,
    90-92, 94, 100-101, 110,
    113-114, 121, 134-136,
    149, 151-153, 160, 162-
    164, 175, 184-185, 189,
    192, 198-199, 207, 221,
    237, 245, 291, 295; God of,
    190
Abram. *See* Abraham
Adam, 17, 51, 128, 139-140,
    146, 161, 206, 235
Adam and Eve, Book of, 143
afternoon prayers, and Isaac, 98
agricultural setting, 239, 257

Akiba, Rabbi, 127-129, 131
Akkadian(s), 41-42
Alamogordo, New Mexico, 315
Alexander the Great, 233-234
Alice in Wonderland, 236
aliyah, 54-55
allegorical dreams, 77, 80
American Indian, 177. *See
    also* Native American Indi-
    ans; Native Americans
Amnon, 40
Amorites, 49
angel(s), 17-18, 23, 104-105,
    131, 141, 144-148, 161-
    162, 165, 185, 187-188,
    191, 194-199, 200-201,
    204, 206-207, 209-210,
    215, 222, 235, 271-272,
    274-275, 286, 295, 292,
    320; as intercessors, 146;
    as messages from God,
    148; as metaphorical, 147;
    as mysterious visitors, 184;
    camp of, 196; created daily,

B

E

F

G

M

Q

R

T

About the Author

𝄟

Seymour Rossel is the Director of Pathways Foundation, an advocacy program for Jewish dreams and Jewish teens. He is the author of twenty-eight books and the editor of more than 300.

Rabbi Rossel studied at the Jerusalem Institute for Youth Leaders, Southern Methodist University, and New York University. He formerly served the Jewish Reform movement as Director of the Department of Education of the Union of American Hebrew Congregations and Coordinator of the School of Education of Hebrew Union College-Jewish Institute of Religion in New York. He directed education for Temple Shalom of Dallas and Temple Beth El of Chappaqua, was Curriculum Coordinator for Temple Emanuel of Great Neck, and Headmaster of Solomon Schechter Academy of Dallas. He was President of Rossel Books and Executive Vice-President of Behrman House, Inc.

Presenting lectures, workshops, and retreats on Judaism and spirituality, Bible, and Bible dreams for Jewish and Christian groups, he has traveled extensively throughout North America, Great Britain, and Israel. His web site, which includes a fuller biography, may be found at *www.rossel.net*.